P9-EKT-744

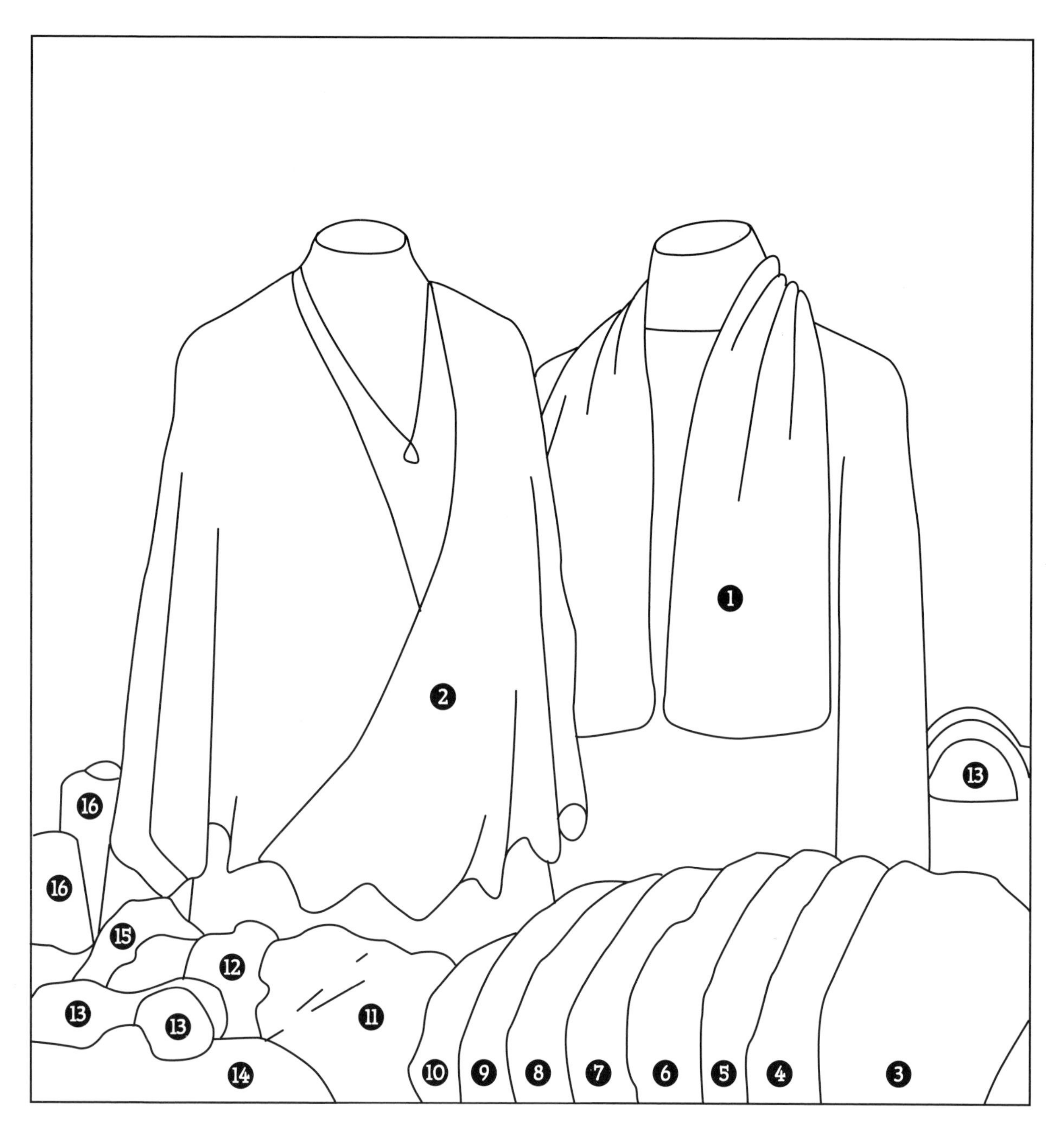

Cover Photo Legend

1. Walter Seamen's Scarf, Haneke Select 75% merino, 25% alpaca medium weight, fawn.
2. Josephine Shawl, Haneke Exotics 50% super fine alpaca, 50% tencel fingering weight, white.
3. Alka Shawl, JaggerSpun 50% merino, 50% silk lace weight, white.
4. Alka Shawl, Euroflax 4/14 linen, eggplant.
5. Alka Shawl, Haneke Select 75% merino, 25% alpaca fingering weight, white.
6. Alka Shawl, Hayfield Exquisite Shimmer, 61% acrylic, 39% nylon sport weight, emerald.
7. Alka Shawl, Haneke Select 75% merino, 25% alpaca, sport weight, fawn.
8. Alka Shawl, Cotton Clouds, 3/2 pearle cotton sport weight, deep blue.
9. Alka Shawl, Haneke Select 75% merino, 25% alpaca medium weight, cocoa.
10. Alka Shawl, Haneke 100% merino three-ply bulky, chocolate.
11. Skeins of Haneke Select 75% merino, 25% alpaca fingering, sport, medium and bulky weight yarn.
12. Skeins of MOCO hand spun 100% qiviut fingering weight, cranberry.
13. Seamen's scarf in progress using MOCO 100% qiviut fingering weight.
14. Frances Shawl, Haneke Select 75% merino, 25% alpaca fingering weight, pewter.
15. Skein of Margaret Stove's Artisan New Zealand lace weight yarn.
16. Cones of New Zealand lace weight 100% merino yarn.

Stahman's

Shawls & Scarves

Lace Faroese-Shaped Shawls From the Neck Down

and Seamen's Scarves

Myrna A.I. Stahman

Boise, Idaho

Copyright ©2000 by Myrna A.I. Stahman dba Rocking Chair Press

All rights reserved. No part of this publication may be reproduced, stored in a retrieval system, or transmitted in any form or by any means without the prior permission of the copyright holder. Direct all inquiries to Rocking Chair Press, 2814 Tartan Place, Boise, ID 83702-1429.

Permission is granted, to the purchaser of this book, to make one personal working copy of the charts for the shawl or scarf being knit. Permission is also granted to the purchaser to copy and share with friends, for non-commercial use only, the Matthew, Matt, Columbine I, Columbine II, and Columbine III Seamen's scarf patterns in the section titled "Let's Make the World a Better Place for All."

The Traditional Seamen's Scarf pattern and the Watch Cap pattern of Appendix F may be copied and used for knitting scarves and caps to be donated to the Seamen's Church Institute of New York and New Jersey Christmas-at-Sea project, 241 Water Street, New York, NY 10038-2016.

This book is available for special purchase from Rocking Chair Press, 2814 Tartan Place, Boise, ID 83702-1429. stahman@aol.com; 208-342-6690.

First published January 2000.
Fourth printing December 2007.
Printed by The Caxton Printers, Ltd., Caldwell, Idaho.

Library of Congress Cataloging-in-Publication Data

Stahman, Myrna A. I.
Stahman's Shawls and Scarves: Lace Faroese-Shaped Shawls From the Neck Down and Seamen's Scarves / by Myrna A.I. Stahman
168 p. 22 cm
Includes bibliographical references and index.
ISBN 0-9675427-0-7 (pbk.)
1. Knitting – Patterns. 2. Shawls – Faroe Islands. 3. Scarves. 4. Knitted Lace
I. Stahman, Myrna A.I. II. Title
TT820. 1998
746.2'2-dc21 99-96028
CIP

Photographer: Mark VanderSys
Book Designer: Peter E. Wilson, DesignWorks, Inc.
Production Artist: Kelly G. Mitchell, DesignWorks, Inc.
Graphic Artist: Ralph R. Blount
Copy Editor: Jeanette Germain
Wardrobe: Ragtime; Haneke Wool Fashions; Diana Goslin; Kathy Estes

Contents

Chapter 6. Knitting from a Chart

Chapter 7: The Lace Border

Chapter 8: Customizing the Faroese Shawl Patterns

Chapter 9: After the Knitting Is Done

Illustrations and Photos

Foreword

Knitting is a journey – designing, an evolutionary process. The evolution of my lace Faroese-shaped shawls began when I discovered Barbara G. Walker's works, including *A Treasury of Knitting Patterns* and *Knitting from the Top*. Several years later, while attending Meg Swansen's knitting camp, I purchased *Foroysk Bindingarmynstur*, a book I could not read, but with which I fell in love. My journey continued when, as a student in Cheryl Oberle's Faroese shawl class at Stitches West '95, I met Marilyn van Keppel, who also has a great love for Faroese shawls. Thanks to Marilyn's inquisitive genius, *Foroysk Bindingarmynstur* was translated into English as *Faroese Knitting Patterns – Knitted Shawls*, now available as a set from Schoolhouse Press.

After knitting three beautiful Faroese shawls from Marilyn's translations, each beginning at the bottom with hundreds of stitches which magically disappear in the wonderful decrease shapings, I decided to reverse the engineering and begin a shawl from the top. Because I love lace, I use stockinette lace stitches, rather than the traditional garter stitch, for many of my designs. Because I fall in love with beautiful yarn, purchase it, and knit it only after allowing it to "properly mature" in my yarn stash for a time, I sometimes question whether I have sufficient yarn to finish my desired project. Knitting a shawl from the top down permits me always to finish the shawl, although sometimes the recipient must be a short friend!

My knitting journey continued. Using the classic scarf pattern of the Seamen's Church Institute's Christmas-at-Sea program as my inspiration, I developed what have become known as Seamen's scarves. "The Elegant Seamen's Scarf," published in the Fall 1998 issue of *Interweave Knits*, received a wonderful reception, so I decided to include in this book many of my Seamen's scarf designs.

XRX, Inc. published "Lace Shawl Knitting Tips," an article based upon materials from the draft of this book, and "Catharina," a lace Faroese-shaped shawl I designed. They appeared in the Spring 1998 issue of *Knitter's Magazine*, and have been reprinted in *The Best of Knitter's Magazine: Shawls and Scarves* (1999).

Acknowledgments

Thanks to Jeanne Schaub, my sister Marialis' fifth grade teacher, who planted the seed for knitting which resulted in my mother and her three daughters learning to knit; to my mother, who knit thereafter during her entire life; to my biological sisters Iloise and Marialis, with whom I learned to knit; to our ancestors who passed on the knitting gene; to my very special "knitting sister" Pat Stevens; to Gracie Larsen, the founder of the Lacy Knitters Guild; to all the knitters who have gone before me and provided inspiration – Barbara G. Walker, Mary Walker Phillips, Anne L. Macdonald, Elizabeth Zimmermann, Meg Swansen, and Margaret Stove to name just a few; to Marilyn van Keppel and her genius for her English translation of the wonderful book of Faroese shawls; to Dolores Hanson, who introduced me to the Seamen's scarf; and to Beth Rountree who inspired me to design the elegant Seamen's scarves.

A special thanks to all the wonderful knitters who assisted by proof-knitting my designs: Linda L. Antill, Virginia Bird, Esther S. Bozak, Cathlene Burk, Barbara A. Burri, Sue Cathey, Debra Chinn, Anna E. Conley, Bev Dillon, Petra Doerfling, Ruth Donahue, Cynthia M. Douglass, Shelda Eggers, Yvonne Eyer, Beverley Francis, Sally A. Fuhrmann, Polly R. Garvey, Barbara George, Karen Gott, Terry Harris, Susan Hope, Donna Hunt, Mary Serena Hunt, Darlene Ihrig, Anya Konzi-Ashburn, Caroline Laudig, Susan M. Lewis, Linda Loeffelholz, Janet Lynn, Ginger L. Meeker, Sharon Meeuwsen, Michele Miller, Carole Morain, Edward Myatt, Karen Officer, Shaunet Olsson, Daphne Page, Alicia Plotkin, Elizabeth Powers, Maggie Putnam, Karen Raz, Rochelle Ribeiro, Evelyn Ann Rude, Donna L. Russell, Karen L. Sanders, Betty Sargent, Maureen Sorenson, Connie Spann, Gayle Surrette, Rebecca H. Taaffe, Maria E. Valcarcel, Dine Varen, Lester Vaughn, Wendy Watson, Janet B. W. Williams, and Kate Winkler. Thanks also to Pat Stevens for knitting the Susan shawl pictured and to Tommie Tank for knitting the Idella Seamen's scarf pictured. I am indebted to Susan Stacy, Ginger L. Meeker, Sandy Rich and Mary Anne Thompson for their editorial assistance.

A very special thank you to Kathy Haneke and Haneke Wool Fashions, without whose support this book would never have come into existence. "Heavenly Haneke" merino and merino blend yarns have played a major role in my designing journey and have been used for the majority of the shawls and scarves in this book. Kathy's request that I design for her, and her wonderful fibers, have made my designing journey a fantastic adventure.

I am especially appreciative of my husband Bob, who cooked many a meal and accepted my knitting fantasies, my children Kayla and Jeff and our dog Waldo, who all gave me the support I needed while designing, knitting, and writing.

Preface

by Marilyn van Keppel

Myrna Stahman and I both love Faroese shawls, and it was this love that brought us together in 1995. I was working on an English translation of a book of traditional Faroese shawl patterns at the time. Myrna – who has been knitting for 40 years and has extensive experience with lace – volunteered to test knit some of my translated patterns. With that, she began her journey of exploration, the fruits of which you hold in your hands.

The traditional Faroese shawl is worked in garter stitch from the bottom up, shaped by decreases and usually incorporating a band of lace or an all-over lace pattern. The bottom edge is finished with fringe or crochet. After knitting a few shawls in the traditional way, Myrna was inspired to try a shawl starting at the top and working down, using a stockinette ground instead of garter stitch and knitting a lace edge onto the bottom.

Myrna has unvented a variation of the Faroese shawl, incorporating the traditional shape, with the shoulder shaping and unique center back gusset, but with the advantages of working from the top down. The ability to make one of these shawls without worrying about running out of yarn is one of these advantages. If one runs low on yarn, one can simply end the shawl at a convenient place. Another advantage is that the shawl has no inflexible cast-on edge, and if a sideways lace border is knitted onto the shawl, there is no cast-off edge either.

In *Knitting Workshop*, Elizabeth Zimmermann wrote, "Knitting has been a comfort and an inspiration to people for hundreds – perhaps thousands – of years, and during this time methods have been discovered, forgotten, distorted, improved upon, forgotten again, and re-discovered to be improved upon yet again." A new generation of knitters will thank Myrna for this method of making a Faroese shawl.

Marilyn van Keppel
Kansas City, Missouri
September, 1999

Introduction

This book is divided into three major parts. Part I sets forth the techniques I use in constructing lace Faroese-shaped shawls from the neck down and Seamen's scarves. Part II provides specific instructions for 14 Faroese-shaped shawls and variations, with matching lace Seamen's scarves. Part III provides instructions for an additional 28 Seamen's scarves and instructions on designing your own Seamen's scarves.

I have strived to make this book knitter-friendly. If you are an experienced knitter, you may have no need or desire to use portions of Part I – skip those portions, with my blessing. Use what is helpful, ignore the rest at will.

To assist my knitting friends world-wide, both U.S. and metric measurements are provided; Canadian needle sizes are also provided. To assist you in using your handspun and/or stash yarn I have included wraps per inch/2.5 cm; yards per ounce and meters per 50 grams for the yarns used. These details are found in the section titled "Yarns Used For Shawls and Scarves Pictured" found at pages 142-146. Hints for determining the amount of yarn needed for the pattern, yarn and needle you select, and your personal knitting gauge are also provided.

Most stitch patterns are provided in chart form. I grant permission to the purchaser of this book to make one personal working copy of the charts for the shawl or scarf being knit. I recommend that you enlarge the charts to the size necessary to make it easy for your eyes to follow.

I grant the purchaser of this book permission to copy, and share with friends for non-commercial use only, the patterns in the section titled "Let's Make the World a Better Place for All" Seamen's Scarves. These scarves I have created in memory of Matthew Shepard, and the teacher and students who died at Columbine High School. Each time you use one of these patterns, please take some action to foster the understanding of people who are different from yourself. Knit an extra scarf and donate it to a worthy cause. Offer your help, your hope, and your heart to make the world a better place for all.

Part I

Hints and Techniques for Knitting Fabulous Lace Faroese-Shaped Shawls From The Neck Down and Seamen's Scarves

Chapter 1. The Magnificent Shaping of Faroese Shawls

The wearing of a Faroese-shaped shawl is pure joy, due to the magnificent shaping developed by the shawl knitters of the Faroe Islands. Through the dedication of Elsa Baerentsen, the Faroese Home Industries Council and many knitters of the Faroe Islands, the secrets of the wonderfully shaped shawls of the Faroe Islands were published in 1983 in *Foroysk Bindingarmynstur*. Thanks to the genius of Marilyn van Keppel, this great work was translated into English and published by Schoolhouse Press, enabling a much larger segment of the knitting world to enjoy the traditional Faroese shawl. *Foroysk Bindingarmynstur*, and its English translation, *Faroese Knitting Patterns – Knitted Shawls*, are a great investment for any knitter who loves knitting beautiful shawls. My admiration for the wonderful Faroese shaping, my love of lace pattern stitches and my preference for knitting from the top down led me to use the Faroese shawl shaping as the basis for my shawl designs.

Traditional Faroese Shawls

In the "Forward to the English Translation" of *Foroysk Bindingarmynstur*, Marilyn van Keppel explains the characteristics of the traditional Faroese shawl, which include:

- Cast on at the bottom
- Worked in garter stitch
- Knit with a center back panel which is often shaped by the use of decreases
- Narrowed as the shawl is worked up to the shoulders
- Shaped by using decreases in the side panels and in the shoulders
- Sometimes decorated with a lace bottom band
- Commonly edged with crocheting for everyday use; sometimes fringed
- Often lined with a contrasting color knit lining to show off the lace
- Generally knit from yarn of natural sheep colors or dyed from plants and lichens of the area.

In a section titled "Knitted Shawls" in *Foroysk Bindingarmynstur* we are told:

- The finest shawls had fringe and were made of a very lightweight yarn
- The usual lace pattern was of diamonds in different shapes
- It was important that the shawl could be tied behind the back so it could be worn while working
- The usual needle size was 4.5 to 5 mm which is U.S. #7 to 8
- Approximately 350 stitches were cast on to make a medium-sized shawl.

The distinctive Faroese shaping is explained:

- The decreases made every other row at the four fixed points (on both sides of the center panel and at both outer edges) are the distinguishing feature which gives a Faroese shawl its shape.
- The shawl fits so well at the shoulders because of extra decreases before the shoulders and towards the top in the center panel.
- A line of eyelets is placed along the edge strips to enhance the beauty of the shawl. This edge strip is usually five to seven stitches in width, but sometimes it begins with up to 15 stitches and narrows to five.

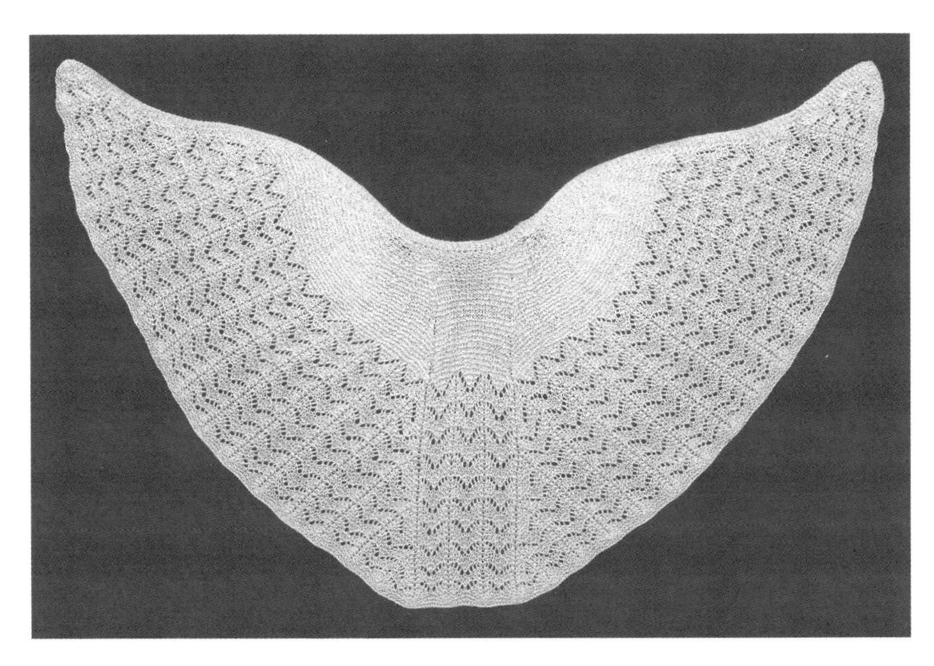

Photo 1: *The Anna shawl from "Foroysk Bindingarmynstur," a traditional Faroese shawl worked from the bottom up.*

Characteristics of a Stahman Lace Faroese-Shaped Shawl

Although the traditional Faroese shawls are knit from the bottom up, all the shawls in this book are knit from the top down. I have designed several shawls worked with a garter stitch base, which is so characteristic of traditional Faroese shawls. Using a garter stitch, rather than stockinette stitch, makes a wonderful working shawl. The additional width resulting from the use of garter stitch allows for tying the shawl behind one's back, and the garter stitch thickness provides warmth.

Photo 2: *The GS Gracie working shawl, with the ends tied in the back, is great for a crisp morning walk with my dog.*

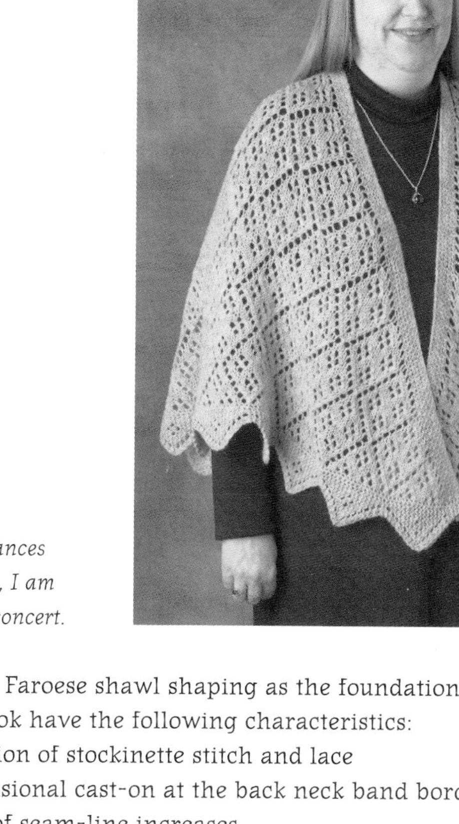

Photo 3: *Wearing the Frances shawl over a black dress, I am ready for dinner and a concert.*

Using the traditional Faroese shawl shaping as the foundation, the majority of the shawls in this book have the following characteristics:

- Knit in a combination of stockinette stitch and lace
- Begun with a provisional cast-on at the back neck band border
- Shoulder shaping of seam-line increases
- Neck band/front border of six stitches of seed stitch, with the first stitch slipped to form a chain selvedge
- Increases evenly spaced on both edges of each side panel
- Increases at the top edges of the center back panel for a portion of the shawl
- Knit-on lace border or seed stitch border.

Chapter 2. Seamen's Scarves

More than 100 years ago, during the Spanish-American War, a wonderful tradition began. Through the efforts of a concerned citizen and a military chaplain a program which now involves over 3,000 knitters and serves over 13,000 seamen was born. From those early efforts came the traditional and ageless Seamen's neck scarf.

I first adapted the traditional Seamen's scarf when a friend asked for help in knitting a "candy cane" scarf. She was interested in Barbara Walker's Fish Hooks pattern from *A Second Treasury of Knitting Patterns*. We incorporated the 4x4 ribbing of the traditional Seamen's scarf with the upside-down Fish Hooks for the scarf tails and created the wonderful scarf now known as Beth's Candy Canes (pattern on page 111). This led to experimentation with many other stitch patterns. These designs lend a new elegance to the ageless Seamen's neck scarf.

The History of the Traditional Seamen's Neck Scarf

The Reverend Walter A.A. Gardner, chaplain of the North River Station, noted in his annual report of 1898 that a lady named Mrs. E.A. Gardner "conceived the idea of supplying 'our' warships with 'just what they needed.'" As a result of this idea, "Noble-hearted friends came to her assistance. The *New York Herald* and the *Associated Press* took it up, and thousands of (comfort) bags, medical supplies, delicacies, Bible prayer books, testaments, and many cases of literature were sent to our men."

The seeds of the current Christmas-at-Sea Program were planted. Soon the Seamen's Benefit Society, a ladies' auxiliary of the Seamen's Church Institute of New York and New Jersey, was established. One of the many functions of this auxiliary was providing knitted articles to the seafarers who stopped at the Institute.

By 1941 approximately 2,000 volunteers, including many from churches of all denominations throughout the United States, provided approximately 5,000 gift boxes containing hand knit sweaters, socks, hats, mufflers, and mittens. Volunteers of the Seamen's Church Institute distributed these gift boxes to the crews of freighters and tankers who spent Christmas Day at sea. In 1996, nearly 3,000 volunteers knit approximately 17,000 garments, including 6,000 scarves, as gifts for merchant mariners who were at sea on Christmas Day.

The Christmas-at-Sea Program of the Seamen's Church Institute of New York and New Jersey provides volunteer knitters with patterns for knitting scarves, watch caps, sweaters and socks. Please join this very worthwhile program; the traditional Seamen's scarf pattern is on page 103 and the matching watch cap in Appendix F. For more information write to: Christmas-at-Sea, The Seamen's Church Institute, 241 Water Street, New York, NY 10038 or call 212-349-9090 extension 257.[1]

The Stahman Adaptation of the Traditional Seamen's Neck Scarf

The traditional Seamen's scarf is knit from end to end by knitting 14 inches of garter stitch, followed by 18 inches of knit four, purl four ribbing, followed by another 14 inches of garter stitch. The garter stitch tails provide warmth to the chest of the wearer, and the knit four, purl four neck ribbing provides both a wonderful fit and warmth as it hugs the neck of the wearer.

Photo 4: *The I.J. Seamen's scarf, in the style of the traditional scarf of the Seamen's Church Institute.*

[1] Leah Robinson Rousmaniere. *Anchored Within the Vail: A Pictorial History of the Seamen's Church Institute* (New York: The Seamen's Church Institute, 1995), 120-121.

Using the traditional Seamen's scarf as my inspiration, my designs generally have the following characteristics:

- Begun with a provisional cast-on
- Tails knit down from the neck, using a pattern stitch
- Side and bottom borders of the tails done in seed stitch
- Neckline ribbing of 4x4, 3x3, or a combination of the two
- Width of tails measuring from 6 inches/15 cm to 10 inches/25 cm
- Total length of scarf between 50 inches/127 cm and 63 inches/160 cm

By using a provisional cast-on and working each tail from the neck down, the pattern stitch in each tail is identical. This is of utmost importance when using a lace stitch or any other stitch that is not horizontally reversible. This construction method is a great help when your yarn is limited, as you can knit the two tails at the same time until you have exhausted your yarn supply.[2]

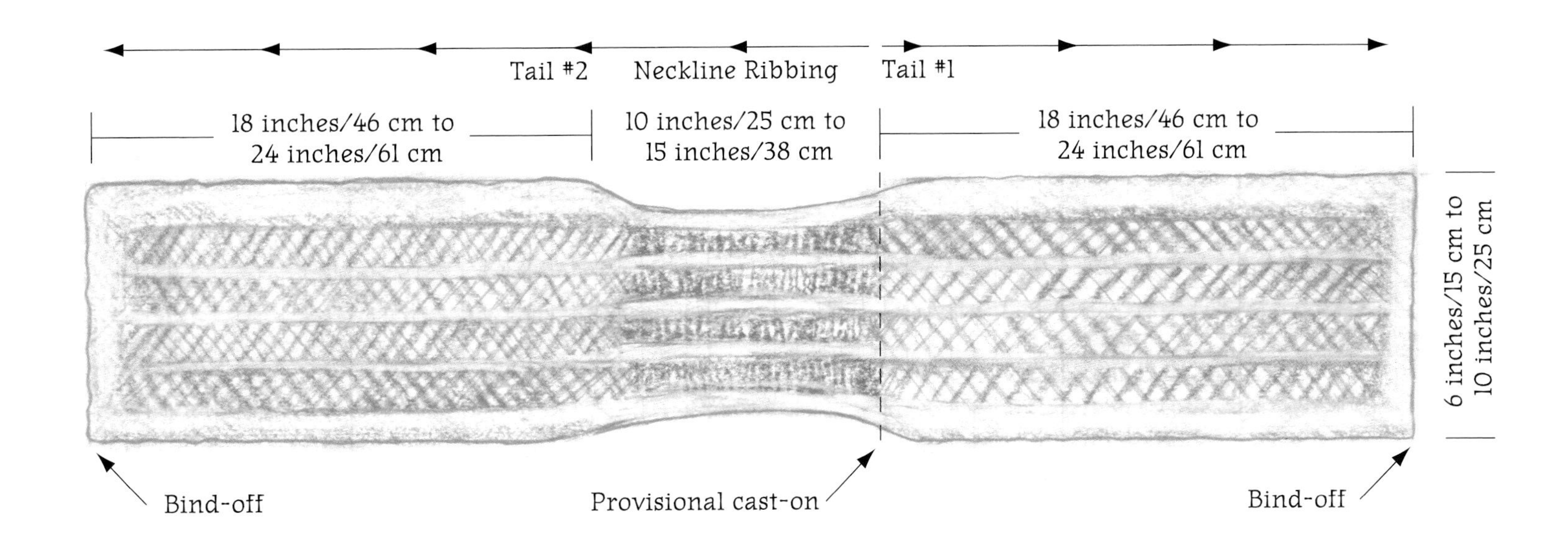

Illustration 1: *Schematic of the Stahman adaptation of the traditional Seamen's scarf.*

[2] Parts of this chapter were published in "The Elegant Seamen's Scarf," *Interweave Knits* (Fall 1999): 44-47.

Chapter 3. Knitting Properly Practiced

In *Knitting Without Tears*, Elizabeth Zimmermann writes, "Properly practiced, knitting soothes the troubled spirit ... [that is, when] executed in a relaxed manner, without anxiety, strain, or tension, but with confidence, inventiveness, pleasure and ultimate pride."[3] The following techniques will assist you in "properly practicing" your knitting of the beautiful Faroese-shaped shawls and Seamen's scarves in this book.

What Works for You is the Right Way to Knit

I am a firm believer that the right way for you to knit is the way that is most comfortable and works best for you. Yet, I also agree with Montse Stanley who said, "Hand knitting often looks more homemade than handmade. The subtle difference hinges on an equally subtle choice of techniques that distinguishes the outstanding from the mediocre."[4]

This chapter includes the techniques I use while "properly practicing" my knitting of lace Faroese-shaped shawls and Seamen's scarves. I hope these techniques will assist you in many hours of enjoyable knitting. If you have a technique that works better for you than the one recommended, by all means, use it. What is important is that you understand the array of possibilities and select the techniques which give the results you desire. This is your knitting, so you have the final word on which techniques to use.

The Vast Knitting Universe

How many techniques for casting on do you know? When I learned to knit more than 40 years ago, I was taught how to cast on. And for 30 years I used that same technique for casting on. In 1992 I attended Elizabeth Zimmermann's and Meg Swansen's knitting camp, and my knitting world exploded – the vastness of the knitting universe became apparent to me! I learned long-tail cast-on and Elizabeth's provisional cast-on, among others. A quick review of knitting books now available reveals at least 40 different techniques for casting on. Wow! What an array of techniques to choose from. We now have the tools to assist us in selecting the most appropriate techniques for the project at hand.[5]

"I'm having lots of fun with this! I tend to be a 'jump-right-in' person, in that I follow the directions one-by-one as I read them. I think it would have been helpful to have a specific 'directive' in the first part of the general instructions that encouraged me to read through all the instructions before I began knitting. Now, whether I would have followed the directive or not isn't certain ☺, but I spent some time kicking myself later because I hadn't read through everything first."

– Shelda Eggers

[3] Elizabeth Zimmermann, *Knitting Without Tears* (New York: Charles Scribner's Sons, 1971) 2.

[4] Montse Stanley, "Knitting a Perfect Rib," *Hand-Knitting Techniques from Threads Magazine* (Newton, CN: The Tauton Press, Inc, 1991) 8.

[5] Two great sources for different ways of casting on are Montse Stanley, *The Handknitter's Handbook* 2nd ed. (New York: Sterling Publishing Co., Inc. 1990); and June Hemmons Hiatt, *The Principles of Knitting* (New York: Simon & Schuster 1988).

Chapter 4. Gauge – Determining the Size of Your Shawl or Scarf

Taking the Mystery Out of Gauge

A long scarf I knit more than forty years ago in the "Feather and Fan," also know as "Old Shale," lace pattern began my love of knitting. I progressed from scarves to afghans to shawls, knitting a sweater, mittens, or socks only now and then. It was not until recently that I came to an understanding of why I have such a strong preference for knitting scarves, afghans, and shawls over sweaters and socks – with these items I don't have to be much concerned with gauge.

Knitting a lace shawl is very different from knitting a garment using a non-lace stitch pattern. A fantastic factor of knitting a lace Faroese-shaped shawl from the neck down is that gauge, although important, is not nearly as critical as in the knitting of a sweater, mittens or socks. Still, there are a number of principles relating to gauge that you must take into account.

Selecting the correct needle size for the look you desire is an interesting challenge which greatly depends upon (1) the yarn you have selected, (2) the needle you will use, and (3) your personal knitting tension. This challenge is offset by the fact that (a) neither a shawl nor a scarf requires the exacting fit of a sweater, (b) the beauty of a lace shawl or a lace scarf can be varied by changing the needle size without changing the yarn (see the Josephine shawls at page 9), (c) the size of a shawl or a scarf can be varied by the "dressing process," and (d) when knitting a shawl or scarf from the neck down, the knitter has control over the length of the shawl or scarf – i.e., you can decide when your shawl or scarf is long enough so that you can stop knitting.

Because of different knitting styles and tensions, a dozen knitters, each using the same brand knitting needle and wool and the same shawl pattern, will produce a dozen beautiful, but different, shawls. For this and other reasons, the patterns in this book are written without including exact instructions as to the number of pattern repeats required for each. Rather, it is left to the knitter to determine, after doing the appropriate gauge swatch, how many pattern repeats are necessary for a shawl or scarf of the length desired. Each shawl pattern can be customized (Chapter 8).

Yarn Selection

Are you a knitter who decides upon a project and then purchases the yarn? Or, are you a knitter who falls in love with yarn, buys it, and after it has properly matured in your yarn stash, finds it crying to be knit up, so you begin your hunt for just the right pattern? Lace Faroese-shaped shawls and Seamen's scarves are suitable for either type of yarn purchaser.

To demonstrate the adaptability of these patterns I have knit shawls and scarves from many weights and fibers. The finer the yarn, the more yardage and less yarn by weight is necessary; the heavier the yarn, the less yardage and more yarn by weight is necessary.

Any weight yarn may be used for the shawls and scarves in this book. What is important is that you select the needle size and the pattern stitch to complement the yarn you have chosen. Even bulky yarn can make a beautiful shawl or scarf– with an appropriate pattern and needle size. See the Alka shawls pictured in "Customizing the Faroese Shawl Patterns," Chapter 8, page 33.

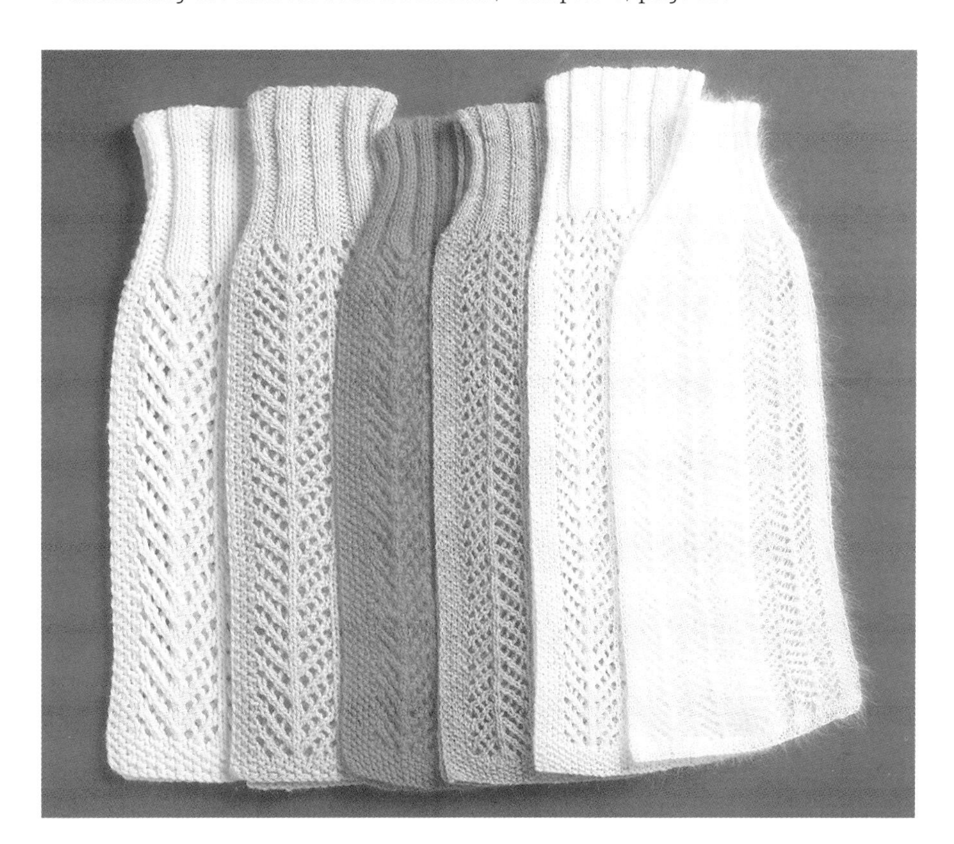

Photo 5: *The Robert Seamen's scarf is beautiful when knit from 3-ply bulky, medium, sport, fingering, lace, or cobweb weight.*

I highly recommend the use of natural fiber yarns – wools, cotton, linen, silk, etc. Because of the "memory" characteristics of most synthetic yarns, I recommend the use of synthetic yarns only if you are knitting a fringed garter stitch Faroese-shaped shawl. Synthetics have minds of their own so often do not dress out nicely.

A Circular Needle is a Must for Shawls and Recommended for Scarves

When knitting lace, a circular needle with a nice point, rather than a blunt tip, works best. A 24 inch/60 cm or 27 inch/70 cm circular needle is sufficiently long for holding all the stitches of any shawl in this book. A longer connector tends to get in my way. Select the circular needle which permits you to "properly practice" your knitting.

For knitting a Seamen's scarf, use your favorite needle(s). I use a circular needle for all my knitting. Using a circular needle rather than straight needles has been advocated by some doctors, as with a circular needle the weight of your project is always evenly distributed, rather than being on one needle or the other. Having the weight evenly distributed is less demanding on your hands and your entire body.

Needle Size – An Approximate Suggestion

Elizabeth Zimmermann offers great advice not to take needle size too seriously, and to regard the recommended needle size in any pattern as an approximate suggestion. I wish I had received that advice 40 years ago when I began knitting. Because I am a loose knitter, I never "knit to gauge" using the recommended needle size in most commercial patterns.

Generally, when knitting lace, a knitter should use a needle two sizes larger than that recommended for knitting that same yarn or fiber in stockinette stitch for a sweater or socks. Other factors that affect gauge are the fiber used, the degree of relaxation of the knitter, the material from which the needle is made, and the brand of needle used. Do realize that needle sizes vary from brand to brand and the needle size recommended is "an approximate suggestion."

Yarn Weights and Recommended Needle Size

A universal system for classifying yarns by thickness has not been adopted. Yarn that one manufacturer calls fingering weight may be similar to what a second manufacturer calls lace weight and a third manufacturer calls sport weight. For this reason I have adopted the most common measure of thickness used by spinners – wraps per inch/2.5 centimeters. For more information on wraps per inch, see Rita Buchanan, "Measuring Yarn - Part 2: Thickness," *Spin-off* (Fall 1993): p.54.

My general recommendations when selecting the needle size to use in knitting a shawl or scarf from this book are:

Cobweb weight
- Approximately 36 to 50 wpi/2.5 cm
- American 0, 1, 2 or 3; metric 2, 2.25, 2.5, 2.75, 3 or 3.25; Canadian 14, 13, 12, 11 or 10

Lace weight
- Approximately 21 to 35 wpi/2.5 cm
- American 2, 3, 4 or 5; metric 3, 3.25, 3.5 or 3.75; Canadian 12, 11, 10 or 9

Fingering weight
- Approximately 17 to 20 wpi/2.5 cm
- American 3, 4, 5, 6 or 7; metric 3.25, 3.5, 3.75, 4 or 4.5 mm; Canadian - size 10, 9, 8 or 7

Sport weight
- Approximately 15 to 17 wpi/2.5 cm
- American 5, 6, 7, 8 or 9; metric 3.75, 4, 4.5 5 or 5.5; Canadian 9, 8, 7, 6 or 5

Medium/worsted weight
- Approximately 12 to 14 wpi/2.5 cm
- American 7, 8, 9, 10 or 10 1/2; metric 4.5, 5, 5,5, 6 or 7; Canadian 7, 6, 5, 4 or 3

Bulky weight
- Approximately 10 wpi/2.5 cm
- American 9, 10, 10 1/2, 11 or 13; metric 5.5, 6, 7, 8 or 9; Canadian 5, 4, 3, 2, 1, 0 or 00

Use the above as a reference, but don't be tied to the recommendations – be adventurous. One of the beauties of knitting lace is that many different needle sizes can be used appropriately with the same fiber. A lace-weight yarn which is beautiful when knit on small needles has a totally different beauty when knit on much larger needles. Compare the Josephine shawl knit using size American 3/metric 3.25/Canadian 10, with the Josephine shawl knit using the very same fiber (Haneke alpaca/tencel fingering) on an American 7/metric 4.5/Canadian 7.

Photo 6: *Josephine knit with Haneke alpaca/tencel fingering weight yarn and American 3/ metric 3.25/Canadian 10 needle.*

Photo 7: *Josephine knit with Haneke alpaca/tencel fingering weight yarn and American 7/ metric 4.5/Canadian 7 needle.*

Knitting a Swatch to Check the Fabric and Determine Rows Per Inch/ 2.5 Centimeters – A Necessary Exercise

What is most important is that your hands are comfortable when knitting and you are happy with the fabric produced by the yarn, the needle size you have chosen and your individual knitting tension. To accomplish this it is very important to knit a good-sized swatch.

Once you have selected the yarn from which to knit your shawl or scarf, go to the section on "Yarn Weights and Recommended Needle Size" (page 8). If you are a loose knitter, begin with the smallest size needle recommended; if you are a tight knitter, begin with the largest size recommended. Then adjust as required to get a fabric which pleases you.

For most of the lace shawls a triangular swatch chart, Chart B, is provided. For all lace shawls the matching Seamen's scarf pattern, Chart S, is provided. Use either Chart B or Chart S to knit a swatch.

When using Chart B, I recommend you border your swatch with the same border you intend to use for your shawl. All garter stitch shawl patterns are written using a five-stitch garter stitch border. All stockinette stitch lace shawl patterns are written using a six-stitch, seed stitch border.

Use your favorite cast-on to cast on the border stitches plus the number of stitches needed for the lace pattern. Work eight rows of garter or seed stitch, always slipping the first stitch as if to purl, knitting the second stitch, and knitting the last stitch. Work using Chart B, the swatch chart provided, for the shawl you have selected.

If, after knitting a few inches, you decide you are not totally happy with the fabric produced, take a new ball of yarn and begin again with a different needle size – but DO NOT tear out your first swatch. Keep that first attempt and compare it to the fabric you produce on your subsequent swatches. Compare your results and decide which you like best. I recommend that you knit as many pattern repeats as necessary for a swatch at least six inches in height.

If you intend to knit a lace border onto your shawl, I recommend that you place your live stitches on a good-sized piece of cotton waste yarn so you can later practice knitting on the lace border. If you intend to finish your shawl with a seed stitch border, knit eight rows of seed stitch, binding off in pattern on the ninth row (page 21).

After knitting your swatch, measure it before you dress it; record that measurement. Use a copy of the swatch, scarf or shawl record forms found in Appendices B, C and D. Dress your swatch (page 34, "Dressing Your Shawl or Scarf for Maximum Beauty"). Measure again and record that measurement.

The most important measurement in knitting a lace Faroese-shaped shawl from the top down or a Seamen's scarf is the **rows to the inch/2.5 centimeters**, not the stitches to the inch/2.5 centimeters. The rows per inch/2.5 centimeters determine the length of your shawl, and it is length that is most important in determining the fit of a lace Faroese-shaped shawl.

It is very important to measure your swatch both before and after dressing it. Lace knit with fine fiber, especially merino wool, grows in the dressing process. Knowing how much your fabric grows is necessary if you wish to get a finished shawl of a specific size. I love shawls of all sizes. I confess – I rarely swatch in my designing process!

Keep your swatch handy so you can use it to practice knitting on the lace border.

Every lace pattern used for a lace Faroese-shaped shawl is also presented as a lace Seamen's scarf. An excellent method of trying out a lace pattern, and becoming comfortable with the pattern stitch, is to knit a Seamen's scarf. The stitch pattern for the Seamen's scarf is very similar to the pattern for the back center panel of the lace Faroese-shaped shawl.

Size – Width of Back Panel at Neckline

Both the rows per inch and the stitches per inch are factors in determining the width of the back panel. The stitches you pick up using the selvedge of the neck band, and which become the first row of the back panel, should measure approximately 40% - 45% of the shoulder-to-shoulder measurement of the person for whom the shawl is made. If the yarn and needle size you select give a gauge of six or more stitches per inch you may wish to change your yarn, your needle size or adjust the number of stitches in the back panel. Chapter 8 provides instructions for customizing your shawl.

"I'm someone who very rarely leaves a pattern alone or doesn't at least ponder about how it all goes and how it could go differently. I'm a large woman and must continually be aware of fit and upsizing. How do I adjust the shoulder shaping, which is the real claim to fame of Faroese shawls?"

– Shelda Eggers

Chapter 8, "Customizing the Faroese Shawl Patterns" provides guidance on adjusting the pattern for different body frames and different yarn selections.

– Myrna

Size – Length

The size of your shawl is determined by your gauge in rows per inch/2.5 cm and the number of pattern repeats you knit. Shawls are sized according to the measurement from the top of the back neck to the bottom of the shawl. The measurements used in this book for classifying the size of a shawl are:

- Small - 22 inches/56 cm to 24 inches/61 cm
- Medium - 25 inches/63 cm to 28 inches/71 centimeters
- Large - 29 inches/74 cm to 32 inches/81 centimeters

"How long should a Faroese shawl be? To the waist? To the bottom of the buttock?"

– Janet Williams

Make it the length that is most comfortable for the individual wearing the shawl. I like my garter stitch working shawls to be large so I can tie them in the back and have my hands free. I like my dressy shawls to come down to my wrist.

– Myrna

You have the opportunity to determine the length of your shawl by selecting the appropriate number of pattern repeats you knit.

In determining the length of your shawl, do keep in mind the geometrics of the pattern you have selected. If you are knitting on a lace border, you will get the best looking shawl if the pattern of the center back panel is completed on the recommended row. By so doing, the lace pattern of the shawl will match up with the pattern in the lace border.

> *"As I was knitting and trying to determine length and whether I had enough yarn, I questioned whether I could stop halfway through the pattern repeat, as that did complete a triangle. Luckily, I didn't because the edging really is a continuity of the pattern, so the instructions for the row on which to end really need to be followed."*
>
> *– Yvonne Eyer*

Planning Your Shawl

Select the yarn and pattern stitch for your shawl and determine the needle you will use (page 9, "Knitting a Swatch to Check the Fabric and Determine Rows Per Inch/2.5 Centimeters – A Necessary Exercise"). Decide how large you wish your finished shawl to be. Determine how many pattern repeats you must knit in the back panel to reach your desired length.

Because of the nature of the lace patterns used and the increase shaping of a Faroese shawl, one full pattern repeat in the back panel is equal in number of rows to what appears to be two pattern repeats in the side panels.

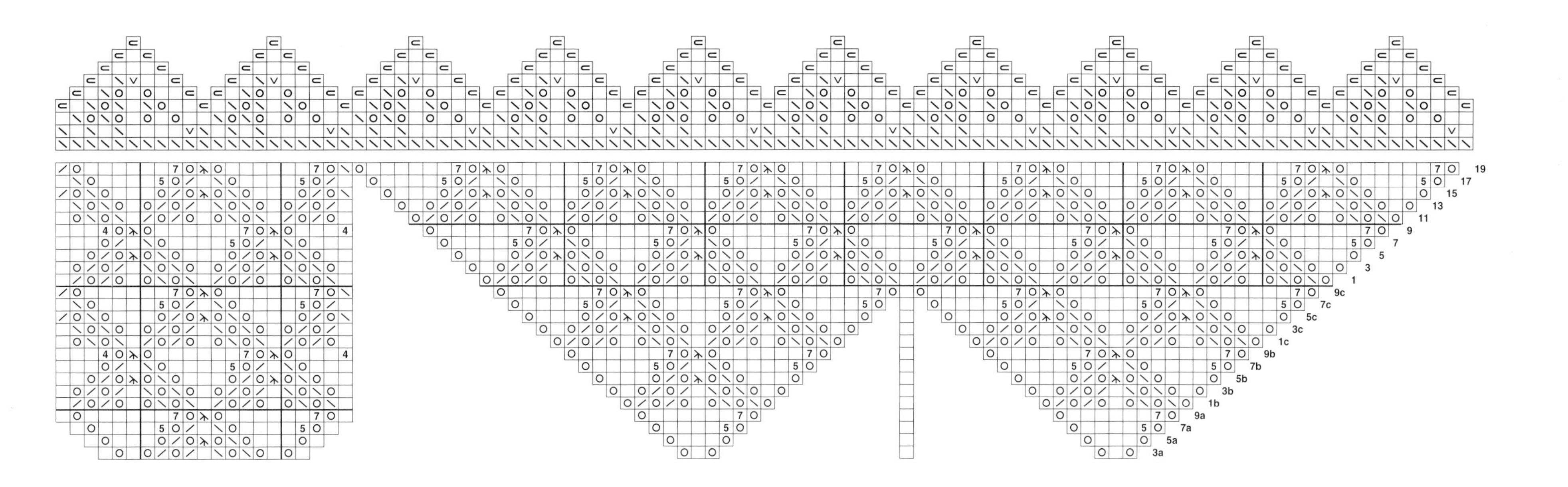

Illustration 2: *Although one full repeat of the Barbara pattern consists of 20 rows, because of the increase shaping used for these shawls, row 1 of the side panels is the same as row 11, row 3 is the same as row 13, et seq. By ending your shawl after working row 20, the knit-on lace border will complete the smiling diamond.*

Is that Yarn in My Stash Enough? Determining the Amount of Yarn Needed

If you are using a yarn different from those used in this book for the shawl, you likely will enjoy your knitting most if you determine, before you begin, that you indeed have a sufficient amount of that now discontinued yarn to complete the shawl you have selected. The amount of yarn you will need depends upon the fabric you produce by the needle size and yarn weight you have selected and the size shawl you wish to make. Now that you have made those decisions on the yarn to use, the needle size, and the pattern stitch, you can estimate the amount of yarn you will need to complete your shawl.

Method #1: Compare the wpi/2.5cm and yards per ounce or meters per 50 grams of your stash yarn with the yarn used for the shawl you have selected. How different are they? If your yarn is heavier, or if you wish to make a larger shawl, you will need more yarn by weight. If there is much difference in wpi or yardage, go to method #2.

Method #2: Using the yarn you have selected and the appropriate needle size for that yarn, cast on the number of stitches needed for a nice sized swatch which does not include a seed stitch border. From the last stitch you cast on, measure out five yards or five meters of yarn and tie a slip knot. Knit a swatch, in pattern, until you reach the slip knot. (Hint: Place the slip knot on your little finger when you begin knitting to insure that you don't knit past it.) Now, determine the number of stitches you knit from that length of yarn.

Next, determine the approximate number of stitches in your finished shawl by using the charts and the following formula.

R = number of rows in the side panel after shoulder increases have been completed

X = number of stitches in the first row of the side panel after shoulder increases have been completed

The number of stitches in the side panel in question = R times (R plus X -2) = $R(R+X-2)$

To the above you must add the number of stitches in the back panel, the number of stitches in the side panels for the shoulder shaping, the stitches in the back neck band, and the stitches in the border you have selected.

Have you done all that? If so, you now know approximately how many yards or meters you need to complete your shawl. Do you think I have ever used this formula? Absolutely not, I just happily knit away, knowing that I will be happy with my shawl no matter how large or small it turns out. ☺

Chapter 5. Techniques

Casting On – the Provisional Cast-On

The American College Dictionary defines "provisional" as "pertaining to or of the nature of a temporary arrangement." Every shawl and almost every scarf in this book begins with a provisional cast-on, a technique for casting on that I believe is very helpful in "properly practicing" the knitting of these shawls and scarves. This cast-on, which is temporary, is known by various names, with different methods for accomplishing the same purpose.

The "Stahman Method" of Provisional Cast-On

Use cotton waste yarn of a weight a bit heavier than the yarn you are using for your shawl or scarf and a crochet hook larger than the needle with which you are knitting. Crochet a chain of about six stitches more than the number of stitches you are to cast on. Cut your yarn and pull the last stitch through the loop to fasten. Turn the crocheted chain so that the "bumps" are on top - facing you. Using your knitting needle and the yarn you are using to knit your shawl or scarf, insert your needle in the second bump and pick up a stitch. Continue in this manner until you have "knit up" the necessary number of stitches for beginning your shawl or scarf. Properly done, this cast-on can later be removed by "unzipping" like the top of a sugar or feed sack once the waste yarn is removed from the very first stitch.

Illustration 3: *A crocheted chain.*

Illustration 4: *The crocheted chain, showing the bumps used for the provisional cast-on.*

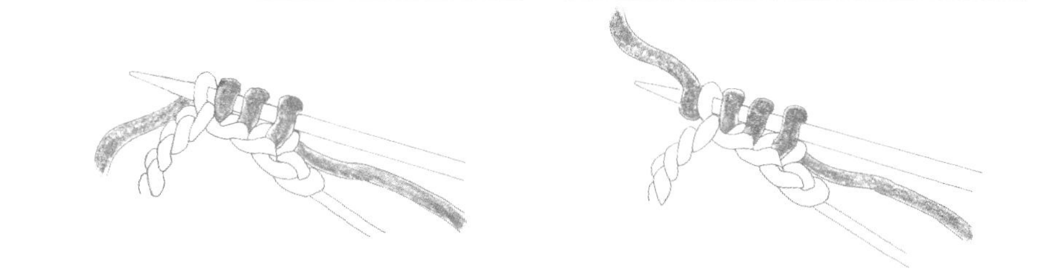

Illustration 5: *The provisional cast-on using the right hand.*

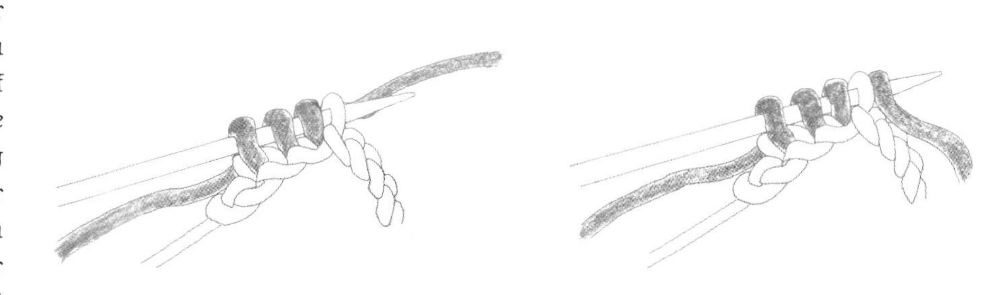

Illustration 6: *The provisional cast-on using the left hand.*

Other Methods of Provisional Cast-On

Detailed directions for different methods of provisional cast-on are found in the following books:

Hiatt, June Hemmons, *The Principles of Knitting*, Simon and Schuster, Inc., New York (1988), called "stranded cast-on," pages 138-139.

Stanley, Montse, *The Handknitter's Handbook*, David & Charles Craft (1990), called "provisional cast-on," with directions for three variations – "two-strand provisional cast-on," "crochet provisional cast-on," and "looping provisional cast-on," pages 68-70.

Vogue Knitting, Pantheon Books, New York (1989), called "Open cast-on," page 28.

Zimmermann, Elizabeth, *Knitting Without Tears*, Charles Scribner's Sons, New York (1971), called "Invisible casting-on," pages 20-22.

The Chain Selvedge – Always Slipping the First Stitch and Always Knitting the Last

The selvedge finish of your shawl and your scarf is very important, as the selvedges grace your front as you wear your shawl or scarf. My favorite finish is the "chain" selvedge. A "chain" selvedge is obtained by always slipping the first stitch of every row as if to purl, and always knitting the last stitch of every row. Slipping as if to purl is done by holding the yarn to the front of the needle and slipping the stitch from the left needle to the right needle as if to purl (Illustration 7), then lifting the yarn up and putting it to the back by placing it between your needles, pulling rather firmly (Illustration 8).

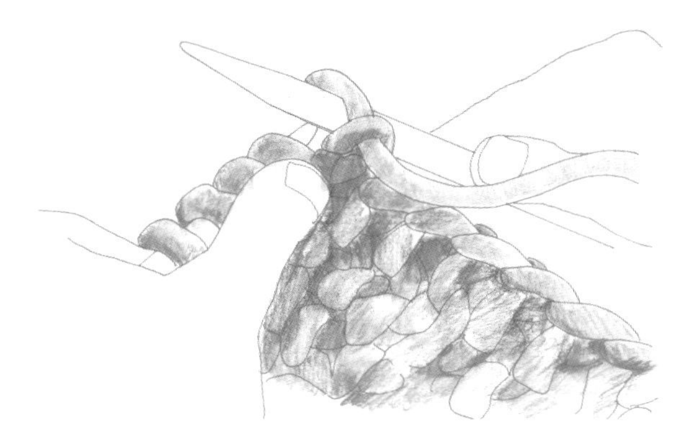

Illustration 7: *With your yarn in front, put the needle into the first stitch of every row as if to purl.*

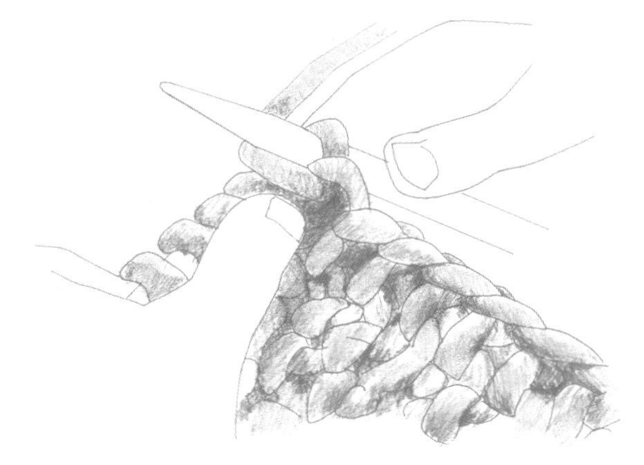

Illustration 8: *After slipping the first stitch as if to purl, move the yarn to the back of your work by placing it between your needles.*

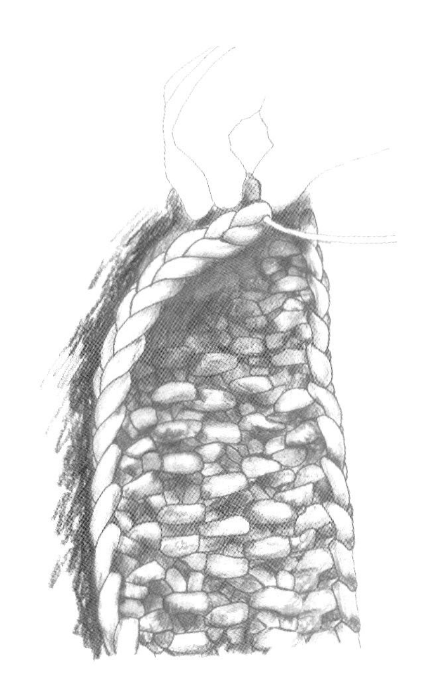

Illustration 9: *A uniform chain is developed on the selvedge by always slipping the first stitch as if to purl and always knitting the last stitch.*

Slipping the first stitch of each row as if to purl, with the yarn in front and always knitting the last stitch of the row gives a nice "chain" look to the selvedges (Illustration 9). Work on developing an appropriate tension in using this technique. This stitch should be neither so loose that it is sloppy nor so tight that it distorts the edge. Practice this selvedge technique on your swatch.

Neck Band/Front Border Selection – Knitter's Choice: Garter Stitch, Seed Stitch or Mock Ribbing

Every shawl begins with the back neck band border, which turns into the front borders. I refer to this as the neck band/front border. All shawls done with a garter stitch base are designed with a garter stitch neck band/front border. For the Faroese lace shawls worked in stockinette stitch, I have provided instructions using my favorite neck band/front border, the seed stitch border. If you wish, you may adapt the patterns by using a mock-rib, I-cord, or garter stitch neck band/front border.

Beginning Your Shawl with a Garter Stitch Neck Band/Front Border

Cast on: Using a provisional cast-on (page 13), cast on six stitches.

Set-up row 1: Knit across.

All following rows: Slip the first stitch as if to purl, knit across.

Knit as many rows as specified in the pattern. This is equal to twice the number of stitches to be picked up for the first row of the shawl, plus three.

Beginning Your Shawl with a Seed Stitch Neck Band/Front Border

Cast on: Using a provisional cast-on (page 13), cast on seven stitches.

Set-up row: K2, p1, k1, p1, k2.

All following rows: Slip the first stitch as if to purl, k1, p1, k1, p1, k2.

Repeat the above row for as many rows as specified in the pattern. This is equal to twice the number of stitches to be picked up for the first row of the shawl, plus three.

Beginning Your Shawl with a Mock Rib Neck Band/Front Border

Cast on: Using a provisional cast-on (page 13), cast on seven stitches.

Set-up row 1: K2, (p1, k1) two times, k1.

Set-up row 2: With the yarn in front, slip the first stitch as if to purl, p 5, k1.

Row 1: With the yarn in front, slip the first stitch as if to purl, (k1, p1) two times, k2.

Row 2: With the yarn in front, slip the first stitch as if to purl, p 5, k1.

Repeat the above two rows for as many rows as specified in the pattern. This is equal to twice the number of stitches to be picked up for the first row of the shawl, plus three. End after completing row 1.

Ensuring that the Back Panel is the Correct Size for a Well-Fitting Shawl

For the best fitting shawl, the length of the neck band should equal 40% to 45% of the shoulder-to-shoulder measurement of the intended wearer. If your neck band is less than this measurement, you may wish to change your yarn, your needle size or adjust the number of stitches in the back panel. See Chapter 8 for assistance in customizing your pattern.

Picking up Neck Band Stitches for the Body of Your Shawl

By always slipping the first stitch of every row as if to purl, and always knitting the last stitch, when you work the neck band of your shawl you creat a "chain" selvedge. Each link of your chain covers two rows of the worked border. The links of your chain are what you pick up to begin the first row of the body of your shawl.

Picking up by Purling

This is the method likely most comfortable for right-handed people. Holding your knitting so that:

a. the stitches are on your right needle,
b. the neck band you have just knit is to the left,
c. the yarn "tail" from the beginning of your knitting is at the top, and
d. the yarn you are knitting with is at the top right of your work,

place your needle, from back to front, into the second link of the selvedge chain and purl one stitch. Continue picking up by purling the specified number of stitches.

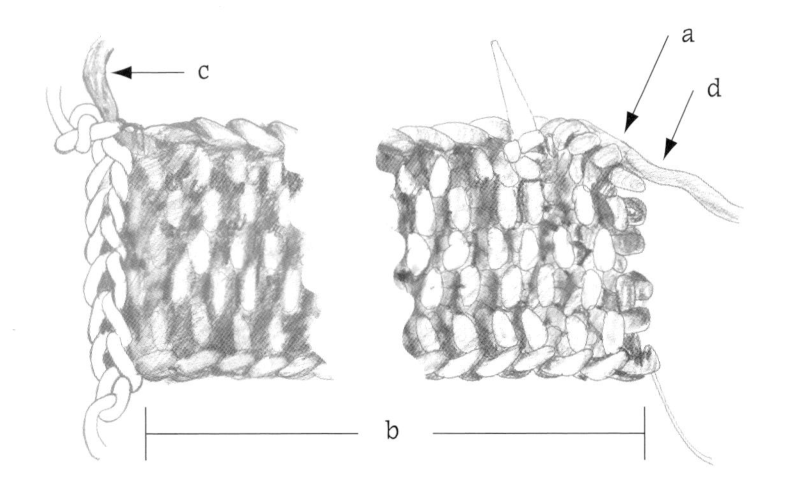

Illustration 10*: Using the right hand for picking up, as if to purl, the neck band stitches for the body of your shawl.*

Picking up by Knitting

Although I knit "right-handed," I am left-handed. This is the method I use and believe likely to be most comfortable for left-handed people. Holding your knitting so that:

a. the stitches are on your left needle,
b. the neck band you have just knit is to the right,
c. the yarn "tail" from the beginning of your knitting is at the top, and
d. the yarn you are knitting with is at the top left of your work,

place your needle, from front to back, into the second link of the selvedge chain and knit one stitch. Continue picking up by knitting the specified number of stitches.

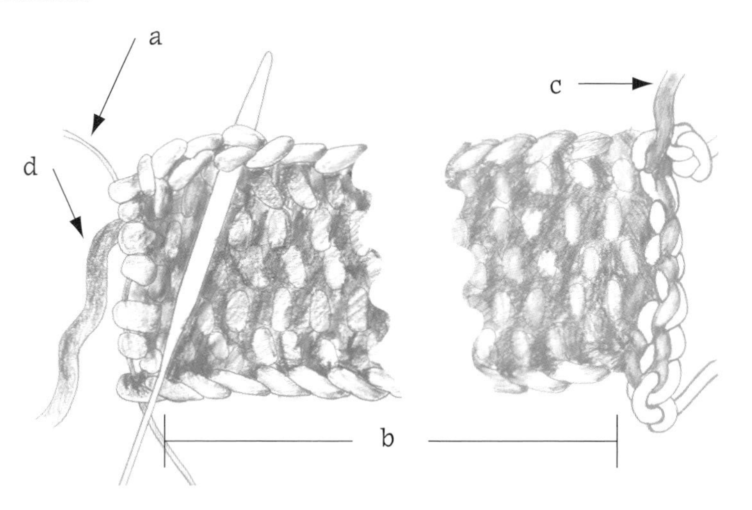

Illustration 11: *Using the left hand for picking up, as if to knit, the neck band stitches for the body of your shawl.*

> *"When picking up the stitches along the edge of the neck, I found it more comfortable to 'knit-up' the stitches and make the next row a wrong side set-up row, beginning the pattern on the second working row."*
>
> *– Karen Raz*

When "knitting up" or "purling up" the stitches, it is "knitters choice" as to whether to pick up both parts of the chain link or just one part of the link. When using lace weight or fingering weight yarn, I generally knit through both parts of the link; when using sport weight, medium weight, or bulky yarn I generally knit through one part of the link – the "top" part. Experiment and see which you prefer.

Illustration 12: *Picking up by purling through both parts of the chain selvedge.*

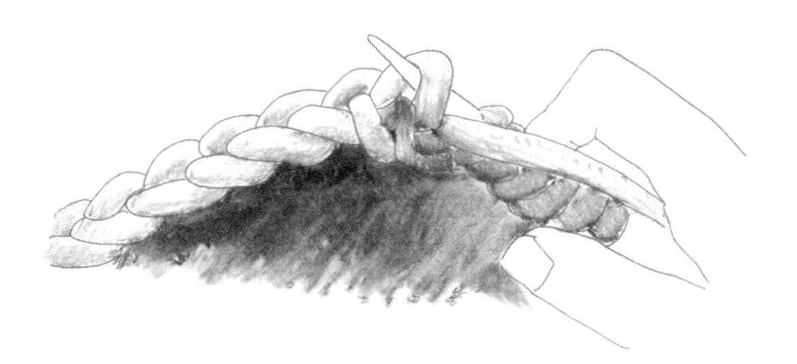

Illustration 13: *Picking up by purling through just one part of the chain selvedge.*

In "knitting up" or "purling up" these stitches, skip the first link of the chain, and begin by using the second link of the chain. Likewise, don't pick up the last link of the chain. If you have knit the correct number of rows, you should have on your needle the stitches from the neck band you worked (6 stitches if doing a garter stitch; 7 stitches if doing a seed stitch), followed by the number of stitches you were to pick up for the first row of your shawl. The waste yarn holding the stitches created by the provisional cast-on should be hanging down from the needle.

Recovering Stitches from the Provisional Cast-On

Using the free end of your circular knitting needle, carefully insert the tip of your needle into the first stitch of the provisional cast-on, going from the back to the front in the same direction that the waste yarn will flow when pulled out. Remove the waste yarn from that first stitch. This makes one twist in that first stitch as you pick it up with your needle, gives you your first stitch and prevents that first stitch from being too loopy.

The waste yarn should now unzip from the remaining stitches like the string of a sugar or flour sack. Carefully remove the waste yarn, picking up each live stitch before it is released from the waste yarn.

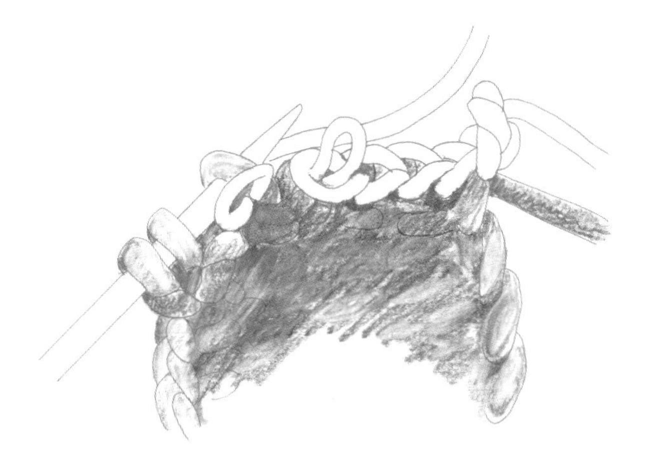

Illustration 14: *Picking up a live stitch as it is released from the waste yarn.*

Notice that the stitches you have just picked up are 1/2 stitch off. This is because you are now knitting those stitches in the opposite direction. If you are using a garter stitch border you should now have six stitches on your left needle; if you are using a seed stitch border, you should have seven stitches on your left needle.

Hold your work so that the stitches from the provisional cast-on are on the needle to your left, with the needle to your right holding the neck border piece with all the stitches you have either knit up or purled up. The private/wrong side of your shawl will be facing you.

Knit together the first two stitches that are on your left needle. If you are using a garter stitch border, knit the remaining four stitches; if you are using a seed stitch border, p1, k1, p1, k2. Turn; the public/right side of your work should now be facing you. You are now ready to begin the first row of the body of your shawl.

> *"I thought that when you pick up from a provisional cast-on you always have one fewer stitch."*
>
> *– Shelda Eggers*
>
> *If you carefully follow the instructions as written you will pick up the same number of stitches you cast on. What some would regard as a half-stitch becomes the very first stitch you put on your needle as you begin to unzip the waste yarn.*
>
> *– Myrna*

Beginning the Body of Your Shawl

Shawls Worked from Charts

Go to the instructions for the shawl you have selected and Chapter 6, "Knitting from a Chart," for detailed instructions on how to proceed.

Shawls Worked from Written Instructions

Go to the written instructions for the shawl you have selected.

Increasing

Many different methods of increasing exist. The selection of the increase method depends upon the result desired. The increase method given in the pattern instructions is the one I have selected to give the result I determined best for that pattern. If you prefer a different result, feel free to select your own method of increasing; do realize your selection of increase method will affect the final look of your shawl.

Yarnover Increases

The four prominent increases for which Faroese-shaped shawls are known are done with a simple yarnover (yo) increase. Put the yarn under your needle from back to front and over, creating a new stitch. On the return row be sure that you do not twist the stitch you created with your yarnover.

Yoke Increases - Twisted Yarnover Increases[6] *- m1R and m1L*

For the increases in the yoke of the garter stitch shawls, I recommend the twisted yarnover increases. These increases are made by using the working yarn and making a twisted yarnover. For the finest finished look, you will want to make "mirror image" increases. Elizabeth Zimmermann in *Knitting Without Tears* calls this a "Make One" increase, explaining:

> *This is quite simply achieved by putting a firm backward loop over the right needle (A). The result is the same as that accomplished by picking up the running thread between the stitches and knitting into the back of it (twisting it), which produces the effect of the stitch having been made a row sooner. I think my way is faster, and anyway I like it, and I'm used to it. It is the best increase for pairing that I know, as it is a totally separate stitch, made independently of any other and standing all by itself between its neighbors. If you are a perfectionist, you may make the loop as above for the first increase of a pair, and then reverse it for the second (B) — then your shaping will be absolutely symmetrical. But this is, as I said, sheer perfectionism. Try it out and see if you think it is worth it.*

I definitely think it is worth it. My way of doing it is to use my right thumb to make a loop and place it on the needle; knit one stitch; then I make a loop using my left thumb, which results in twisting the yarn so that it is the mirror image of my first increase. Call one m1R; call the other m1L. As long as you use the mirror images it makes no difference which one you do first.

[6] June Hemmons Hiatt, in *The Principles of Knitting*, page 75, calls this the "left crossed yarnover increase" and "right crossed yarnover increase." Montse Stanley, in *The Handknitter's Handbook*, page 99, refers to this as the "closed eyelet increase."

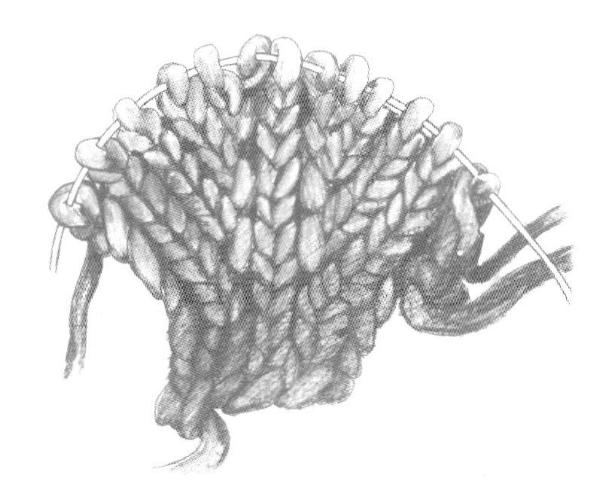

Illustration 15: *Mirror image twisted yarn over increases, separated by one stitch. These are referred to as m1R and m1L in the shawl instructions..*

When working the new stitches on the following row, always work into the right leg of the loop; for half of these increases, the right leg will be to the front of the needle. For the other half, the right leg will be to the back of the needle. By working into the right leg of the loop, you will avoid putting an extra twist into the new stitch you made in the previous row.

Illustration 16: *When purling on the return row, be sure to put your needle in the correct "leg" of the m1L yarnover increase to avoid adding an extra twist.*

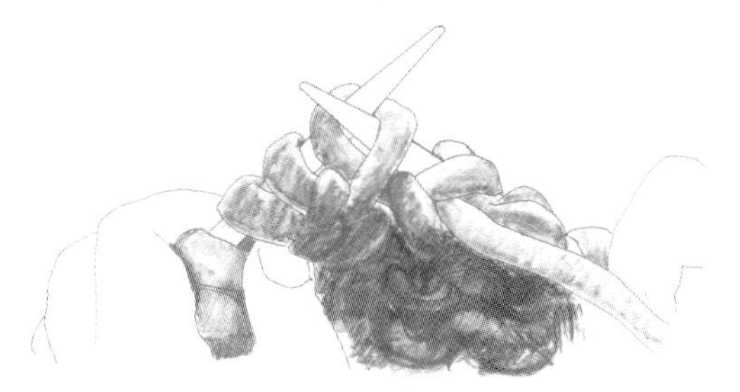

Illustration 17: *When purling on the return row, be sure to put your needle in the correct "leg" of the m1R yarnover increase to avoid adding an extra twist.*

Splicing Yarns for Smooth Sailing

The best way to avoid problems in joining yarn is to knit from a cone! But even then, a knot is sometimes encountered, which must be removed and the ends nicely joined. When working with wool, I prefer to splice the ends of my yarn. When approximately 10 inches of the working yarn remain, separate this 10-inch length into two separate plys. Do the same for the first 10-inch length of yarn from the new skein to be joined, beginning the separation 10 inches in, rather than at the end of the yarn. Now overlap, right next to the last stitch knit, one section of the working yarn with one section of the yarn from the skein you are beginning. Re-ply, by wrapping one strand around the other for about six inches, plying the fibers for a fiber just like the yarn you are using. This leaves four "tails" hanging out. Resume knitting, knitting up the six-inch section of yarn you have spliced. Leave the "tails" hanging for now. Later go back and carefully weave each of the four tails into the fabric for a few stitches, each in a different direction. Clip off the remainder of the tails.

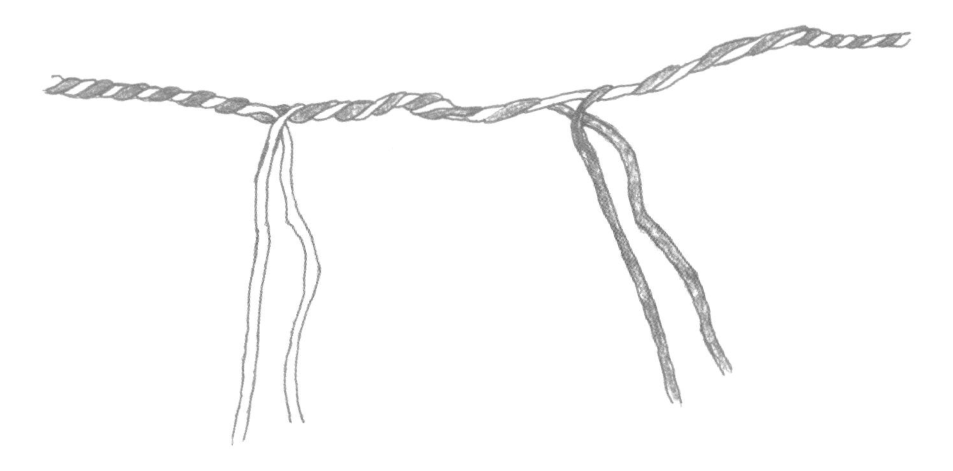

Illustration 18: *A completed splicing of the two ends of your yarn. Be sure to splice in the middle of a row.*

Using Stitch Markers

I use stitch markers on my needle between the neck band/front borders and between each of the lace panel sections. My favorites are the small round rubber stitch markers and the elegant silver rings now available, with a fine thread tail to prevent the marker from migrating to the incorrect side of the yarnover.

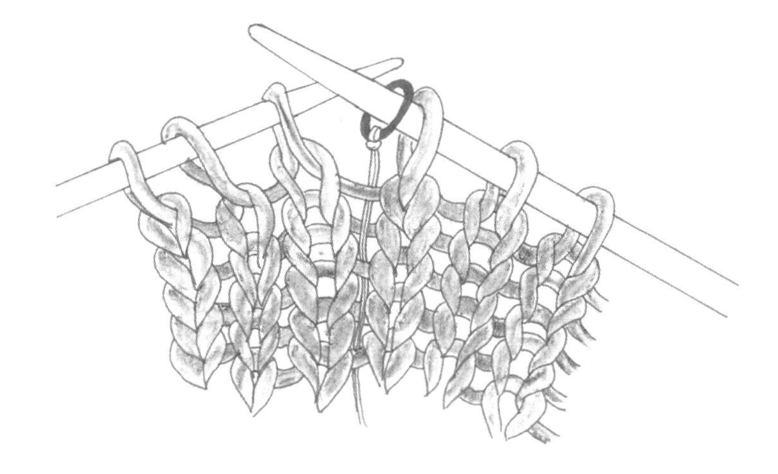

Illustration 19: *Attaching a length of thread to an O-ring stitch marker helps to keep the O-ring stitch marker from moving between the stitches and from jumping off your needle.*

Bottom Border Selection

Bottom Border Same as Neck Band/Front Border

Do you wish to have an easy finish to your shawl? If so, finish with the same pattern used for the neck band/front border – seed stitch, garter stitch, mock ribbing or I-cord.

Knitting on a Lace Border

If you wish to have an elegant and more challenging finish, knit on a lace border. For this you will use Chapter 7 and Chart E of the shawl you are knitting.

Bind-Off Selections

For the Seamen's scarves and the shawls for which you choose not to knit a lace border, I have two favorite bind-offs: One I call the knit-in-pattern bind-off; the second I call the Icelandic bind-off, which is a must for the Marialis shawls and scarves. The curves of the Feather and Fan, also known as Old Shale, pattern used for the Marialis shawls and scarf need the stretch of the Icelandic bind-off. When an I-cord border is used, the I-cord bind-off should also be used.

Knit-in-Pattern Bind-Off

For shawls and scarves knit with a seed stitch bottom border, except for Marialis, the knit-in-pattern bind-off works great, as it produces a finish very similar to the chain selvedge produced by slipping the first stitch of every row. For the shawls and scarves which are completed with a seed stitch bottom border, do the following: On the last row, slip the first stitch as if to purl, kl, psso, *pl, pass the knit stitch over, kl, pass the purled stitch over, repeating from *.

Icelandic Bind-Off

Eugen Beugler introduced me to this bind-off he learned from a book of Icelandic shawls so I call it the Icelandic bind-off. This is my version of this bind-off. With all of the stitches on your left needle and the yarn in back, insert your right needle through the first stitch on your left needle, catch second stitch and knit the front loop of it, slipping both stitches off your left needle – this leaves one stitch on your right needle. Make sure this stitch is fairly loose. Move this loose stitch from your right needle and place it back on your left needle and repeat the process you have just completed. This gives a very nice, somewhat stretchy, bind-off. With very little practice this becomes one step, which is simply knitting the second stitch on the left needle through the first stitch and dropping it off. For my right needle I generally use a needle two sizes larger than the needle I have used for knitting the shawl or scarf I am binding off.

What you call "Icelandic" bind-off I learned from my grandma, who was from Czechoslovakia and she learned from her mum. Oma called it "elastischer Abkettrand fuer Rollkragen" (elastic bind-off for polo necks). I use it regularly on polo neck and crew neck jumpers.
– Petra Doerfling

I-Cord Bind-Off

To work the I-cord bind-off, you will work one row of I-cord for each stitch being bound off. When using a four stitch I-cord, knit the first three stitches, slip the fourth stitch, knit one stitch from the final row of your shawl or scarf, pass the slipped stitch over. For more detailed information on I-cord, refer to the books by Elizabeth Zimmermann and Meg Swansen, the experts on I-cord.

Correcting Mistakes

There may be a time when you realize that you forgot to do a yarnover, you knit two together when you should have simply knit two, or made a similar error. Don't panic. It is sometimes possible to correct such a mistake with less drastic means than tearing out, "frogging," "tinking," or whatever you call your "unknitting." The beauty of knitting with Haneke merino and merino blends or any fine wool is that it is very forgiving.

- Did you forget to do a yarnover in the pattern a row or two below? If you are knitting with wool, just pick up the yarn where you forgot your yo. You just created the yo you previously missed.

- Did you, 10 rows down, forget to slip the first stitch as if to purl? Get your crochet hook and your courage. Drop that selvedge stitch down to the row below the mistake. Using your crochet hook, "chain-up" the selvedge stitches, twisting once with each stitch.

- Did you make a "big goof" in just one pattern repeat eight rows earlier? If you are courageous, I suggest you try dropping down as many stitches as are involved in the mistake and reknitting them. This is not a task for the faint-hearted.
  - Determine the number of stitches you must work with to correct the error.
  - Isolate those stitches by removing them from your working needle and putting a point protector on each end of your working needle.
  - Get out two of your double-pointed needles of the same size as the needle you are using for your shawl.
  - Take out (drop) all the stitches you have isolated to the row above the row with the mistake.
  - Carefully take out the stitches from the row with the mistake; with one double-pointed needle, pick up each stitch as it is taken out.
  - With the public side of your shawl facing you and using the second double pointed needle, carefully select the correct strand of yarn for the row and reknit your stitches, one row at a time, while carefully following the pattern. **Good luck!**

As I was knitting on the lace border of the GS Catharina shawl, I discovered that while knitting the back center panel my marker had gotten off by 1/2 a pattern – I had repeated rows 1-18 twice, so instead of having a smiling diamond I had a rather strange design. Rather than tearing out the last 36 rows of my entire shawl, I "unknit" the 36 rows of the back center panel and reknit according to the directions above. It was a challenge – but was better than reknitting the one-half of the lace border and the last 36 rows of the entire shawl!

Chapter 6. Knitting from a Chart

I believe that knitting lace generally is easiest when done from a chart. If you are not comfortable knitting from a chart, you will be happy to know that the Marialis and GS Fenna shawls and several of the Seamen's scarves have no charts. Many scarf patterns have both charts and written instructions.

You may wish to be adventurous and try GS Gracie or GS Catharina, which can be done with just one repeat of a charted pattern. If you have never knit from a chart I invite you to do so. I hope that you will learn to enjoy knitting lace from charts.

Establishing a Rhythm – The Music of Lace Knitting

Every lace pattern in this book consists of a sequence of repeats of a group of knitting maneuvers. Look for the repeats and discover the rhythm of the pattern you have selected. Once you get the rhythm in your mind and fingers, the pattern flows like great music.

Symbols

The charts consist of rectangles which contain symbols. A blank rectangle means knit one. A number within a rectangle tells you how many plain knit stitches are shown; thus, you don't have to count the blank rectangles. Whenever there are three or fewer plain knit stitches, no number will be shown. In the majority of charts, whenever there are four or more plain knit stitches, a number is inserted in the first rectangle.

The symbols are

(blank) = k = knit one

O = yo = yarn over

– = p = purl one

∩ = slip as if to purl with yarn in front

/ = k2tog = knit two stitches together

\ = ssk = slip one stitch as if to knit, slip the second stitch as if to knit, knit the two stitches together

ℓ = twisted stitch = knit into the back of the stitch

ℓ/ = twisted stitch k2tog

ℓ\ = twisted stitch ssk

< > = twisted yarnover = make one stitch with a left thumb loop (mlL) or make one stitch with a right thumb loop (mlR); when these are used in close proximity, be sure to make mirror-image thumb loops; see page 19

⟍ Slip the first stitch onto a cable needle and hold in front, knit the next two stitches, knit the stitch from the cable needle.

⟋ Put two stitches on a cable needle and hold in back, knit the next stitch, knit the two stitches from the cable needle.

⋌ = 3-to-1 = k3tog = knit three together

⋋ = 3-to-1 = Sl1-k2tog-psso = slip the first stitch as if to knit, knit two together, slip the first stitch over the k2tog. This method produces a "crossed" look, which reminds me of chicken feet.

↑ = 3-to-1 = slip the first two stitches at the same time as if to knit, knit the third stitch, slip the two slipped stitches over. This gives a very vertical look to the pattern.

= the border stitches, knitter's choice of seed stitch, garter stitch, mock ribbing, or I-cord

B5 = the five border stitches when working in garter stitch

- B5 at the beginning of the row when knitting a shawl in garter stitch = slip the first stitch as if to purl, k 4
- B5 at the end of the row when knitting a shawl in garter stitch = k5
- B5 at the beginning of the row when knitting a garter stitch Seamen's scarf = slip the first stitch as if to purl, k3, k2tog, yo
- B5 at the end of the row when knitting a garter stitch Seamen's scarf = yo, ssk, k4

B6 = the six border stitches when working in seed stitch

- B6 at the beginning of the row when working in seed stitch is slip the first stitch as if to purl, kl, pl, kl, pl, kl
- B6 at the end of the row when working in seed stitch is kl, pl, kl, pl, k2

m1R = increase one stitch with a twisted yarnover increase; see page 19

m1L = increase one stitch with a twisted yarnover increase of a mirror image of the mlR; see page 19

Photo 8: This close-up of two Robert scarves shows the result of two different ways of working the 3-to-1 decrease. The scarf on the left has a crossed look, and was done with the sl1-k2tog-psso method. The scarf on the right has a much more vertical look, having been done with the slip the first two stitches at the same time as if to knit, knit the third stitch and slip the two slipped stitches over.

Knitting Terms

Knitting to and fro: Working the stitches first from your left needle to your right needle, which is sometimes referred to as right-handed knitting; then, instead of turning your work, work the stitches from your right needle to your left needle, which is sometimes referred to either as left-handed knitting or knitting back backwards.

Public side: The side of your knitting which will be seen when the item is worn, which is sometimes referred to as the "right side" or the "outside."

Private side: The side of your knitting which will not be seen when the item is worn, which is sometimes referred to as the "wrong side" or the "inside."

Work in pattern: When instructed to work an even-numbered row in pattern, work the stitches as they present themselves – i.e., knit the stitches that look like knit stitches from the side you are looking at and purl the stitches that look like purl stitches from the side you are looking at.

Knitting from a Chart

Enlarge the Chart as Necessary

Permission is granted for making a working copy of the charts for the shawl or scarf you are knitting. I recommend enlarging the charts for ease of reading. I like to place the paper copy of the chart on a metal craft board and insert both in a plastic sleeve. I use a magnetic strip, placing it over the plastic sleeve and above the pattern row I am working. Another great idea, offered by a knitting friend, it to use a metal music stand to hold your chart and use a magnetic strip in a similar fashion.

A knitting chart is a picture of the "public" or "right" side of your knitting.

> *I copied the charts and had them laminated. This kept my charts neat, and I could write on them with wash-off pens or use white correction tape to mark my rows as I completed them.*
>
> *– Gayle Surrette*

Learning to Read Your Knitting

Learn to "read" your knitting as you read your chart – the public/right side of your knitting looks just like the "picture" on the chart. Once you learn to read your knitting and knit from a chart, it will be much easier to locate a mistake you may have made.

Charts Showing Every Other Row

Most, but not all, charted patterns in this book have a "plain" row between the pattern rows. For the patterns which have a plain row between the pattern rows, only the pattern rows are shown, and all pattern rows shown have an uneven number, i.e., 1, 3, 5, etc. For these patterns the chart is read exactly as your knitting proceeds. Begin with row 1 at the bottom right corner and read to the left. Work row 2 as instructed. For row 3 move up one row of the chart, and again begin at the right and read to the left. To keep track of the row you are knitting, use a metal board and a magnetic strip, and place your magnetic strip above the row you are working.

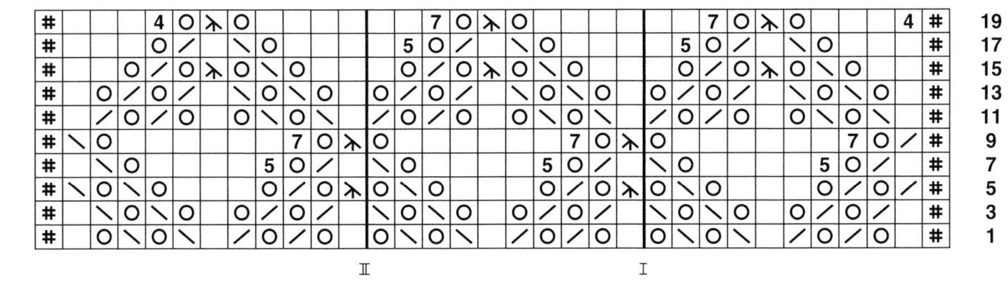

Illustration 20: *The chart of the Barbara stitch pattern, which has a plain row between the pattern rows, shows only the odd-numbered rows.*

The first five rows of the Barbara Seamen's scarf are:

Row 1: B6 (which, at the beginning of the row when doing a seed stitch border, is slip the first stitch as if to purl, k1, p1, k1, p1, k1), (k1, yo, k2tog, yo, k2tog, k1, ssk, yo, ssk, yo) three times, k1, B6 (which, at the end of the row when doing a seed stitch border, is k1, p1, k1, p1, k1).

Row 2 and all even-numbered rows: B6, purl across, B6.

Row 3: B6, (k1, k2tog, yo, k2tog, yo, k1, yo, ssk, yo, ssk) three times, k1, B6.

Row 5: B6, k2tog, (yo, k2tog, yo, k3, yo, ssk, yo, sl1-k2tog-psso) three times, ending the third repeat with ssk rather than sl1-k2tog-psso, B6.

Charts Showing Every Row

Several Seamen's scarf patterns have every row charted. These charts show every row from the public/right side of your scarf.

When knitting from a chart which shows every row of the pattern, the even-numbered rows are worked reading the chart from left to right AND working the stitches opposite of how they are shown. When you are working an even-numbered row, you are working on the "private/wrong" side of your garment: what is shown as a purl stitch on the chart will actually be knit and what is shown as a knit stitch on the chart will actually be purled.

The even-numbered rows are (a) numbered on the left of the chart and (b) shaded gray to help you remember (a) to knit from left to right and (b) to work the stitches opposite to that shown. You will discover that many of the patterns are mirror images, so the chart reads the same from the left to the right as from the right to the left; but, you must remember to work the stitches of the shaded, even-numbered rows opposite to that shown.

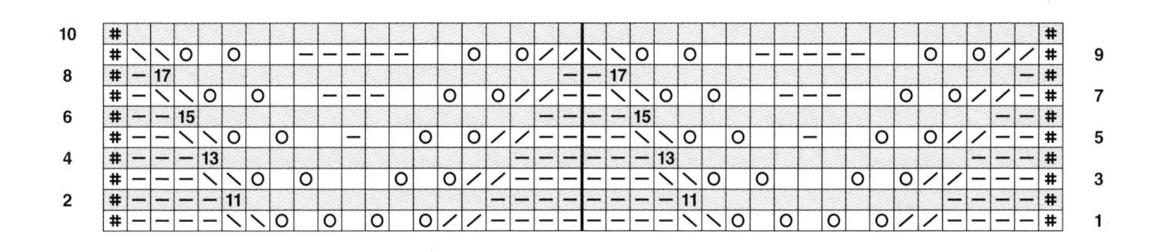

Illustration 21: *Every row of the Ginger Seamen's scarf is charted.*

Row 1: [B6, which at the beginning of the row is slip the first stitch as if to purl, k1, p1, k1, p1, k1] [(purl 4, k2tog, k2tog, yo, k1, yo, k1, yo, k1, yo, ssk, ssk p4) twice] [B6, which at the end of the row is k1, p1, k1, p1, k2].

Row 2: B6, (k4, p 11, k4) twice, B6.

Row 3: B6, (p3, k2tog, k2tog, yo, k1, yo, k3, yo, k1, yo, ssk, ssk, p3) twice, B6.

Row 4: B6, (k3, p 13, k3) twice, B6.

Row 5: B6, (p2, k2tog, k2tog, yo, k1, yo, k2, p1, k2, yo, k1, yo, ssk, ssk, p2) twice, B6.

Row 6: B6, k2, p 15, k2) twice, B6.

Row 7: B6, (p1, k2tog, k2tog, yo, k1, yo, k2, p3, k2, yo, k1, yo, ssk, ssk, p1) twice, B6.

Row 8: B6, (k1, p 17, k1) twice, B6.

Row 9: B6, (k2tog, k2tog, yo, k1, yo, k2, p5, k2, yo, k1, yo, ssk, ssk) twice, B6.

Row 10: B6, p 38, B6.

Using the Charts for a Faroese-Shaped Shawl

For each lace Faroese-shaped shawl, five charts are provided with the shawl instructions.

- Chart A is the "building block," showing one repeat of the lace pattern when knit as a rectangle.
- Chart B is a triangular-shaped swatch.
- Chart C is one side panel.
- Chart D is the back panel.
- Chart S is the scarf.

Chart E for the lace border is provided in chapter 7.

The charts do not include the neck band/front border; remember to work this border in the pattern you have selected as you begin each and every row and as you end each and every row.

Although there are separate charts for the side panels and the back panel, both Chart C and Chart D are used in knitting every pattern row of your shawl. Please note that the whole of Chart C is used twice in working your shawl. Work using the whole of Chart C for the first side panel, then use Chart D for the back panel, and then use the whole of Chart C again, this time for the second side panel.

You will begin using Charts C and D after you have picked up the stitches for your shawl ("Picking up Neck Band Stitches for the Body of Your Shawl," page 16). Every shawl pattern includes written instructions for working the first two rows of the body of the shawl.

The hardest part was staring at the shoulder shaping in the chart. That single column of stitches confused me, and I stared at it a long time trying to figure out what I was supposed to do. Finally, I took a deep breath and just followed the chart and the stitches worked out. It was so simple. When in doubt, just follow the chart — the stitches will work out.

The only problems I ran into were of my own making when I tried to read into the instructions more than was given. Once I took a deep breath and did as I was told it all fell into place and I'd have an ah-hah experience — so that's what she meant. Then I'd re-read the directions and sure enough, it was so plain that I couldn't figure out what was so confusing.

– Gayle Surrette

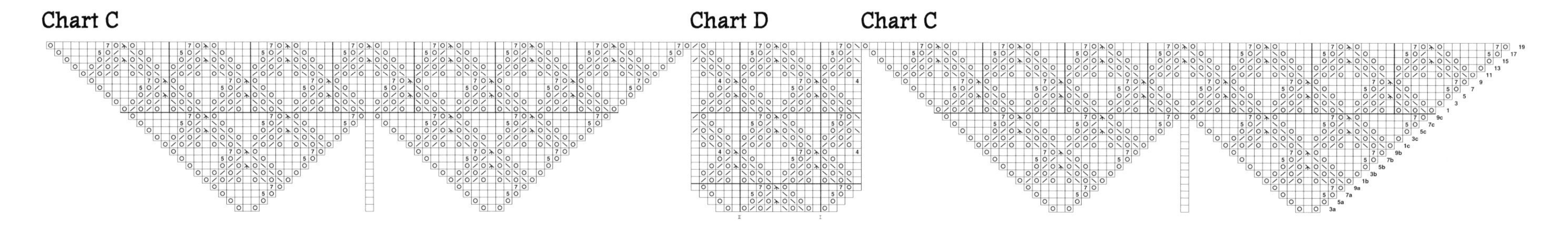

***Illustration 22**: When knitting a lace Faroese-shaped shawl from the charts in this book, you will always begin by working your neck/front band border stitches, followed by Chart C all the way across, then Chart D, then Chart C again all the way across, followed by your neck/front band border stitches.*

Chapter 7: The Lace Border

"Knitting To and Purling Fro"

Knitting on the lace border provides a wonderful opportunity for you to develop your skill at "knitting to and purling fro," Joyce Williams' name for the technique also known as "purling back backwards" or "left-handed" purling. Rather than constantly turning your garment to work the even-numbered rows, simply put your yarn to the front and purl your stitches from your right needle to your left needle. This technique takes some practice to perfect, but is a great skill to master. For further instruction on this technique, see the books listed in the Bibliography under Knitting To and Purling Fro, also know as Knitting Back Backwards and Left Handed Knitting.

The "Stahman Method" of "Knitting To and Purling Fro"

Hold your work with the public side facing you and with all the shawl stitches on the left portion of your circular needle. The following instructions are for knitting the lace border on the Barbara shawl done with a six-stitch seed stitch border:

Row 1a: Slip the first stitch as if to purl, k1. Do not turn your work.

Row 2a: With the yarn in back, slip the point of your left needle into the first stitch on your right needle and remove it from your right needle; place the yarn in front by going between the needles; insert the point of your left needle into the back loop of the stitch on your right needle and purl that stitch.

Row 3a: Slip the first stitch as if to purl, move the yarn to the back, k2tog.

Row 4a: Same as row 2a.

Row 5a: Slip the first stitch as if to purl, make a twisted yarn over, k2tog.

Row 6a: Same as row 2a, except you purl two stitches.

Row 7a: Slip the first stitch as if to purl, k1, k2tog.

Row 8a: Same as row 6a.

/		∩	7a
/	<	∩	5a
/	∩		3a
	∩		1a

Note that as you work the lace border pattern toward the body of the shawl, you will always knit together the last stitch of the lace border with one stitch from the shawl, "eating up" one shawl stitch every pattern row of the lace border.

After working the very last row of the lace border you will have two stitches on your right needle. Pass the right stitch over the left stitch, pull the yarn through and cut your yarn.

Turning Your Work Instead of "Knitting To and Purling Fro"

If you do not wish to "knit to and purl fro" you may turn your work for every row when knitting on the lace bottom border.

Set-up row 1 and all odd-numbered rows: Work as charted; turn.

Set-up row 2 and all even-numbered rows: With your yarn in front, slip the first stitch as if to purl, put your yarn in back and knit to the end.

Alternate Methods of Attaching the Lace Border to the Shawl

Although the k2tog method of attaching the lace border to the shawl is my favorite, the following methods work and give a different look.

- Join the last stitch of the lace border with the first stitch of the shawl by doing a ssk – slip the last stitch of the lace border, slip the first stitch of the shawl, knit the two stitches together (or sl1, k1, psso, which results in the same look).
- Purl together the last stitch of the lace border with the first stitch of the shawl.

Charts for the Lace Borders of the Faroese-Shaped Shawls

GS Gracie Lace – Chart E

Gracie Lace – Chart E

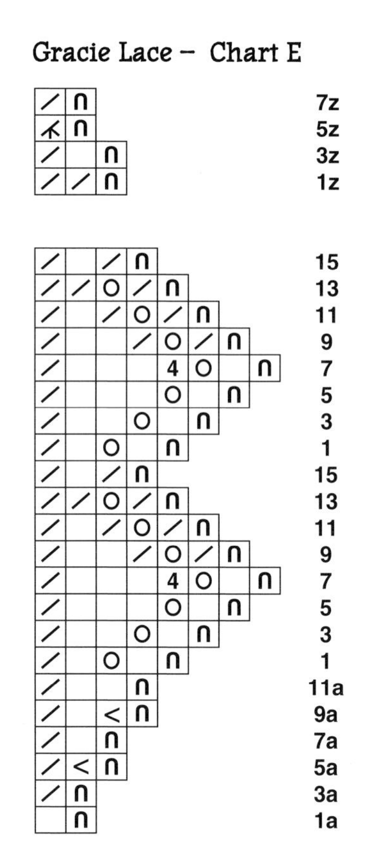

Idella Lace – Chart E

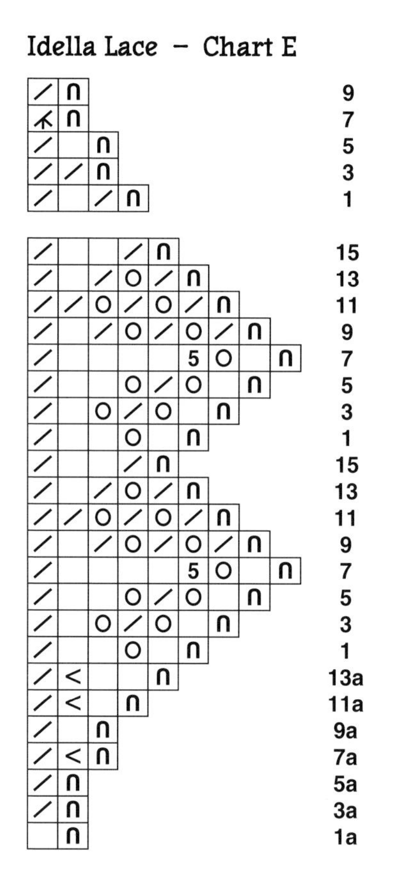

Alka Lace – Chart E

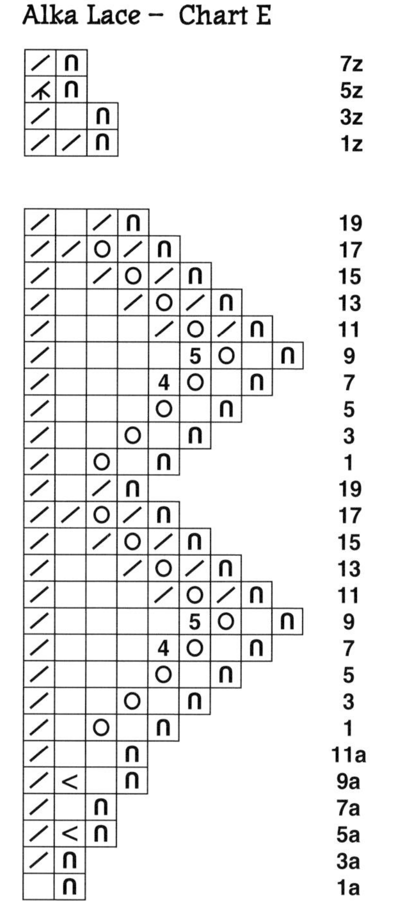

Anne Lace – Chart E

Alberta Lace – Chart E

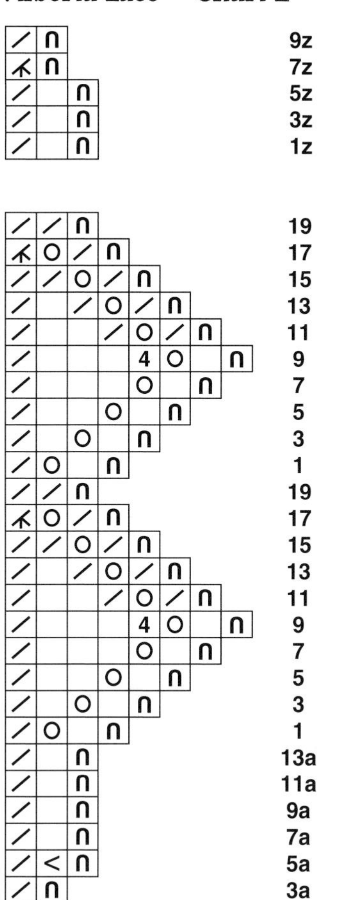

Barbara Lace – Chart E

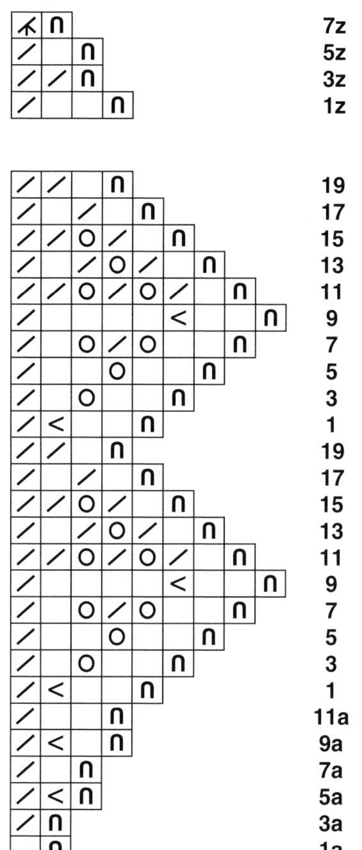

Susan Lace – Chart E

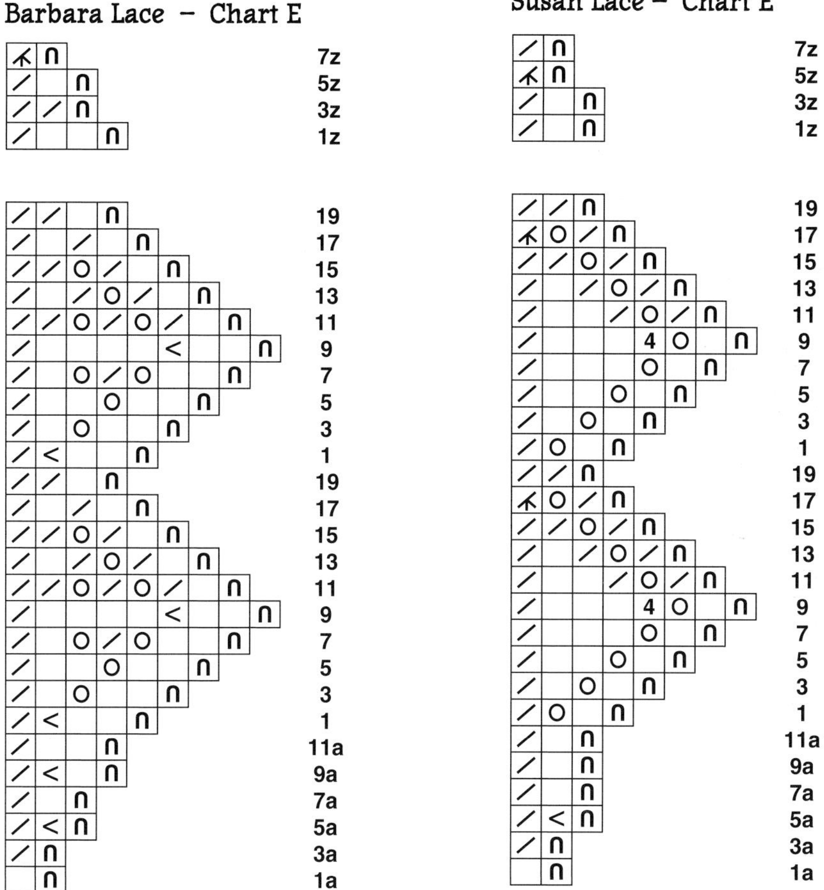

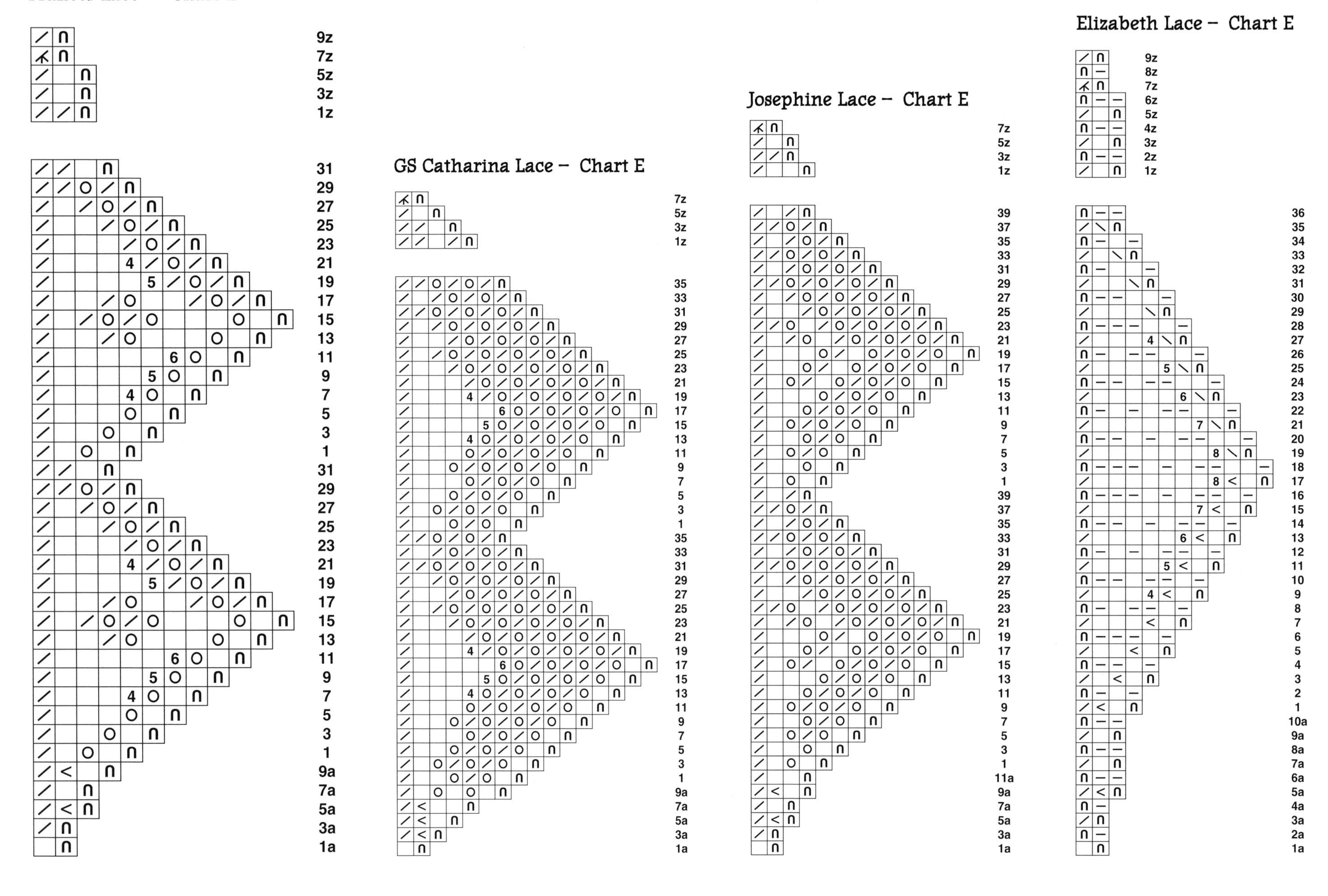
Frances Lace – Chart E
GS Catharina Lace – Chart E
Josephine Lace – Chart E
Elizabeth Lace – Chart E

Chapter 8: Customizing the Faroese Shawl Patterns

Although one of the beauties of a Faroese-shaped shawl is how well the same shawl fits many different body sizes, I recommend customizing any shawl pattern in this book for a tiny body frame or a large body frame or when using a very fine or a very heavy yarn.

The charts for the shawl patterns have bold horizontal and vertical lines and have some rows numbered followed by a letter. The charts for the back panel have the Roman Numerals I and II. These are to assist you in adapting the patterns for a different yarn or a different body frame.

If you are knitting for a larger body frame or if you are using a very fine yarn, you will need to increase the number of rows in the back neck band, the number of stitches in the back panel and the number of rows worked in doing the shoulder shaping. If you are knitting for a smaller body frame or if you are using a bulky yarn, you may need to decrease the number of rows in the back neck band, the number of stitches in the back panel and the number of rows worked in doing the shoulder shaping.

General Principles for Sizing a Faroese-Shaped Shawl

The length of the neckband, from which you pick up the stitches for the first row of the shawl, should measure approximately 40% - 45% of the shoulder-to-shoulder measurement of the intended wearer. In determining how many rows to knit for the neckband, coordinate this percentage with the number of stitches needed for beginning each pattern repeat in the center back panel. This will help you decide how many pattern repeats to use when you begin your back panel.

The distinctive touch of a Faroese-shaped shawl is the shoulder shaping. The column of stitches, with an increase on each side of the column which creates the shoulder shaping, should be approximately the length of the intended wearer's shoulder from the base of the neck to the tip of the shoulder. A great deal of latitude may be exercised here. The length of the shoulder shaping in the majority of the shawls I have knit ranges from 5 inches to 7.5 inches (13 centimeters to 19 centimeters), but the shoulder shaping in one shawl is 10.5 inches (26.5 centimeters). The longer you continue the shoulder shaping, the fuller your shawl will be.

Customizing, Using Alka (pages 68-69) as an Example

I have made the Alka shawl using many different fibers, including Jaggerspun merino/silk blend at 35 wpi/2.5cm and Haneke two-ply bulky at 10 wpi/2.5cm, making just a few adjustments to the Alka charts.

Adjusting the Charts for a Fine Yarn or a Large Body Frame

Adjusting the Back Panel

Look at Alka Chart D, the chart for the back panel (page 68). Note that this chart begins at the base with two repeats of the "building block" plus the increase stitches. You may increase the width of the back panel by adding one or more "building block(s)" by repeating the stitches in each row between the bold lines labeled I and II one or more times. For my Alka shawl knit from Jaggerspun, I added one repeat in the back panel. See Photo 9, page 33.

Adjusting the Number of Neck Band Rows and the Number of Stitches Picked Up When Beginning Your Shawl

When you increase the width of the back panel of your shawl, you will need to increase the number of neck band rows you knit and the number of stitches you pick up when beginning your shawl. For every stitch in width you increase the back panel of your shawl, you will pick up one stitch when beginning your shawl. You must add two rows of neck band stitches for every additional stitch you add to the center back panel. Note that the Alka shawl pattern begins in row la with eight stitches in each repeat and two yarnovers. Note that the yarnover in row la is added as you work row la, and does not use up a stitch picked up from the neck band.

Adjusting the Shoulder "Seam" Increases

Look at Alka Chart C, the chart for the side panels (page 69). Note that the first 30 rows of the chart are labeled 1a through 9c. To increase the length of the shoulder "seam," you will need to do one more sequence of increase rows, as charted in Illustration 23.

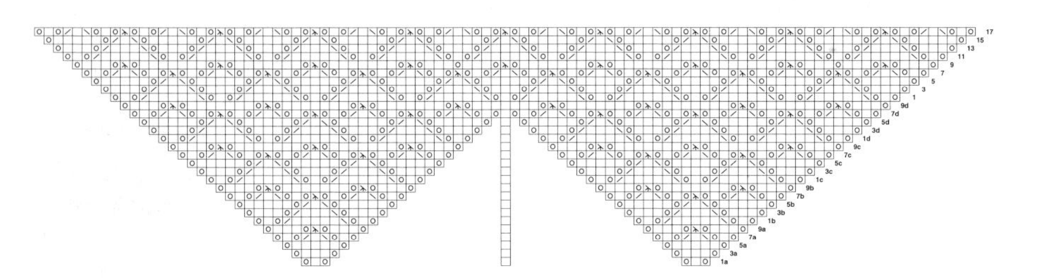

***Illustration 23**: Alka shawl side panel Chart C adjusted for finer yarn or a larger body frame.*

Adjusting the Charts for a Heavy Yarn or a Small Body Frame

Adjusting the Back Panel

Turn to Alka Chart D, the back panel chart (page 68). Note that this chart begins with two repeats of the "building block." To decrease the size of the back panel, delete one of the "building blocks." Simply cut out the columns of stitches between the bold lines labeled I and II. For the Alka shawl knit from Haneke three-ply bulky merino, I deleted one repeat in the back panel. See Photo 10, page 33.

Adjusting the Number of Neck Band Rows and the Number of Stitches Picked Up When Beginning Your Shawl

When you decrease the width of the back panel of your shawl, you will need to decrease the number of neck band rows you work and the number of stitches you pick up when beginning your shawl. For every stitch in width you decrease the back panel of your shawl, you will subtract an equal number of stitches to be picked up when beginning your shawl. Delete two rows of neck band stitches for every stitch you delete from the center back panel. Note that the Alka shawl pattern begins in row 1a with eight stitches in each repeat, not nine; the yarnover in row 1a is added as you work row 1a, and does not use up a stitch picked up from the neck band.

Adjusting the Shoulder "Seam" Increases

Because of the nature of these shawls, for most patterns it will not be necessary to shorten the shoulder seam. With some patterns, shortening it will be a real challenge.

Look at Alka Chart C, the side panel chart (page 69). Note the rows labeled with an a, b, or c following the number. To decrease the length of the shoulder "seam," work rows 1a through 10b. Cut and paste Chart C vertically to eliminate the "building block" directly above the shoulder "seam" column of stitches. Work row 1c, adjusting by eliminating the yo directly to the left of where you "seamed" your chart by folding. Continue in pattern.

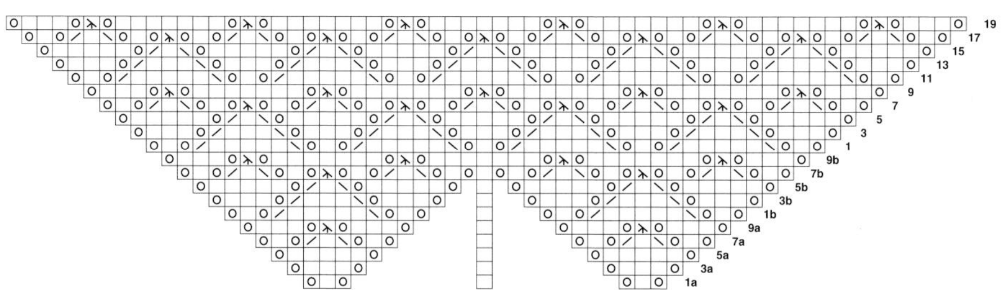

***Illustration 24:** Alka shawl side panel Chart C adjusted for heavier yarn or a smaller body frame.*

The Alka Shawls Adjusted

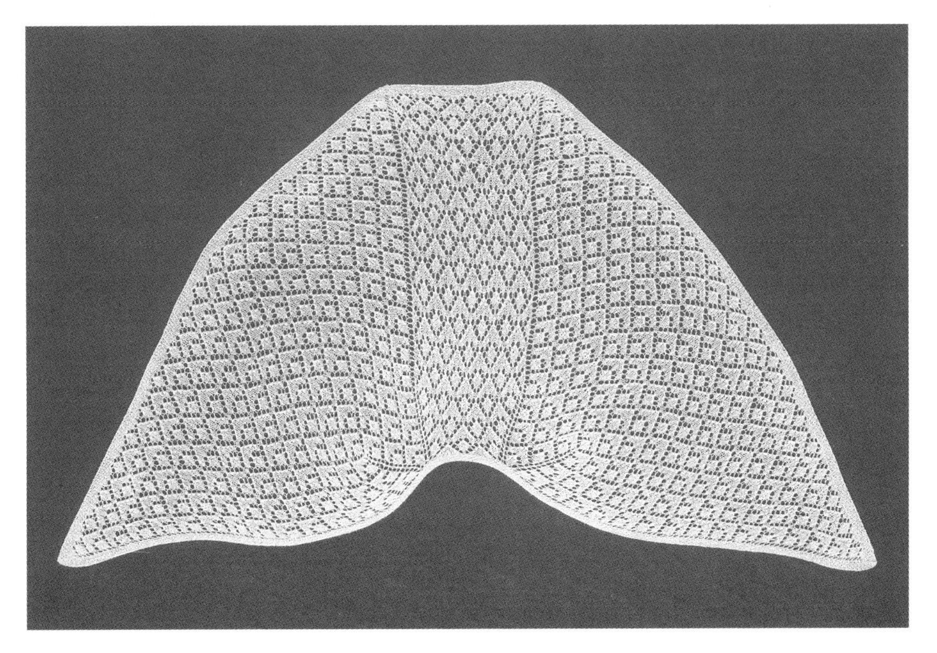

Photo 9: *The Alka shawl made from JaggerSpun merino/silk lace weight wool.*

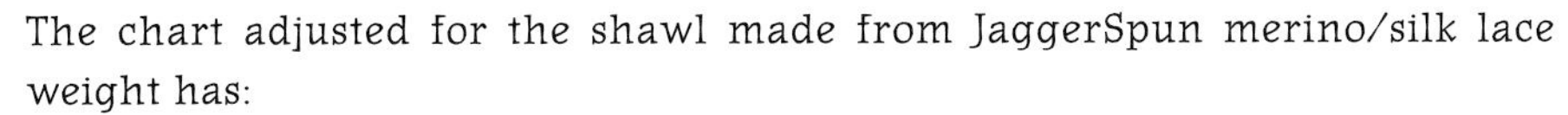

The chart adjusted for the shawl made from JaggerSpun merino/silk lace weight has:

(1) an increase of one building block in the center back panel;
(2) the lengthening of the shoulder seam by continuing the increasing by one pattern; and
(3) working eight full pattern repeats in length.

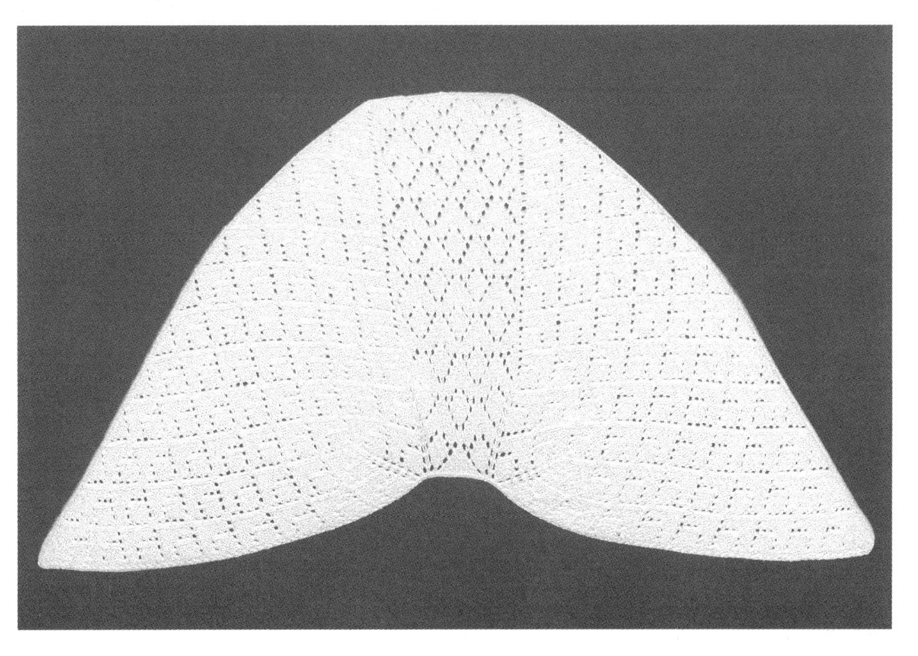

Photo 10: *The Alka shawl made from three-ply bulky merino wool.*

The adjustments for the shawl made from Haneke three-ply bulky 100% merino include:

(1) a decrease of one building block in the center back panel; and
(2) the shortening of the shoulder seam increase by discontinuing increasing after row 10b; and
(3) working five full pattern repeats in length.

Chapter 9. After the Knitting Is Done

Dressing Your Shawl or Scarf for Maximum Beauty

It is important to properly dress your beautiful hand knit shawls and scarves. I prefer to use the term "dressing," rather than "blocking," as blocking brings to mind the use of a steam iron, lots of pins, and force. "Dressing" is a gentle process, such as the dressing of your new baby.

Your home washing machine, which you can control, is perfect for the first step in the dressing process. Also needed is a bed sheet, a floor space, bed, or dressing board on which to lay your shawl or scarf while it is drying, and a set of "Handworks Northwest Dressing Wires."[7]

Fill the washing machine with sufficient warm water so that you can later completely immerse your beautifully hand knit shawl or scarf. Be sure to fill the machine with water **before** putting your shawl or scarf in the machine, as the water should not run directly on your hand knit work of art. While the machine is filling, put in a capful or two of a gentle wool-friendly washing product. Turn the machine off. With the machine off, put in your hand knit shawls and scarves. After letting them soak for 5 to 10 minutes, turn the machine to the last spin cycle and spin the water out. Do not let the machine go through the entire spin cycle; when you no longer hear water draining out, stop the machine. Remove your shawls and scarves from the machine. If a rinse is required, repeat the process without adding the wool-friendly washing product.

A plaid or large-checked bed sheet laid on a carpeted floor is ideal for the final step in dressing your shawls and scarves. A dressing board may be made from styrofoam building insulation covered with a large-checked bed sheet.

Dressing Your Shawl

Using the dressing wires, select eight 36" wires and two 18" wires of the appropriate gauge for the yarn from which you have knit your shawl. Weave a 36" dressing wire through the outer-most purl bumps of each seed stitch front border of your shawl; do not put a wire in the purl bumps of the back neck border.

Weave an 18" dressing wire through the first pattern row of the back panel, where it meets the seed stitch neck band border.

Weave dressing wires through the stitches joining the lace border to the bottom of your shawl, using two 36" wires for each side panel and one 18" or 36" wire for the back panel.

You may wish to weave a 36" wire in the yo's between the back panel and each side panel.

Lay the shawl on the sheet and gently pull the shawl into the beautiful butterfly shape of a Faroese-shaped lace shawl. You may wish to use a measuring tape to insure that your shawl is dressed the same length throughout; this is where a sheet with 3" blocks is so helpful. Fasten the wires in place with rust-proof T-pins.

Because of the shaping of a Faroese-shaped lace shawl, the gauge of stitches to the inch varies greatly – there are more stitches to the inch closer to the neckline than around the bottom. But the gauge of rows to the inch stays relatively constant.

Pull out each point of the lace border and use a rust-proof T-pin to fasten it in place.

Let your beautiful shawl dry, permitting the pattern to "set" overnight.

[7] Dressing wires for lace projects may be purchased from HandWorks Northwest. Go to handworksnw.com for details. A portion of the proceeds from Handworks Northwest dressing wires is donated to the Susan G. Komen Breast Cancer Foundation.

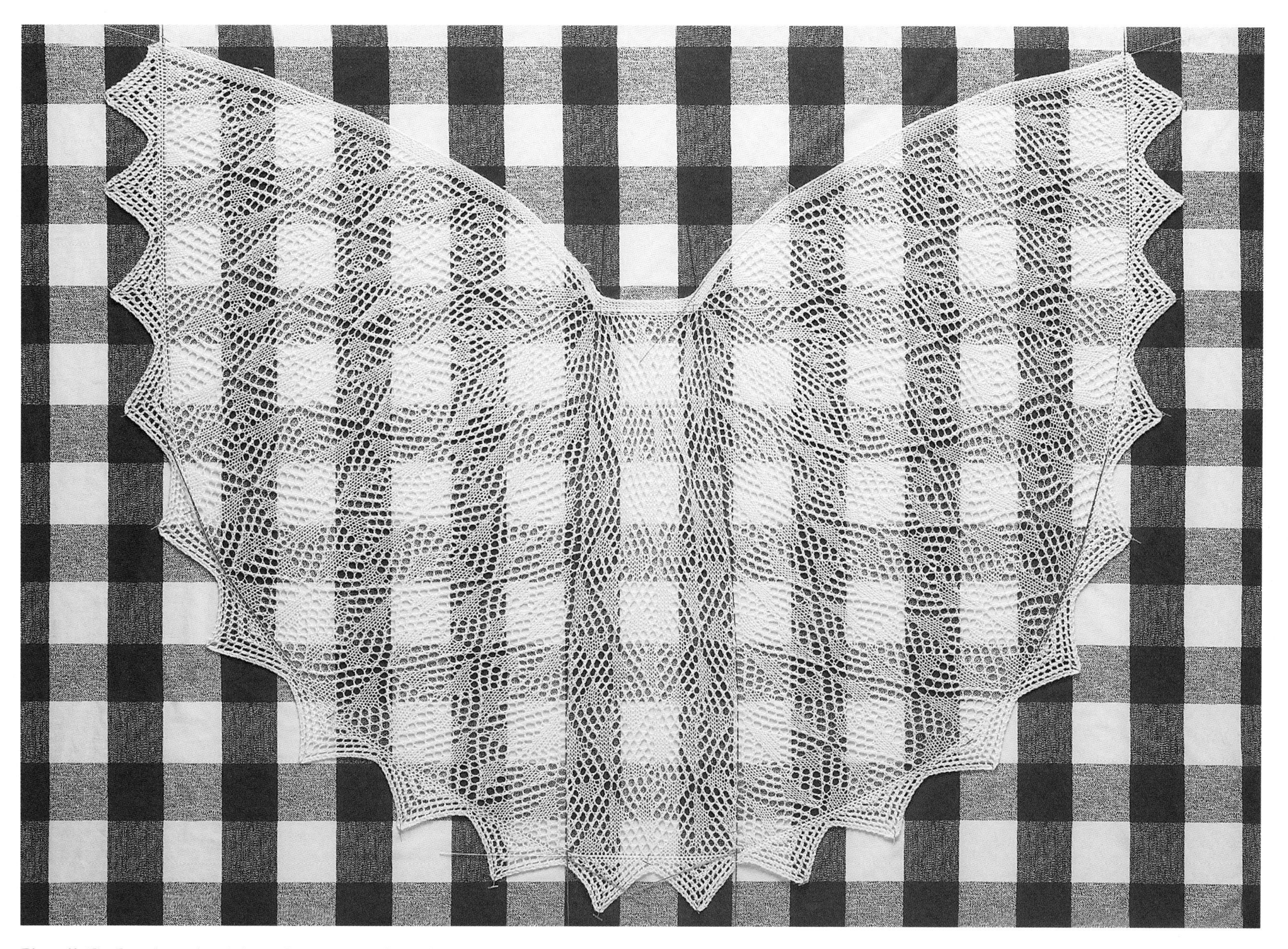

Photo 11: *The Josephine shawl dressed on a piece of styrofoam building insulation covered with a checked bed sheet. Note the T-pins and Zonta Dressing Wires.*

Dressing Your Seamen's Scarf

For just one scarf the bathroom or kitchen sink works well for the first stage of dressing. Fill the sink with sufficient warm water so you can later immerse your scarf. Add a capful of a wool-friendly washing product. Soak for 5 to 10 minutes. Rinse as necessary. Remove your scarf, gently squeezing out the excess water. Wrap your scarf in a large terry towel to blot out the remaining water.

Select four 36" and two 18" Zonta Dressing Wires of the appropriate gauge for the yarn from which you have knit your scarf.

Weave one 36" Zonta Dressing Wire into the outer-most purl bumps of each side of each tail. Do not put wires in the neckline ribbing. Weave one 18" Zonta Dressing Wire in the purl bumps of each bottom border.

Lay your scarf on the sheet and gently pull the scarf into the size desired, fastening the wires in place with rust-proof T-pins. Because of the nature of lace, a lace Seamen's scarf can easily be varied in length and width in the dressing process.

Fasten the ends of the Zonta Dressing Wires under the neckline ribbing with one T-pin so that the wires form a gentle curve to the top of each lace tail of your scarf.

Let your beautiful scarf dry, permitting the pattern to "set" overnight.

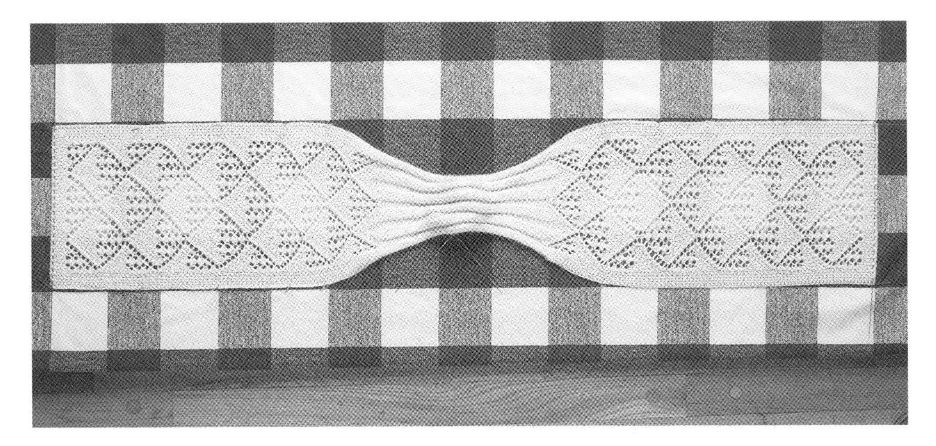

Photo 12: *The Elizabeth Seamen's scarf dressed on a piece of styrofoam building insulation covered with a checked bed sheet.*

Wearing Your Beautiful Lace Faroese-Shaped Shawls and Seamen's Scarves

When you put on your shawl, appreciate how nicely it sits on your shoulders. Enjoy the wonderful way your Seamen's scarf hugs your neck and the beauty of the pattern you selected for the tails of your scarf. Enjoy wearing the fruits of your knitting properly practiced – your beautiful hand knit shawls and scarves.

Caring for Your Hand Knit Shawls and Scarves

Keep several yards of the fiber used with your shawl or scarf record. If, for some reason, repair is needed in the future, you have the fiber necessary.

Wear, wear, wear and enjoy your works of art. Each time you put away your shawl or scarf, fold it differently. When your shawl or scarf gets soiled, wash it using a fine wool wash. Following the directions provided above, dress it after each washing. Don't put your shawl or scarf away to save it for a "special occasion" – wear and enjoy it often.

> *My shawl has been dressed and now rests on the arm of my rocking chair for me to pet and smile over!*
>
> *– Debra Chinn*

Part II

The Shawl Patterns and Matching Lace Seamen's Scarves

Fenna

Knit totally in garter stitch, this shawl is a wonderful introduction to the shoulder shaping used by the knitters of the Faroe Islands. Select a yarn whose beauty you wish to accent when knitting Fenna, a shawl named in honor of my mother.

Ozark Carding Mill
Hand spun by Gail White
Romney top medium weight

Fenna Shawl

Select the yarn and needle size to give you the fabric you desire (Chapter 4).

Using a provisional cast-on (page 13), cast on six stitches.
Set-up row 1: Knit across.
Rows 2-45: Slip the first stitch as if to purl, knit 5. [6 sts]

Following the instruction for "Picking up Neck Band Stitches for the Body of Your Shawl" (page 16), pick up 21 stitches.
Pick up the stitches from your provisional cast-on by following the instructions for "Recovering Stitches from the Provisional Cast-On" (page 18). [32 sts]

Set-up row 1: B5, yo, k3, yo, k 15, yo, k3, yo, k2tog, k4. [35 sts]
Set-up row 2: B5, knit across.
Row 1: *1st increase row* B5, [yo, k2, m1L, k1, m1R, k2, yo], [k1, m1L, k 13, m1R, k1], [yo, k2, m1R, k1, m1L, k2, yo], k5. [45 sts]
Row 2 and all even-numbered rows: Always slipping the first stitch as if to purl, k across.
Row 3: *2nd increase in shoulder* B5, [yo, k4, m1L, k1, m1R, k4, yo], [k 17], [yo, k4, m1R, k1, m1L, k4, yo], k5. [53 sts]
Row 5: *3rd increase in shoulder; 2nd and final increase in back panel* B5, [yo, k6, m1L, k1, m1R, k6, yo], [k1, m1L, k 15, m1R, k1], [yo, k6, m1R, k1, m1L, k6, yo] k5. [63 sts]
Row 7: *4th increase in shoulder* B5, [yo, k8, m1L, k1, m1R, k8, yo], [k 19], [yo, k8, m1R, k1, m1L, k8, yo] k5. [71 sts]
Row 9: *5th increase in shoulder* B5, yo, [k 10, m1L, k1, m1R, k 10, yo], [k 19], [yo, k 10, m1R, k1, m1L, k 10, yo] k5. [79 sts]
Row 11: *6th increase in shoulder* B5, [yo, k 12, m1L, k1, m1R, k 12, yo], [k 19], [yo, k 12, m1R, k1, m1L, k 12, yo] k5. [87 sts]
Row 13: *7th and final increase in shoulder* B5, [yo, k 14, m1L, k1, m1R, k 14, yo], [k 19], [yo, k 14, m1R, k1, m1L, k 14, yo], k5. [95 sts]
Row 15 and all following odd-numbered rows until the shawl is approximately one inch shorter than desired final length: B5, yo, knit side panel, yo, knit center panel, yo, knit side panel, yo, k5.
When shawl is approximately one inch shorter than desired length, B5, *yo, k2tog, Repeat from * across to the last five stitches, yo, k5.
Work eight rows of garter stitch. Bind off using either the Icelandic bind-off (page 21) or the knit-in-pattern bind-off (page 21).

Dress your shawl (page 34). Enjoy wearing your beautiful hand knit work of art!

B5 = Slip the first stitch as if to purl, knit the next 4 stitches.

Brackets are used to show [side panel] [back panel] [side panel].

With each odd-numbered row you are increasing the number of stitches on your needle by four stitches.

This pattern works great when knit at a gauge of four or five stitches per inch/2.5 cm. If you are working at a gauge of six or more stitches per inch/2.5cm with the yarn and needle you have selected, I recommend you use a heavier yarn, use a larger needle or make an adjustment to the pattern. The length of the neck band, from which you pick up the stitches for the first row of the shawl, should measure approximately 40% - 45% of the shoulder-to-shoulder measurement of the intended wearer.

GS Gracie

Made using a worsted weight wool, mainly solid garter stitch, with several pattern repeats near the bottom, GS Gracie is great when tied in the back as a traditional working shawl, leaving your hands free to do the task at hand. Made with more pattern stitch and an added lace border, GS Gracie is a beautiful dress shawl.

GS Gracie building block Chart A

O					5	O	⋏
	O	/		\	O		
O	/				\	O	
					6	\	O
		O	⋏	O			
\	O				O	/	
	\	O		O	/		
		\	O				

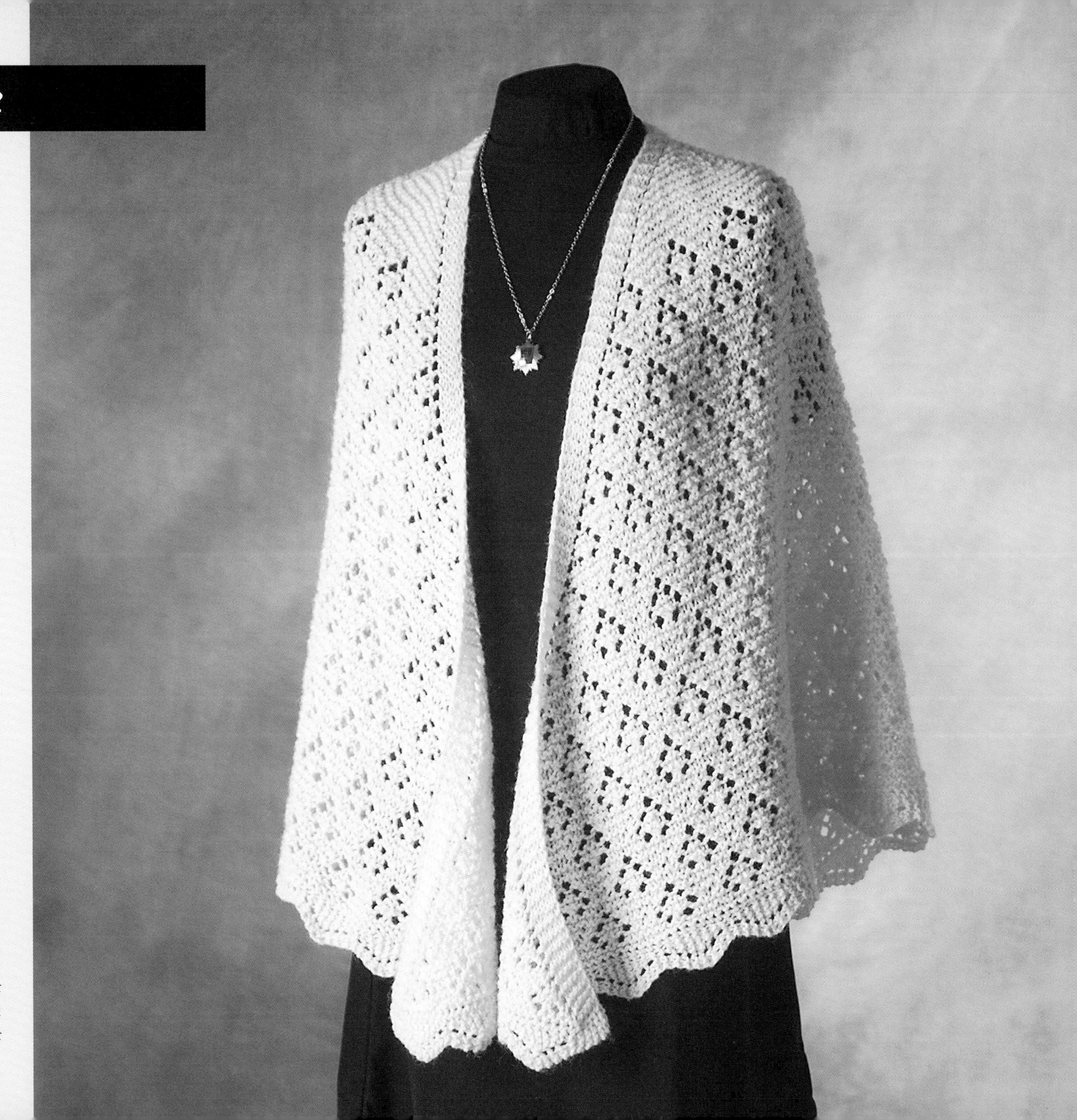

Haneke Select merino/alpaca sport weight

The GS Gracie Seamen's Scarf

Tail #1:

Using a provisional cast-on (page 13), cast on 37 stitches.

Set-up row: K across.

Using GS Gracie Chart S, work as many repeats of rows 1-16 as necessary to make the scarf the length you desire.

Finish Tail #1 by working the following bottom border:

Row 1: Slip the first stitch as if to purl, k3, (k2tog, yo) 7 times,k1, (yo, ssk) 7 times, k4.

Rows 2-10: Slip the first stitch as if to purl, knit across.

Bind off on the eleventh row, using either the knit-in-pattern bind-off (page 21) or the Icelandic bind-off (page 21).

Neckline ribbing:

Remove the provisional cast-on, picking up the 37 stitches.

Set-up row: With the private/wrong side of your scarf facing you, slip the first stitch as if to knit, p4, k4, p4, k4, p3, k4, p4, k4, ending p4, k1.

Row 1: Slip the first stitch as if to purl, k4, p4, k4, p4, k3, p4, k4, p4, k5.

Row 2: Slip the first stitch as if to purl, p4, k4, p4, k4, p3, k4, p4, k4, ending p4, k1.

Repeat Rows 1 & 2 until the neckline ribbing measures approximately 70% of the neck measurement of the intended wearer, between 10 inches/25 cm and 12 inches/30 cm. End after working row 1.

Tail #2:

Set-up row: Slip the first stitch as if to purl, knit across.

Work the same as for Tail #1, beginning with "Using GS Gracie Chart S."

GS Gracie scarf – Chart S

#				O	⋏	O					5	O	⋏	O					5	O	⋏	O				#	15
#		\	O				O	/		\	O				O	/		\	O				O	/		#	13
#			\	O		O	/				\	O		O	/				\	O		O	/			#	11
#				\	O						6	\	O						6	\	O				4	#	9
#	\	O					5	O	⋏	O					5	O	⋏	O					5	O	/	#	7
#			O	/		\	O				O	/		\	O				O	/		\	O			#	5
#		O	/				\	O		O	/				\	O		O	/				\	O		#	3
#							7	\	O						6	\	O								8	#	1
#				O	⋏	O					5	O	⋏	O					5	O	⋏	O				#	15
#		\	O				O	/		\	O				O	/		\	O				O	/		#	13
#			\	O		O	/				\	O		O	/				\	O		O	/			#	11
#				\	O						6	\	O						6	\	O				4	#	9
#	\	O					5	O	⋏	O					5	O	⋏	O					5	O	/	#	7
#			O	/		\	O				O	/		\	O				O	/		\	O			#	5
#		O	/				\	O		O	/				\	O		O	/				\	O		#	3
#							7	\	O						6	\	O								8	#	1

II I

Haneke Select merino/alpaca fingering weight

at the beginning of the row = slip the first stitch as if to purl, k3, k2tog,yo

at the end of the row = yo, ssk, k4

Row 2 and all even-numbered rows: Slip the first stitch as if to purl, knit to the end.

GS Gracie Shawl

This pattern works best when knit at a gauge of four or five stitches per inch/2.5 cm.

Select the yarn and needle size to give you the fabric you desire (Chapter 4).

Using a provisional cast-on (page 13), cast on six stitches.

Set-up row 1: Knit across. [6 sts]

Rows 2-45: Slip the first stitch as if to purl, knit 5. [6 sts]

Following the instruction for "Picking up Neck Band Stitches for the Body of Your Shawl" (page 16), pick up 21 stitches.

Pick up the stitches from your provisional cast-on by following the instructions for "Recovering Stitches from the Provisional Cast-On" (page 18). [32 sts]

Brackets are used to show [side panel] [back panel] [side panel].

Set-up row 1: B5, yo, k3, yo, k 15, yo, k3, yo, k2tog, k4. [35 sts]

Set-up row 2: B5, knit across.

Row 1: *1st increase in shoulders and in back panel* B5, [yo, k2, m1L, k1, m1R, k2, yo], [k1, m1L, k 13, m1R, k1], [yo, k2, m1R, k1, m1L, k2, yo], k5. [45 sts]

Row 2 and all even-numbered rows: Always slipping the first stitch as if to purl, k across.

Row 3: *2nd increase in shoulder* B5, [yo, k4, m1L, k1, m1R, k4, yo], [k 17], [yo, k4, m1R, k1, m1L, k4, yo], k5. [53 sts]

Row 5: *3rd increase in shoulder; 2nd increase in back panel* B5, [yo, k6, m1L, k1, m1R, k6, yo], [k1, m1L, k 15, m1R, k1], [yo, k6, m1R, k1, m1L, k6, yo] k5. [63 sts]

Row 7: *4th increase in shoulder* B5, [yo, k8, m1L, k1, m1R, k8, yo], [k 19], [yo, k8, m1R, k1, m1L, k8, yo] k5. [71 sts]

Row 9: *5th increase in shoulder, 3rd increase in back panel* B5, [yo, k 10, m1L, k1, m1R, k 10, yo], [k1, m1L, k 17, m1R, k1], [yo, k 10, m1R, k1, m1L, k 10, yo] k5. [81 sts]

Row 11: *6th increase in shoulder* B5, yo, k 12, m1L, k1, m1R, k 12, yo], [k 21], [yo, k 12, m1R, k1, m1L, k 12, yo] k5. [89 sts]

Row 13: *7th and **final** increase in shoulder, 4th increase in back panel* B5, [yo, k 14, m1L, k1, m1R, k 14, yo],[k1, m1L, k 19, m1R, k1], [yo, k 14, m1R, k1, m1L, k 14, yo], k5. [99 sts.]

Row 15: B5, [yo, k 33, yo], k 23, [yo, k 33, yo], k5. [103 sts]

Row 17: *5th and **final** increase in back panel* B5, [yo, k 35, yo], [k1, m1L, k 21, m1R, k1], [yo, k 35, yo], k5. [109 sts; 5 sts in each side border; 37 sts in each side panel; and 25 sts in the center back panel]

Row 19 and all uneven-numbered rows until you are ready to begin the lace: B5, yo, knit side panel, yo, knit center panel, yo, knit side panel, yo, k5.

Row 20 and all even-numbered rows: Knit across.

= B5, which at the beginning of the row = slip the first stitch as if to purl, k4

= B5, which at the end of the row = k5

GS Gracie shawl side panel – Chart C **GS Gracie shawl back panel – Chart D**

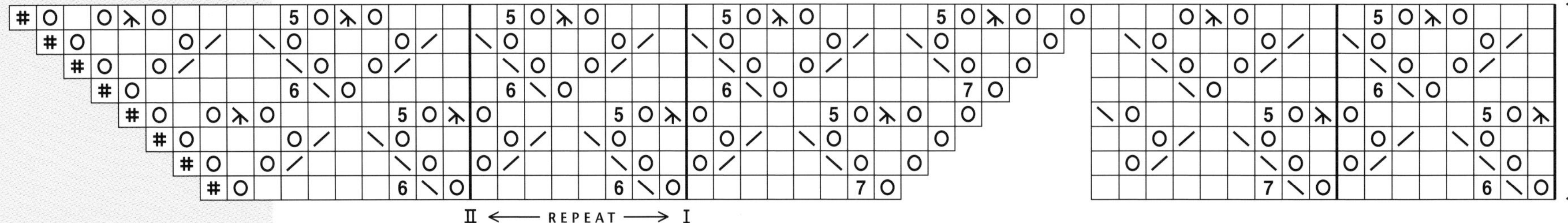

Lace Pattern: To begin the lace pattern you must have a multiple of eight stitches minus one stitch in each of the side panels, excluding the five border stitches. If you wish to have lots of lace, you may begin the lace pattern when you have 39 stitches in each side panel; or you may begin when you have any of the following number of stitches in each side panel: 47, 55, 63, 71, 79, 87, or any other multiple of 8, minus 1. How much or how little lace you wish to have in your shawl determines when you begin the lace pattern.

Using the chart provided, begin your lace pattern on row 21 if you wish to have lots of lace. If you wish to do more garter stitch, follow the directions for Rows 19 and 20 until you have 47, 55, 63, 71, 79, 87, or any other multiple of 8 stitches, minus 1 stitch, in each side panel.

Row 1 of the chart in words: B5, [yo, k7, (yo, ssk, k6) repeat the stitches in parentheses as many times as necessary until you have just 8 stitches before the marker indicating the beginning of the back panel, yo, ssk, k6, yo] [k8, yo, ssk, k6, yo, ssk, k7] [yo, k7, (yo, ssk, k6) repeat the stitches in parentheses as many times as necessary until you have just 8 stitches before the marker indicating the front B5 border, yo, ssk, k6, yo] k5.
Row 2: Slip the first stitch as if to purl, knit across.
Rows 3-16: Work as indicated on the chart.
Repeat rows 1-16 until the shawl, when dressed, is just a bit shorter than the length you desire, ending after knitting row 16.

Knitting on the Lace Border: Go to the instructions on page 27, "The Lace Border." Using GS Gracie Chart E (page 28), work the lace border.
Or, if your prefer a garter stitch border, next row: B5, yo, k2tog, repeat from * across ending yo, k1, yo, k5.
Next eight rows: Knit across. Bind off using the Icelandic bind-off (page 21).

Dress your shawl – Enjoy wearing your beautiful hand knit work of art!

Diane Sullivan's hand spun
Romney medium
Wool Yarns & Fibres
Christchurch, New Zealand

GS Gracie shawl side panel – Chart C

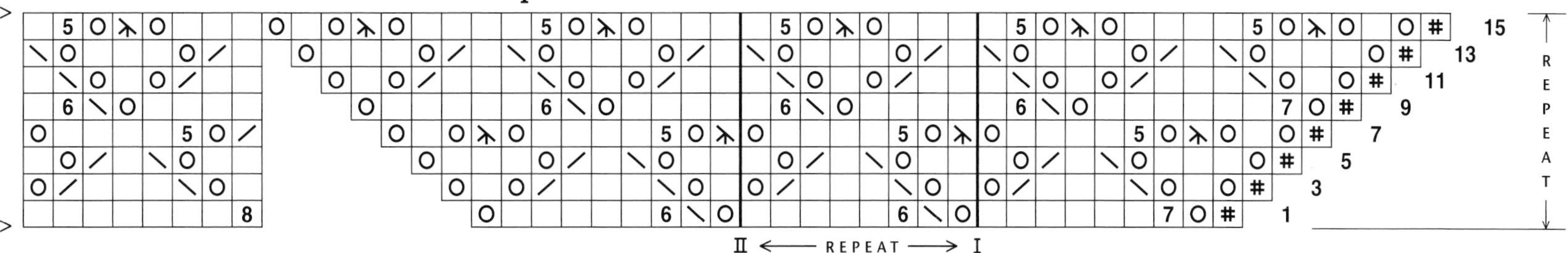

GS Catharina

This garter stitch adaptation of the stockinette stitch Catharina shawl, published in *Knitter's Magazine* (Spring 1998), is a great shawl project for the knitter who loves lace but prefers knitting rather than purling. The use of garter stitch results in a shawl more like the traditional Faroese working shawl, which is tied in the back so one's hands are free to engage in the work at hand.

GS Catharina building block Chart A

							O	⋏	O							
						O	/		\	O						
					O	/	O	⋏	O	\	O					
				O	/	O	/		\	O	\	O				
			O	/	O	/	O	⋏	O	\	O	\	O			
		O	/	O	/	O	/		\	O	\	O	\	O		
	O	/	O	/	O	/	O	⋏	O	\	O	\	O	\	O	
O	/	O	/	O	/	O	/		\	O	\	O	\	O	\	O
	O	/	O	/	O	/				\	O	\	O	\	O	

Haneke Exotics
baby alpaca/merino/angora
sport weight

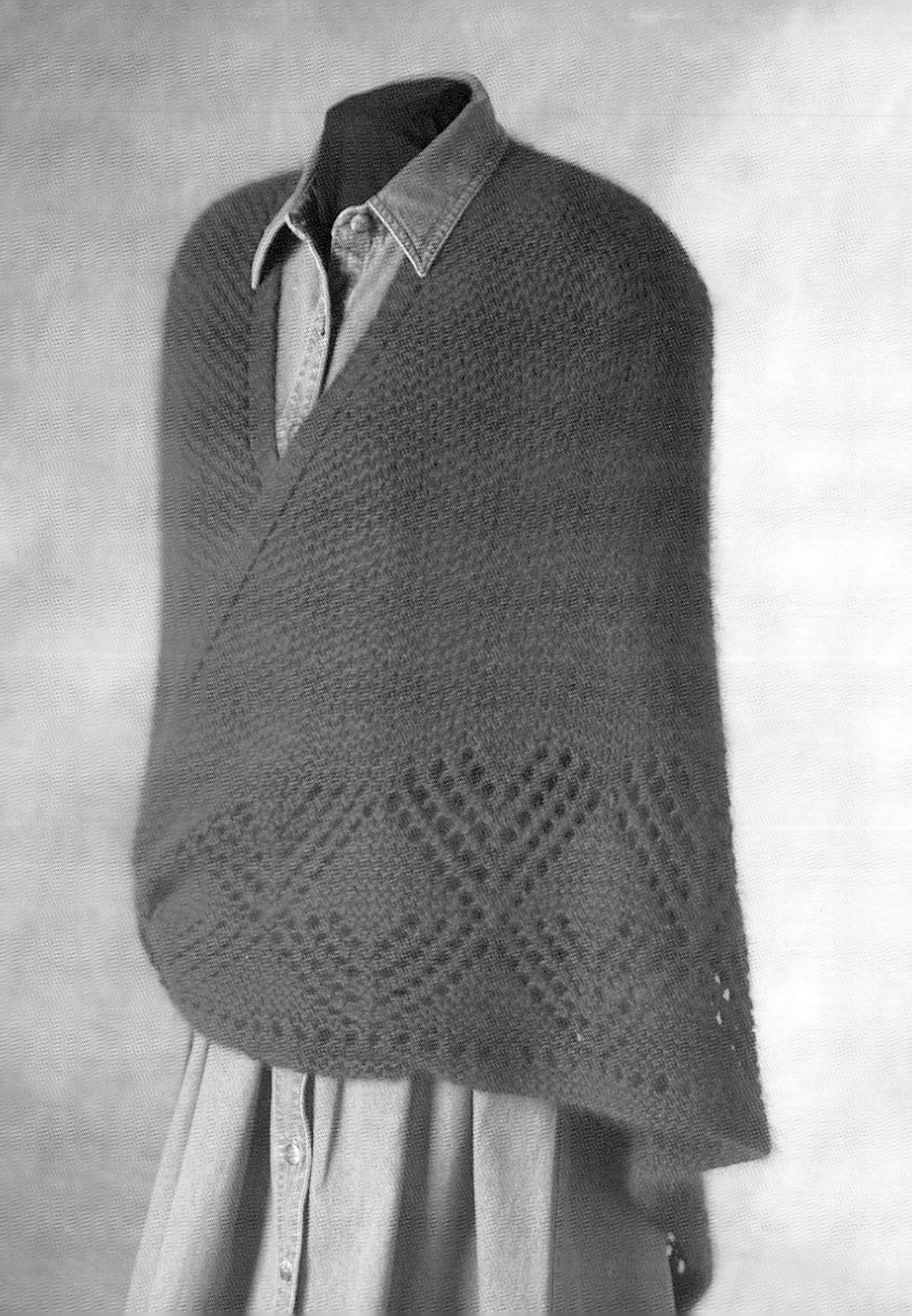

The GS Catharina Seamen's Scarf

Haneke Select merino 2-ply thin spin

Tail #1:

Using a provisional cast-on (page 13), cast on 31 stitches.

Set-up row: K across.

Using GS Catharina Chart S, work as many repeats of rows 1-36 as necessary to make the scarf the length you desire.

Finish Tail #1 by working the following bottom border:

Row 1: Slip the first stitch as if to purl, k3, (k2tog, yo) 5 times, sl1-k2tog-psso, (yo, ssk) 5 times, k4.

Rows 2-10: Slip the first stitch as if to purl, knit across.

Bind off on the eleventh row, using either the knit-in-pattern bind-off (page 21) or the Icelandic bind-off (page 21).

Neckline ribbing:

Remove the provisional cast-on, picking up the 31 stitches.

Set-up row: With the private/wrong side of your scarf facing you, slip the first stitch as if to knit, p4, k4, p4, k5, p4, k4, p4, k1.

Row 1: Slip the first stitch as if to purl, k4, p4, k4, p5, k4, p4, k5.

Row 2: Slip the first stitch as if to purl, p4, k4, p4, k5, p4, k4, p4, k1.

Repeat Rows 1 & 2 until the neckline ribbing measures approximately 70% of the neck measurement of the intended wearer, between 10 inches/25 cm and 12 inches/30 cm. End after working row 1.

Tail #2:

Set-up row: Slip the first stitch as if to purl, knit across.

Work the same as for Tail #1, beginning with "Using GS Catharina Chart S."

GS Catharina scarf – Chart S

#								8	O	⋏	O								8	#	35
#							7	O	/		\	O							7	#	33
#						6	O	/	O	⋏	O	\	O						6	#	31
#					5	O	/	O	/		\	O	\	O					5	#	29
#				4	O	/	O	/	O	⋏	O	\	O	\	O				4	#	27
#				O	/	O	/	O	/		\	O	\	O	\	O				#	25
#			O	/	O	/	O	/	O	⋏	O	\	O	\	O	\	O			#	23
#		O	/	O	/	O	/	O	/		\	O	\	O	\	O	\	O		#	21
#			O	/	O	/	O	/				\	O	\	O	\	O			#	19
#	\	O															15	O	/	#	17
#		\	O													13	O	/		#	15
#	\	O	\	O											11	O	/	O	/	#	13
#		\	O	\	O									9	O	/	O	/		#	11
#	\	O	\	O	\	O							7	O	/	O	/	O	/	#	9
#		\	O	\	O	\	O					5	O	/	O	/	O	/		#	7
#	\	O	\	O	\	O	\	O				O	/	O	/	O	/	O	/	#	5
#		\	O	\	O	\	O	\	O		O	/	O	/	O	/	O	/		#	3
#			\	O	\	O	\	O				O	/	O	/	O	/			#	1

at the beginning of the row = slip the first stitch as if to purl, k3, k2tog,yo

at the end of the row = yo, ssk, k4

Row 2 and all even-numbered rows: Slip the first stitch as if to purl, knit to the end.

GS Catharina Shawl

B5, at the beginning of the row = slip the first stitch as if to purl, k4
B5, at the end of the row = k5

Brackets are used to show [side panel] [back panel] [side panel].

This pattern works best when knit at a gauge of four or five stitches per inch/2.5 cm.

Using a provisional cast-on (page 13), cast on 6 stitches.
Set-up row 1: Knit across.
Rows 2-45: Slip the first stitch as if to purl, knit 5. [6 sts]

Following the instruction for "Picking up Neck Band Stitches for the Body of Your Shawl" (page 16), pick up 21 stitches.
Pick up the stitches from your provisional cast-on by following the instructions for "Recovering Stitches from the Provisional Cast-On" (page 18). [32 sts]

Row 1: B5, yo, k3, yo, k 15, yo, k3, yo, k2tog, k4. [35 sts]
Row 2 and all even-numbered rows: Slip the first stitch as if to purl, knit across.
Row 3: *1st increase row* B5, [yo, k2, m1L, k1, m1R, k2, yo], [k1, m1L, k 13, m1R, k1], [yo, k2, m1R, k1, m1L, k2, yo], k5. [45 sts]
Row 5: *2nd increase in shoulder*: B5, [yo, k4, m1L, k1, m1R, k4, yo], [k 17], [yo, k4, m1R, k1, m1L, k4, yo], k5. [53 sts]
Row 7: *3rd increase in shoulder; 2nd and final increase in back panel*: B5, [yo, k6, m1L, k1, m1R, k6, yo], [k1, m1L, k 15, m1R, k1], [yo, k6, m1R, k1, m1L, k6, yo] k5. [63 sts]
Row 9: *4th increase in shoulder* B5, [yo, k8, m1L, k1, m1R, k8, yo], [k 19], [yo, k8, m1R, k1, m1L, k8, yo] k5. [71 sts]
Row 11: *5th increase in shoulder*: B5, [yo, k 10, m1L, k1, m1R, k 10, yo], [k 19], [yo, k 10, m1R, k1, m1L, k 10, yo] k5. [79 sts]
Row 13: *6th increase in shoulder*: B5, [yo, k 12, m1L, k1, m1R, k 12, yo], [k 19], [yo, k 12, m1R, k1, m1L, k 12, yo] k5. [87 sts]
Row 15: *7th increase in shoulder*: B5, [yo, k 14, m1L, k1, m1R, k 14, yo], [k 19], [yo, k 14, m1R, k1, m1L, k 14, yo], k5. [95 sts]
Row 17: *8th and final increase in shoulder*: B5, [yo, k 16, m1L, k1, m1R, k 16, yo], [k 19], [yo, k 16, m1R, k1, m1L, k 16, yo] k5. [103 sts]
Row 19 and all odd-numbered rows until you are ready to begin the lace: B5, [yo, knit side panel, yo], [knit center panel], [yo, knit side panel, yo], k5.
Row 20 and all even-numbered rows: Always slipping the first stitch as if to purl, k across.

GS Catharina shawl back panel – Chart D

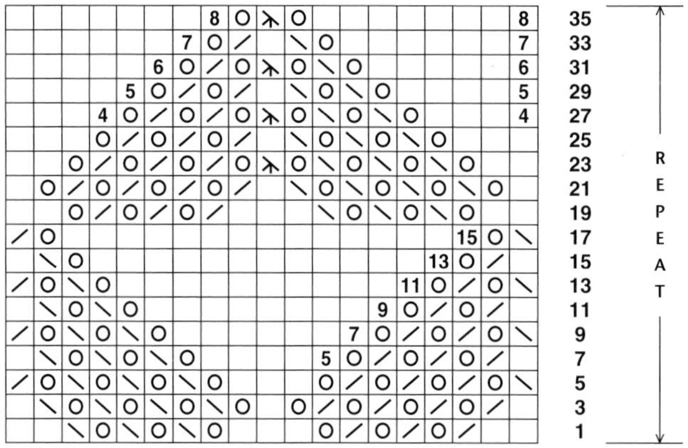

Lace Pattern: To begin the lace pattern you must have a multiple of 18 stitches minus one stitch in each of the side panels, excluding the five border stitches. If you wish to have lots of lace you may begin the lace pattern when you have 53 stitches in each side panel; or you may begin when you have any of the following number of stitches in each side panel: 71, 89, 107, 125, 143, 161, or any multiple of 18, minus 1. How much or how little lace you wish to have in your shawl determines when you begin the lace pattern.

Using Charts C and D, begin the lace portion of your shawl.

Row 1: B5, go to Chart C, row 1, repeating between I and II as many times as necessary for the number of stitches you have in the side panel; go to Chart D and work row 1; go back to Chart C, row 1, and work the same as you did for the first side panel; k5.

Row 2 and all even-numbered rows: Slip the first stitch as if to purl, knit across.

Continue using Charts C and D until the shawl is just a bit shorter than the length you desire, ending after knitting row 18.

Knitting on the Lace Border: Go to the instructions on page 27, "The Lace Border." Using GS Catharina Chart E (page 30), work the lace border.

Or, if you prefer a garter stitch border, next row: B5, yo, k2tog, repeat from * across ending yo, k1, yo, k5.

Next eight rows: Knit across. Bind off using the Icelandic bind-off.

Dress your shawl – Enjoy wearing your beautiful hand knit work of art!

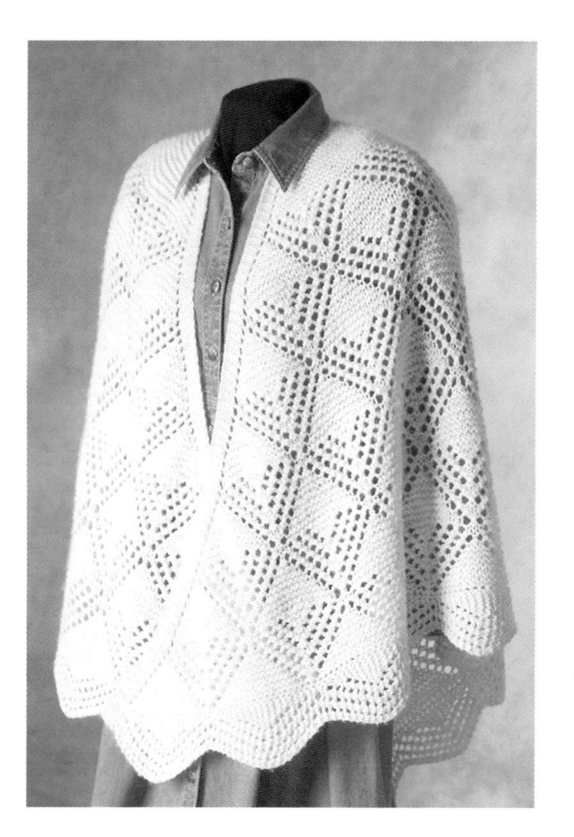

Sirdar Highlands & Islands Balmoral
wool/alpaca/silk
double knitting - sport weight

GS Catharina shawl side panel – Chart C

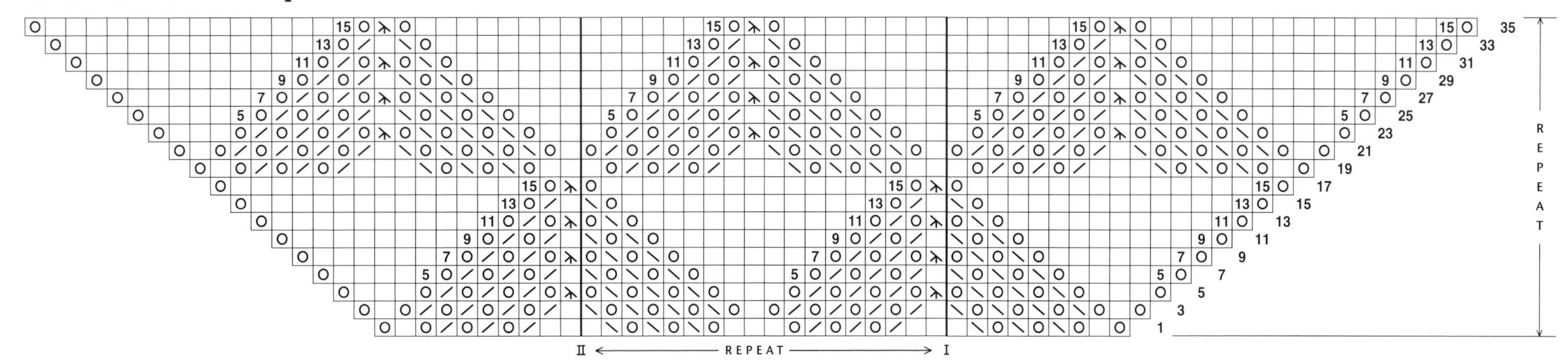

Marialis

As nine and ten year olds, my sister Marialis and I knit long scarves using the beautiful lace pattern known both as "Old Shale" and "Feather and Fan." This is a great pattern for the beginning lace knitter. For knitters who don't like to purl, Variation II is a great choice; only one out of every four rows is a purl row. Try both variations and decide which you prefer – they are both beautiful.

Marialis C: Haneke Select merino/alpaca fingering weight

The Marialis Seamen's Scarf

Variation I Tail #1:

Using a provisional cast-on (page 13), cast on 48 stitches.

Set-up row 1: K2, p1, k1, p1, k1, place a marker on your needle, p 36, place a marker on your needle, B6 (page 23).

Row 1: B6, (k2tog) three times, (yo, k1) six times, (k2tog) six times, (yo, k1) six times, (k2tog) three times, B6.

Row 2: B6, p 36, B6.

Row 3: B6, k 36, B6.

Row 4: B6, p 36, B6.

Work as many repeats of Rows 1-4 as necessary to make the scarf the length you desire. End after working row 2.

Finish Tail #1 as follows:

Row 1: B6, p2tog, (k1, p1) six times, (k2tog, p1) three times, (k1, p1) six times, k2tog, p1, k1, p1, k2.

Rows 2-8: Work in seed stitch. Bind off on the ninth row, using the Icelandic bind-off (page 21).

Neckline ribbing:

Remove the provisional cast-on, picking up the 48 stitches.

Set-up row: With the private/wrong side of your scarf facing you, slip the first stitch as if to knit, p5, (k4, p4) four times, k4, p5, k1.

Row 1: Slip the first stitch as if to purl, k5, p4, (k4, p4) four times, k6.

Row 2: Slip the first stitch as if to purl, p5, (k4, p4) four times, k4, p5, k1.

Repeat Rows 1 & 2 until the neckline ribbing measures approximately 70% of the neck measurement of the intended wearer, between 10 inches/25 cm and 12 inches/30 cm. End after working row 1.

Tail #2:

Set-up row 1: B6, place a marker on your needle, p 36, place a marker on your needle, B6.

Work the same as for Tail #1, beginning with Row 1.

Variation II Tail #1:

Using a provisional cast-on (page 13), cast on 48 stitches.

Set-up row 1: K2, p1, k1, p1, k1, place a marker on your needle, k 36, place a marker on your needle, B6.

Row 1: B6, (k2tog) three times, (yo, k1) six times, (k2tog) six times, (yo, k1) six times, (k2tog) three times, B6.

Row 2: B6, k 36, B6.

Row 3: B6, p 36, B6.

Row 4: B6, k 36, B6

Work as many repeats of Rows 1-4 as necessary to make the scarf the length you desire. End after working row 2.

Finish Tail #1 as follows:

Row 1: B6, p2tog, (k1, p1) six times, (k2tog, p1) three times, (k1, p1) six times, k2tog, p1, k1, p1, k2.

Rows 2-8: Work in seed stitch. Bind off on the ninth row, using the Icelandic bind-off (page 21).

Neckline ribbing:

Remove the provisional cast-on, picking up the 48 stitches.

Set-up row 1: With the public/right side of your scarf facing you, slip the first stitch as if to knit, k5, (p4, k4) four times, p4, k6.

Set-up row 2: Slip the first stitch as if to purl, p5, k4, (p4, k4) four times, p5, k1.

Row 1: Slip the first stitch as if to purl, k5, (p4, k4) four times, p4, k6.

Row 2: Slip the first stitch as if to purl, p5, k4, (p4, k4) four times, p5, k1.

Repeat Rows 1 & 2 until the neckline ribbing measures approximately 70% of the neck measurement of the intended wearer, between 10 inches/25 cm and 12 inches/30 cm. End after working row 2.

Tail #2:

Set-up row 1: B6, place a marker on your needle, k 36, place a marker on your needle, B6.

Work the same as for Tail #1, beginning with Row 1.

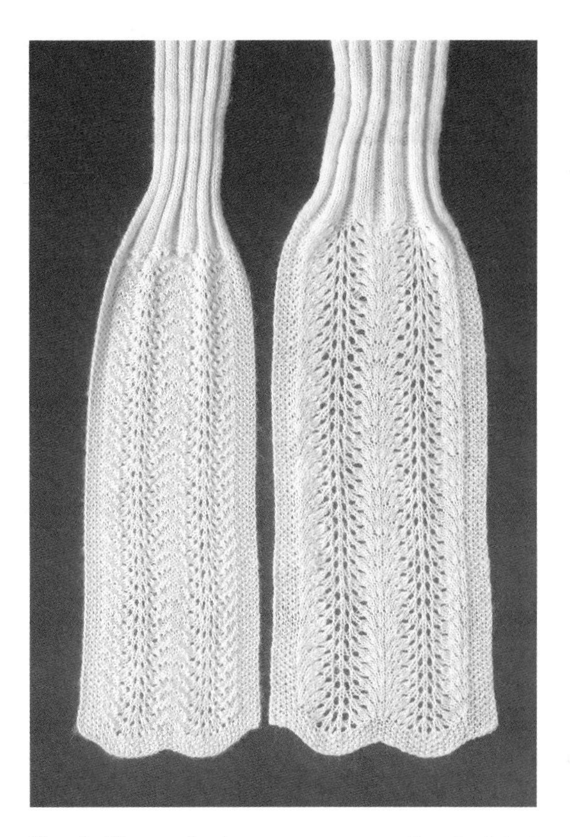

Haneke Heaven Sent alpaca fingering weight Variation II

Haneke Select merino/kid merino lace weight Variation I

This pattern works great when knit at a gauge of four or five stitches per inch/2.5 cm. If you are working at a gauge of six or more stitches per inch/ 2.5cm with the yarn and needle you have selected, I recommend you use a heavier yarn, use a larger needle or make an adjustment to the pattern. The length of the neck band, from which you pick up the stitches for the first row of the shawl, should measure approximately 40% - 45% of the shoulder-to-shoulder measurement of the intended wearer. See page 52 for more information.

Marialis Swatch

Cast on 30 stitches.

Variation I - the pattern row is worked on a public/right side row and produces the smooth stockinette stitch.
Set-up rows 1, 3, 5, 7 and 9: B6, p 18, B6.
Set-up rows 2, 4, 6, 8 and 10: B6, k 18, B6.
Row 11 of your swatch: Begin with row 1 of the pattern.
Row 1: B6, (k2tog) three times, (yo, k1) six times, (k2tog) three times, B6.
Row 2: B6, purl across, B6.
Row 3: B6, knit across, B6.
Row 4: B6, purl across, B6.
Repeat rows 1-4 a total of eight times.

Variation II - the pattern row is worked on a private/ wrong side row and produces a purl ridge.
Set-up rows 1, 3, 5, 7 and 9: B6, p 18, B6.
Set-up rows 2, 4, 6, and 8: B6, k 18, B6.
Row 10 of your swatch – begin with row 1 of the pattern.
Row 1: B6, (k2tog) three times, (yo, k1) six times, (k2tog) three times, B6.
Row 2: B6, knit across, B6.
Row 3: B6, purl across, B6.
Row 4: B6, knit across, B6.
Repeat rows 1-4 a total of eight times.

Work rows 1 and 2 of the pattern, then work the bottom border as follows:
Row 1: B6, p1, k2tog, (p1, k1) 7 times, p1, B6.
Rows 2-8: Work in seed stitch.
Row 9: Bind off using the Icelandic bind-off (page 21).

Measure your swatch, remembering that it is the rows per inch/2.5 cm that is important. Dress your swatch (page 34). Measure your swatch again. The measurements of both the "undressed" and the "dressed" swatches are the important measurements for planning your shawl. These measurements are especially important if you are using multiple colors in your shawl.

Marialis Work Sheet

My gauge in stockinette stitch (set-up rows 2-9), after dressing my swatch, is:
8 rows equal ______________ inches/cm and ________ rows equal 1 inch/2.5 cm

My gauge in pattern stitch (rows 1-4, repeated 8 times), after dressing my swatch, is:
8 pattern repeats equal ______________ inches/cm and ________ rows equal 1 inch/2.5 cm

I wish my finished shawl to be ______________ inches/cm from the top of the neck band to the bottom of the border.

- The six-stitch neck band/front border is ______________ inches/cm wide.
- The yoke of my shawl is 24 rows deep, which according to my stockinette stitch gauge equals ______________ inches/cm.
- The eight row seed stitch bottom border will be ______________ inches/cm deep.
- I need ______________ inches/cm of pattern to have a shawl the length I wish it to be.
- For ______________ inches/cm of pattern I must knit ________ rows of pattern.

Instructions for three different shawl shapings are provided. Each is beautiful in its own way.

Select the shawl shaping you prefer and have a great time knitting your shawl.

Marialis A: Haneke merino thin spin

Marialis A incorporates a doubling of the stitches at two different points in the shawl construction. The pattern stitch is always a repeat of 18 stitches.

Marialis B: Haneke merino lace weight

Marialis B uses a one-stitch increase in each pattern repeat for every pattern row. The first pattern row is a repeat of 18 stitches; four rows later the second pattern row is a repeat of 19 stitches; four rows thereafter the third pattern row is a repeat of 20 stitches. This sequence continues until you have made your shawl as long as you wish it to be.

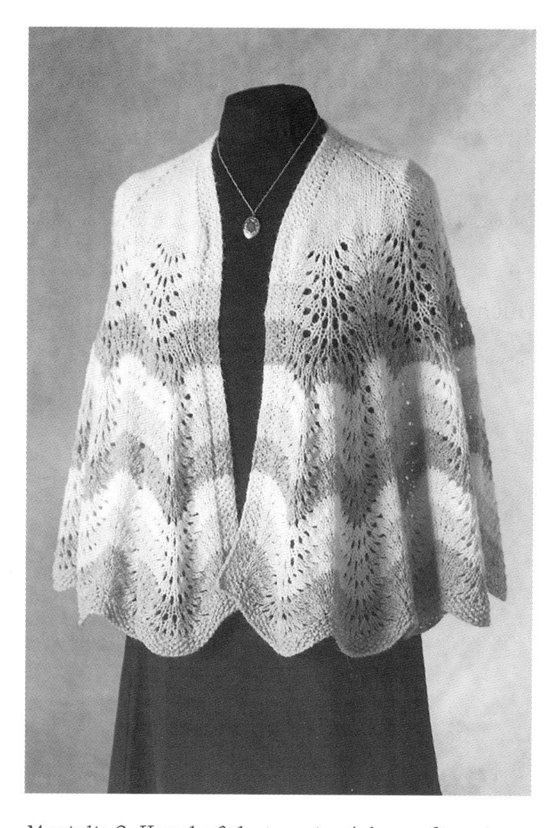

Marialis C: Haneke Select merino/alpaca fingering weight

Marialis C begins the same as Marialis A, with the doubling of stitches for the first increase; thereafter the increase sequence of Marialis B is used, with a one-stitch increase in each pattern repeat until the shawl is the length you desire.

Adjusting Your Pattern For Six or More Stitches Per Inch/2.5 CM

One adjustment I have successfully used for Marialis A and Marialis C is adding 18 stitches to the back center. Using a provisional cast-on, cast on seven stitches, work the set-up row, and then work rows 2-91 for the neck band/ front border. Pick up 44 stitches to begin your shawl. In row 1 of the pattern replace the "k 18" with "k 36." In rows 3-21 add 18 stitches to the middle group of stitches. This changes the the "k 20" to "k 38" in row 3 and the "k 22" to "k 40" in row 5.

For Marialis B try adding 12 stitches to the back center panel, picking up 38 stitches.

Seed Stitch Neck Band/Front Border for Marialis A, B and C

Using a provisional cast-on (page 13), cast on 7 stitches for the seed stitch neck band/front border.
Set-up row: K2, pl, kl, pl, k2.
Rows 2-55: Slip the first stitch as if to purl, kl, pl, kl, pl, k2. [7 stitches]

Shawl Yoke for Marialis A, B. and C

Notation in brackets [ ] indicates the total number of stitches in the row.
Following the instructions for "Picking up Neck Band Stitches for Your Shawl" (page 16), pick up 26 stitches.
Pick up the stitches from your provisional cast-on by following the instructions for "Recovering Stitches from the Provisional Cast-On" (page 18). [39 sts]

Row 1: B6, place a marker on your needle, mlL (page 23), kl, mlR, kl, mlL, kl, mlR, kl, mlL, k 18, mlR, kl, mlL, kl, mlR, kl, mlL, kl, mlR, place a marker on your needle, k2tog, pl, kl, pl, k2. [48]
Row 2 and all even-numbered rows: B6, purl across, B6.
Row 3: B6, mlL, k3, mlR, kl, mlL, k3, mlR, kl, mlL, k 20, mlR, kl, mlL, k3, mlR, kl, mlL, k3, mlR, B6. [58]
Row 5: B6, mlL, k5, mlR, kl, mlL, k5, mlR, kl, mlL, k 22, mlR, kl, mlL, k5, mlR, kl, mlL, k5, mlR, B6. [68]
Row 7: B6, mlL, k7, mlR, kl, mlL, k7, mlR, kl, mlL, k 24, mlR, kl, mlL, k7, mlR, kl, mlL, k7, mlR, B6. [78]
Row 9: B6, mlL, k9, mlR, kl, mlL, k9, mlR, kl, mlL, k 26, mlR, kl, mlL, k9, mlR, kl, mlL, k9, mlR, B6. [88]
Row 11: B6, mlL, k 11, mlR, kl, mlL, k 11, mlR, kl, mlL, k 28, mlR, kl, mlL, k 11, mlR, kl, mlL, k 11, mlR, B6. [98]
Row 13: B6, mlL, k 13, mlR, kl, mlL, k 13, mlR, kl, mlL, k 30, mlR, kl, mlL, k 13, mlR, kl, mlL, k 13, mlR, B6. [108]
Row 15: B6, mlL, k 15, mlR, kl, mlL, k 15, mlR, kl, mlL, k 32, mlR, kl, mlL, k 15, mlR, kl, mlL, k 15, mlR, B6. [118]
Row 17: B6, mlL, k 17, mlR, kl, mlL, k 17, mlR, kl, mlL, k 34, mlR, kl, mlL, k 17, mlR, kl, mlL, k 17, mlR, B6. [128]
Row 19: B6, mlL, k 19, mlR, kl, mlL, k 19, mlR, kl, mlL, k 36, mlR, kl, mlL, k 19, mlR, kl, mlL, k 19, mlR, B6. [138]
Row 21: B6, mlL, k 21, mlR, kl, mlL, k 21, mlR, kl, mlL, k 38, mlR, kl, mlL, k 21, mlR, kl, mlL, k 21, mlR, B6. [148]

Go to the instructions for the shawl you have selected – Marialis A, Marialis B, or Marialis C.

Marialis A – continuation of the Yoke and Lace Body

Row 23: B6, mlL, k 23, mlR, kl, mlL, k 23, mlR, k 42, mlL, k 23, mlR, kl, mlL, k 23, mlR, B6. [156]
You now have a total of 156 stitches on your needle; 144 stitches in the body of the shawl and six stitches in each front band border. You are ready to begin the lace portion of your shawl.
Row 24: B6, purl across, B6.

Variation I [smooth - stockinette stitch]:
Work the following four-row pattern until your shawl measures approximately 10 inches/25.5 cm in length from the outside edge of the B6 neck band border.
Row 1: B6, [place a marker on your needle, (k2tog) three times, (yo, kl) six times, (k2tog) three times] repeat between the brackets a total of eight times, place a marker on your needle B6. [18 st between markers; 156 sts total]
Row 2: B6, purl across, B6.
Row 3: B6, knit across, B6.
Row 4: B6, purl across, B6.

Variation II [ridges - every 4th row is a purl row]:
Row 25: B6, knit across, B6.
Work the following four-row pattern until your shawl measures approximately 10 inches/25.5 cm in length from the outside edge of the B6 neck band border.
Begin row 1 of the pattern on the private/wrong side row, which is row 26 of your yoke.
Row 1: B6, [place a marker on your needle, (k2tog) three times, (yo, kl) six times, (k2tog) three times], repeat between the brackets a total of eight times, place a marker on your needle, B6. [18 sts between markers; 156 sts total]
Row 2: B6, knit across, B6.
Row 3: B6, purl across, B6.
Row 4: B6, knit across, B6.

When your work measures approximately 10 inches/25.5 cm in length from the outside edge of the neck band border after completing row 4 above, work the following increase row in place of row 1 of the pattern stitch:

Increase row: B6, (kl, yo) across, B6. You now have 288 stitches plus six stitches for each of the two side borders, for a total of 300 stitches on your needle. Work row 4, placing a marker on your needle every 18 stitches in the body of your shawl. [18; 300]

Resume the "Old Shale" pattern, repeating rows 1-4 until your shawl, from the outside edge of the neck band border, measures approximately 2/3 the finished length of your shawl. Then again work the increase as above, doubling your stitches. You now have 576 stitches, plus 6 stitches for each of the two side borders, for a total of 588 stitches on your needle. Work row 4, placing a marker on your needle every 18 stitches in the body of your shawl. [18; 588]

Resume the "Old Shale" pattern, repeating rows 1-4 until your shawl is the length you desire minus the width of your six-stitch seed stitch border, ending after working the pattern row plus row 2. [Note: Generally, the six-stitch seed stitch border is equal in width to the depth of eight or nine rows of seed stitch.]

Seed Stitch Bottom Border:

Row 1: B6, pl, k2tog, [(pl, kl) six times, p2tog, k2tog, p2tog), (kl, pl) six times, k2tog, p2tog, k2tog] repeating the stitches in the brackets, with the final repeat ending K2tog, pl; B6.
Rows 2-8: Work in seed stitch.
Row 9: Bind off using the Icelandic bind-off (page 21).

Marialis B – continuation of the Yoke and Lace Body

Row 23: B6, m1L, k 23, m1R, k1, m1L, k 23, m1R, k1, m1L, k 40, m1R, k1, m1L, k 23, m1R, k1, m1L, k 23, m1R, B6. [158]
Row 25: B6, m1L, k 25, m1R, k1, m1L, k 25, m1R, k1, m1L, k 42, m1R, k1, m1L, k 25, m1R, k1, m1L, k 25, m1R, B6. [168]
Row 27: B6, m1L, k 27, m1R, k1, m1L, k 27, m1R, k1, m1L, k 44, m1R, k1, m1L, k 27, m1R, k1, m1L, k 27, m1R, B6. [178]
Row 29: B6, m1L, k 29, m1R, k1, m1L, k 29, m1R, k1, m1L, k 46, m1R, k1, m1L, k 29, m1R, k1, m1L, k 29, m1R, B6. [188]
Row 31: B6, m1L, k 31, m1R, k1, m1L, k 31, m1R, k1, m1L, k 48, m1R, k1, m1L, k 31, m1R, k1, m1L, k 31, m1R, B6. [198]
Row 33: B6, m1L, k 67, m1R, k1, m1L, k 50, m1R, k1, m1L, k 67, m1R, B6. [204]
Row 34: B6, purl across, B6. [204]

Work as many pattern repeats as necessary to make your shawl the length you wish it to be; you very likely will NOT work all 29 pattern repeats unless you are using very fine fiber and very small needles. Remember, a pattern row is done once every four rows.

Variation I [smooth - stockinette stitch]:
Row 34: B6, purl across, B6. [204]
Row 35: Work the first pattern repeat below.
Row 36: B6, purl across, B6.
Row 37: B6, knit across, B6.
Row 38: B6, purl across, B6.
Row 39: Work the second pattern row below, et seq.

Variation II [ridges - every 4th row is garter stitch]:
Row 34: Work the first pattern repeat below.
Row 35: B6, knit across, B6.
Row 36: B6, purl across, B6.
Row 37: B6, knit across, B6.
Row 38: Work the second pattern row below, et seq.

First pattern: B6, *place a marker on your needle, (K2tog) twice, (yo, k1) 4 times, yo, (k2tog) twice; repeat from *, place a marker on your needle, B6. [13 stitches in each repeat; 16 pattern repeats; 208 stitches in the lace portion; 220 stitches total in the row]
Second pattern: B6, *(K2tog) twice, k1, (yo, k1) 4 times, yo, (k2tog) twice; repeat from *, B6. [14; 236]
Third pattern: B6, *(K2tog) twice, k1, (yo, k1) 5 times, (k2tog) twice; repeat from *, B6. [15; 252]
Fourth pattern: B6, *(K2tog) twice, (yo, k1) 5 times, yo, (k2tog) 3 times; repeat from *, B6. [16; 268]
Fifth pattern: B6, *(K2tog) twice, k1, (yo, k1) 5 times, yo, (k2tog) 3 times; repeat from *, B6. [17; 284]
Sixth pattern: B6, *(K2tog) twice, k1, (yo, k1) 6 times, (k2tog) 3 times; repeat from *, B6. [18; 300]
Seventh pattern: B6, *(k2tog) 3 times, (yo, k1) 6 times, yo, (k2tog) 3 times; repeat from *, B6. [19; 316]
Eighth pattern: B6, *(K2tog) 3 times, k1, (yo, k1) 6 times, yo, (k2tog) 3 times; repeat from *, B6. [20; 332]
Ninth pattern: B6, *(K2tog) 3 times, k1, (yo, k1) 7 times, (k2tog) 3 times; repeat from *, B6. [21; 348]
Tenth pattern: B6, *(K2tog) 3 times, (yo, k1) 7 times, yo, (k2tog) 4 times; repeat from *, B6. [22; 364]
Eleventh pattern: B6, *(K2tog) 3 times, k1, (yo, k1) 7 times, yo, (k2tog) 4 times; repeat from *, B6. [23; 380]
Twelfth pattern: B6, *(K2tog) 3 times, k1, (yo, k1) 8 times, (k2tog) 4 times; repeat from *, B6. [24; 396]
Thirteenth pattern: B6, *(K2tog) 4 times, (yo, k1) 8 times, yo, (k2tog) 4 times; repeat from *, B6. [25; 412]
Fourteenth pattern: B6, *(K2tog) 4 times, k1, (yo, k1) 8 times, yo, (k2tog) 4 times; repeat from *, B6. [26; 428]
Fifteenth pattern: B6, *(K2tog) 4 times, k1, (yo, k1) 9 times, (k2tog) 4 times; repeat from *, B6. [27; 444]
Sixteenth pattern: B6, *(K2tog) 4 times, (yo, k1) 9 times, yo, (k2tog) 5 times; repeat from *, B6. [28; 460]
Seventeenth pattern: B6, *(K2tog) 4 times, k1, (yo, k1) 9 times, yo, (k2tog) 5 times; repeat from *, B6. [29; 476]

Eighteenth pattern: B6, *(K2tog) 4 times, kl, (yo, kl) 10 times, (k2tog) 5 times; repeat from *, B6. [30; 492]
Nineteenth pattern: B6, *(K2tog) 5 times, (yo, kl) 10 times, yo, (k2tog) 5 times; repeat from *, B6. [31; 508]
Twentieth pattern: B6, *(K2tog) 5 times, kl, (yo, kl) 10 times, yo, (k2tog) 5 times; repeat from *, B6. [32; 524]
Twenty-first pattern: B6, *(K2tog) 5 times, kl, (yo, kl) 11 times, (k2tog) 5 times; repeat from *, B6. [33; 540]
Twenty-second pattern: B6, *(K2tog) 5 times, (yo, kl) 11 times, yo, (k2tog) 6 times; repeat from *, B6. [34; 556]
Twenty-third pattern: B6, *(K2tog) 5 times, kl, (yo, kl) 11 times, yo, (k2tog) 6 times; repeat from *, B6. [35; 572]
Twenty-fourth pattern: B6, *(K2tog) 5 times, kl, (yo, kl) 12 times, (k2tog) 6 times; repeat from *, B6. [36; 588]
Twenty-fifth pattern: B6, *(K2tog) 6 times, (yo, kl) 12 times, yo, (k2tog) 6 times; repeat from *, B6. [37; 604]
Twenty-sixth pattern: B6, *(k2tog) 6 times, kl, (yo, kl) 12 times, yo, (k2tog) 6 times; repeat from *, B6. [38; 620]
Twenty-seventh pattern: B6, *(k2tog) 6 times, kl, (yo, kl) 13 times, (k2 tog) 6 times, repeat from *, B6. [39; 636]
Twenty-eighth pattern: B6, *(k2tog) 6 times, (yo, kl) 13 times, yo, (k2 tog) 7 times, repeat from *, B6. [40; 652]
Twenty-ninth pattern: B6, *(k2tog) 6 times, kl, (yo, kl) 13 times, yo, (k2 tog) 7 times, repeat from *, B6. [41; 668}
Thirtieth pattern: B6, *(k2tog) 6 times, kl, (yo, kl) 14 times, (k2tog) 7 times, repeat from *, B6. [42; 684]
Thirty-first pattern: B6, *(k2tog) 7 times, (yo, kl) 14 times, yo, (k2tog) 7 times, repeat from *, B6. [43; 700]
Thirty-second pattern: B6, *(k2tog) 7 times, kl, (yo, kl) 14 times, yo, (k2tog) 7 times, repeat from *, B6. [44; 716]
Thirty-third pattern: B6, *(k2tog) 7 times, kl, (yo, kl) 15 times, (k2tog) 7 times, repeat from *, B6. [45; 732]
Thirty-fourth pattern: B6, *(k2tog) 7 times, (yo, kl) 15 times, yo, (k2tog) 8 times, repeat from *, B6. [46; 748]
Thirty-fifth pattern: B6, *(k2tog) 7 times, kl, (yo, kl) 15 times, yo, (k2tog) 8 times, repeat from *, B6. [47; 764]
Thirty-sixth pattern: B6, *(k2tog) 7 times, kl, (yo, kl) 16 times, (k2tog) 8 times, repeat from *, B6. [48; 780]
Thirty-seventh pattern: B6, *(k2tog) 8 times, (yo, kl) 16 times, yo, (k2tog) 8 times, repeat from *, B6. [49; 796]
Thirty-eighth pattern: B6, *(k2tog) 8 times, kl, (yo, kl) 16 times, yo, (k2tog) 8 times, repeat from *, B6. [50; 812]

End your knitting of the body of your shawl after working a pattern row followed by a plain row.

Seed Stitch Bottom Border:

Row 1: Seed stitch is simply a continuation of the kl, pl, in the B6 borders you have been doing, with the appropriate decreases in this row. The decreases of this row are necessary to make the seed stitch border lie flat, rather than ruffle. All the decreasing is done in the portion of the scallop where you have previously done the k2togs. Decrease one stitch for every two "k2togs" from the prior pattern row, but be sure you end up with an odd-number of stitches. If the final pattern row of your shawl is the twenty-fifth repeat, the decrease row is:, B6, *p2tog, k2tog, p2tog, (kl, pl) 12 times, k2tog, p2tog, k2tog repeat from *, ending the last repeat k2tog, p2tog, kl, pl, B6. Note: You must end with an odd-number of stitches; adjust this row as necessary. You are decreasing approximately 1/6 of the stitches in the pattern row.
Rows 2-8: Work in seed stitch.
Row 9: Bind off using the Icelandic bind-off (page 21).

Marialis C – continuation of the Yoke and Lace Body

Row 23: B6, mlL, k 23, mlR, kl, mlL, k 23, mlR, kl, mlL, k 40, mlR, kl, mlL, k 23, mlR, kl, mlL, k 23, mlR, B6. [158]
Row 25: B6, mlL, k 25, mlR, kl, mlL, k 25, mlR, kl, mlL, k 42, mlR, kl, mlL, k 25, mlR, kl, mlL, k 25, mlR, B6. [168]
Row 27: B6, mlL, k 55, mlR,, kl, mlL, k 44, mlR,, kl, mlL, k 55, mlR, B6. [174]
You now have a total of 174 stitches on your needle: 162 stitches in the body of the shawl and six stitches in each front band border.

Variation I [smooth - stockinette stitch]:
Row 28: B6, purl across, B6.
Work the following four-row pattern until your shawl measures approximately 12 inches/30.5 cm in length from the outside edge of the B6 neck band border.
Row 1: B6, [place a marker on your needle, (k2tog) three times, (yo, kl) six times, (k2tog) three times] repeat between the brackets a total of 8 times, place a marker on your needle B6. [18; 174]
Row 2: B6, purl across, B6.
Row 3: B6, knit across, B6.
Row 4: B6, purl across, B6.

Variation II [ridges - every 4th row is garter stitch]:
Work the following four-row pattern until your shawl measures approximately 12 inches/30.5 cm in length from the outside edge of the B6 neck band border.
Begin row 1 of the pattern on the private/wrong side row, which is row 28 of your yoke.
Row 1: B6, [place a marker on your needle, (k2tog) three times, (yo, kl) six times, (k2tog) three times], repeat between the brackets a total of 8 times, place a marker on your needle, B6. [18; 174]
Row 2: B6, knit across, B6.
Row 3: B6, purl across, B6.
Row 4: B6, knit across, B6.

When your work measures approximately 12 inches/30.5 cm in length from the outside edge of the neck band border after completing row 4 above, work the following increase row:

> Increase row: B6, (kl, yo) across, B6. You now have 324 stitches plus six stitches for each of the two side borders, for a total of 336 stitches on your needle. Work row 4, placing a marker on your needle every 18 stitches in the body of your shawl. [18; 336]

Work as many pattern repeats as necessary to make your shawl the length you wish it to be; you very likely will NOT work all 24 pattern repeats unless you are using very fine fiber and very small needles. Remember, a pattern row is done once every four rows. End your knitting of the body of your shawl after working a pattern row plus row 2.
First pattern: B6, *(K2tog) 3 times, (yo, kl) 6 times, (k2tog) 3 times; repeat from*, B6. [18; 336]
Second pattern: B6, *(K2tog) 3 times, (yo, kl) 6 times, yo, (k2tog) 3 times; repeat from *, B6. [19; 354]
Third pattern: B6, *(K2tog) 3 times, kl, (yo, kl) 6 times, yo, (k2tog) 3 times; repeat from *, B6. [20; 372]
Fourth pattern: B6, *(K2tog) 3 times, kl, (yo, kl) 7 times, (k2tog) 3 times; repeat from*, B6. [21; 390]
Fifth pattern; B6, *(K2tog) 3 times, (yo, kl) 7 times, yo, (k2tog) 4 times; repeat from *, B6. [22; 408]
Sixth pattern: B6, *(K2tog) 3 times, kl, (yo, kl) 7 times, yo, (k2tog) 4 times; repeat from *, B6. [23; 426]
Seventh pattern: B6, *(K2tog) 3 times, kl, (yo, kl) 8 times, (k2tog) 4 times; repeat from *, B6. [24; 444]
Eighth pattern: B6, *(K2tog) 4 times, (yo, kl) 8 times, yo, (k2tog) 4 times; repeat from *, B6. [25; 462]

Ninth pattern: B6. *(K2tog) 4 times, kl, (yo, kl) 8 times, yo, (k2tog) 4 times; repeat from *, B6. [26; 480]
Tenth pattern: B6, *(K2tog) 4 times, kl, (yo, kl) 9 times, (k2tog) 4 times; repeat from *, B6. [27; 498]
Eleventh pattern: B6, *(K2tog) 4 times, (yo, kl) 9 times, yo, (k2tog) 5 times; repeat from*, B6. [28; 516]
Twelfth pattern: B6, *(K2tog) 4 times, kl, (yo, kl) 9 times, yo, (k2tog) 5 times; repeat from *, B6. [29; 534]
Thirteenth pattern: B6, *(K2tog) 4 times, kl, (yo, kl) 10 times, (k2tog) 5 times; repeat from *, B6. [30; 552]

Check now to see if your shawl is large enough.

Fourteenth pattern: B6, *(K2tog) 5 times, (yo, kl) 10 times, yo, (k2tog) 5 times; repeat from *, B6. [31; 570]
Fifteenth pattern: B6, *(K2tog) 5 times, kl, (yo, kl) 10 times, yo, (k2tog) 5 times; repeat from *, B6. [32; 588]
Sixteenth pattern: B6, *(K2tog) 5 times, kl, (yo, kl) 11 times, (k2tog) 5 times; repeat from *, B6. [33; 606]
Seventeenth pattern: B6, *(K2tog) 5 times, (yo, kl) 11 times, yo, (k2tog) 6 times; repeat from *, B6. [34; 624]
Eighteenth pattern: B6, *(K2tog) 5 times, kl, (yo, kl) 11 times, yo, (k2tog) 6 times; repeat from *, B6. [35; 642]
Nineteenth pattern: B6, *(K2tog) 5 times, kl, (yo, kl) 12 times, (k2tog) 6 times; repeat from *, B6. [36; 650]
Twentieth pattern: B6, *(K2tog) 6 times, (yo, kl) 12 times, yo, (k2tog) 6 times; repeat from *, B6. [37; 668]
Twenty-first pattern: B6, *(k2tog) 6 times, kl, (yo, kl) 12 times, yo, (k2tog) 6 times; repeat from *, B6. [38; 686]
Twenty-second pattern: B6, *(k2tog) 6 times, kl, (yo, kl) 13 times, (k2 tog) 6 times, repeat from *, B6. [39; 704]
Twenty-third pattern: B6, *(k2tog) 6 times, (yo, kl) 13 times, yo, (k2 tog) 7 times, repeat from *, B6. [40; 722]
Twenty-fourth pattern: B6, *(k2tog) 6 times, kl, (yo, kl) 13 times, yo, (k2 tog) 7 times, repeat from *, B6. [41; 740}

End your knitting of the body of your shawl after working a pattern row followed by a plain row.

Seed Stitch Bottom Border:

Row 1: Seed stitch is simply a continuation of the kl, pl, in the B6 borders you have been doing, with the appropriate decreases in this row. The decreases of this row are necessary to make the seed stitch border lie flat, rather than ruffle. All the decreasing is done in the portion of the scallop where you have previously done the k2togs. Decrease one stitch for every two "k2togs" from the prior pattern row, but be sure you end up with an odd-number of stitches. If the final pattern row of your shawl is the twentieth repeat, the decrease row is: B6, *p2tog, k2tog, p2tog, (kl, pl) 12 times, k2tog, p2tog, k2tog repeat from *, ending k2tog, p2tog, kl, pl, B6. Note: You must end this row with an odd-number of stitches; adjust as necessary. You are decreasing approximately 1/6 of the stitches in the pattern row.
Rows 2-8: Work in seed stitch.
Row 9: Bind off using the Icelandic bind-off (page 21).

Idella

A Norwegian lace doily, charted by Eugen Beugler, served as inspiration for this beautifully lacy shawl, named after my Norwegian mother-in-law. Consisting of just two sequences of eight stitches, as shown in Charts A1 and A2, alternately stacked to form the beautiful lace pattern, this appears more difficult than it is. Rows 1, 5, 9 & 13 are repeats of the eight stitches of Chart A1, while rows 3, 7, 11 and 15 are repeats of the eight stitches of Chart A2.

Idella building blocks
Chart A

	O	/		\	O		
O	/	O	⋏	O	\	O	
	O	/		\	O		
O	/	O	⋏	O	\	O	
\	O				O	/	
O	\	O		O	/	O	⋏
\	O				O	/	
O	\	O		O	/	O	⋏

Chart A2

\	O				O	/	

Chart A1

O	\	O		O	/	O	⋏

Haneke Select merino/mohair fingering weight

The Idella Seamen's Scarf

Tail #1:

Using a provisional cast-on (page 13), cast on 37 stitches.

Set-up row: K2, pl, kl, pl, kl, place a marker on your needle, purl 25, place a marker on your needle, B6 (page 23).

Using Idella Chart S, work as many repeats of rows 1-16 as necessary to obtain the length you desire.

Finish tail #1 by working eight rows of seed stitch. Bind off on the ninth row, using the knit-in-pattern bind-off (page 21).

Neckline ribbing:

Remove the provisional cast-on, picking up the 37 stitches.

Set-up row: With the private/wrong side of your scarf facing you, slip the first stitch as if to knit, p4, k4, p4, k4, p3, k4, p4, k4, ending p4, kl.

Row 1: Slip the first stitch as if to purl, k4, p4, k4, p4, k3, p4, k4, p4, k5.

Row 2: Slip the first stitch as if to purl, p4, k4, p4, k4, p3, k4, p4, k4, ending p4, kl.

Repeat Rows 1 & 2 until the neckline ribbing measures approximately 70% of the neck measurement of the intended wearer, between 10 inches/25 cm and 12 inches/30 cm. End after working row 1.

Tail #2:

Set-up row: B6, place a marker on your needle, purl 25, place a marker on your needle, B6.

Work the same as for Tail #1, beginning with "Using Idella Chart S."

Cashmere America
cashmere
2-ply fingering weight

Idella scarf – Chart S

#		\	O				O	/		\	O				O	/		\	O				O	/		#	15
#	\	O	\	O		O	/	O	⋏	O	\	O		O	/	O	⋏	O	\	O		O	/	O	/	#	13
#		\	O				O	/		\	O				O	/		\	O				O	/		#	11
#	\	O	\	O		O	/	O	⋏	O	\	O		O	/	O	⋏	O	\	O		O	/	O	/	#	9
#			O	/		\	O				O	/		\	O				O	/		\	O			#	7
#		O	/	O	⋏	O	\	O		O	/	O	⋏	O	\	O		O	/	O	⋏	O	\	O		#	5
#			O	/		\	O				O	/		\	O				O	/		\	O			#	3
#		O	/	O	⋏	O	\	O		O	/	O	⋏	O	\	O		O	/	O	⋏	O	\	O		#	1
#		\	O				O	/		\	O				O	/		\	O				O	/		#	15
#	\	O	\	O		O	/	O	⋏	O	\	O		O	/	O	⋏	O	\	O		O	/	O	/	#	13
#		\	O				O	/		\	O				O	/		\	O				O	/		#	11
#	\	O	\	O		O	/	O	⋏	O	\	O		O	/	O	⋏	O	\	O		O	/	O	/	#	9
#			O	/		\	O				O	/		\	O				O	/		\	O			#	7
#		O	/	O	⋏	O	\	O		O	/	O	⋏	O	\	O		O	/	O	⋏	O	\	O		#	5
#			O	/		\	O				O	/		\	O				O	/		\	O			#	3
#		O	/	O	⋏	O	\	O		O	/	O	⋏	O	\	O		O	/	O	⋏	O	\	O		#	1
									II								I										

Variation: Make a wider scarf by adding one pattern repeat.

Using a provisional cast-on, cast on 45 stitches and work as above, repeating once between points I and II of Idella Chart S.

For the neckline ribbing: Remove the provisional cast-on and pick up the 45 stitches.

Set-up row: With the private side of your scarf facing you, slip the first stitch as if to knit, p4, k4, p4, k4, p4, k3, p4, k4, p4, k4, p4, kl.

Idella

Using a provisional cast-on (page 13), cast on 7 stitches for seed stitch neck band/front border.

Set-up row: K2, pl, kl, pl, k2. [7 sts]

Rows 2-45: Slip the first stitch as if to purl, kl, pl, kl, pl, k2. [7 stitches]

Following the instructions for "Picking up Neck Band Stitches for the Body of Your Shawl" (page 16), pick up 21 stitches.

Pick up the stitches from your provisional cast-on by following the instructions for "Recovering Stitches from the Provisional Cast-On" (page 18). [35 sts]

When working the first row, and only the first row of your shawl, when you have just seven stitches left on your left needle, K2tog, pl, kl, pl, k2. [34 sts]

Using Charts C [side panels] and D [back panel], and following the instructions "Using the Charts for a Faroese-Shaped Shawl" (page 26), begin your shawl.

Row 2a and all even-numbered rows: B6, purl across, B6.

Continue, following the charts in the same sequence. Repeat rows 1-16 as necessary to obtain the length you desire, ending after working row 14.

Knitting on the Lace Border: Go to the instructions on page 27, "The Lace Border." Using Idella Chart E (page 28), work the lace border.

Or, if you prefer, finish your shawl by working eight rows of seed stitch. Bind off using either the knit-in-pattern bind-off (page 21) or the Icelandic bind-off (page 21) .

Dress your shawl (page 34). Enjoy wearing your beautiful hand knit work of art!

Idella shawl back panel – Chart D

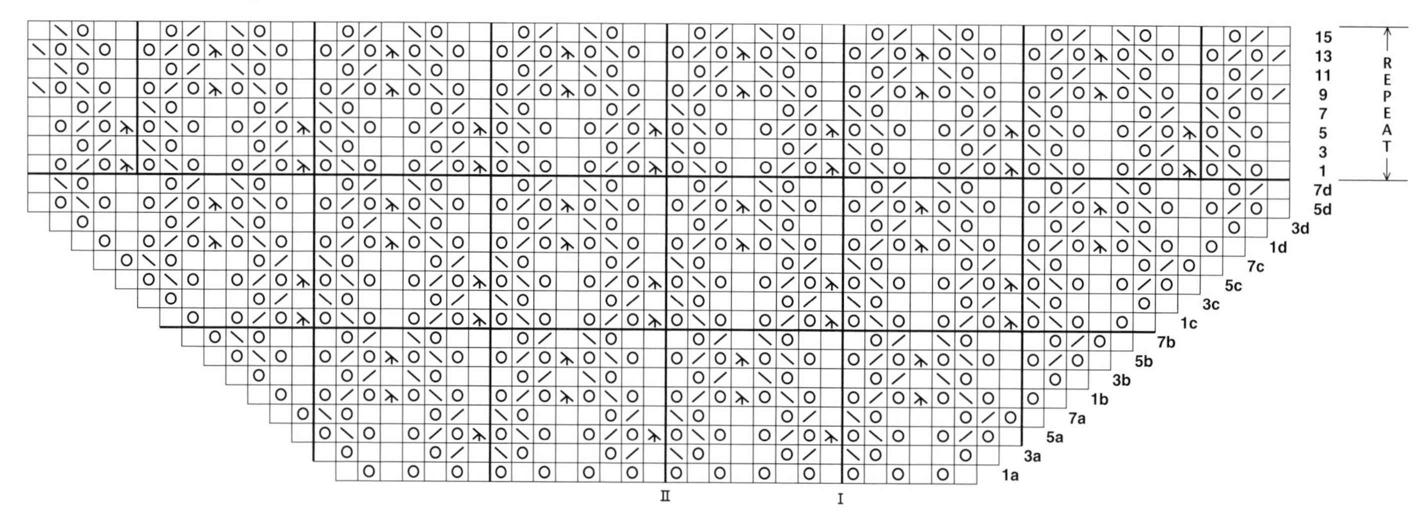

Idella swatch – Chart B

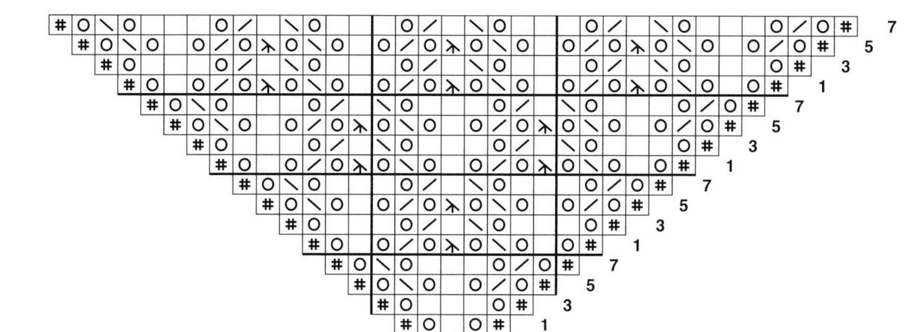

Swatch Chart B rows 1 & 2 in words:

Cast on 13 stitches.

Row 1: B6, yo, k1, yo, B6; or, in other words:

Slip the first stitch as if to purl, k1, p1, k1, p1, k1, yo, k1, yo, k1, p1, k1, p1, k2.

Row 2 and all even-numbered rows: B6, purl across, B6; or, in other words:

Slip the first stitch as if to purl, k1, p1, k1, p1, k1, purl across to the last six stitches, k1, p1, k1, p1, k2.

Idella Shawl Charts C & D, row 1a in words:

Work the six border stitches [B6], which are not shown in the chart and which at the beginning of the row are always worked as slip the first stitch as if to purl, k1, p1, k1, p1, k1; place a marker on your needle;

work the first side panel using Chart C, which is yo, k1, yo, k1, yo, k1, yo; place a marker on your needle;

work the back panel using Chart D, which is (k1, yo) 14 times, k1; place a marker on your needle;

work the second side panel, again using Chart C, which is yo, k1, yo, k1, yo, k1, yo; place a marker on your needle;

work the six border stitches [B6], which are not shown on the chart and which at the end of the row are always worked as k1, p1, k1, p1, k2.

Row 2a and all even-numbered rows:

Slip the first stitch as if to purl, k1, p1, k1, p1, k1, purl across to the last marker, k1, p1, k1, p1, k2.

Idella shawl side panel – Chart C

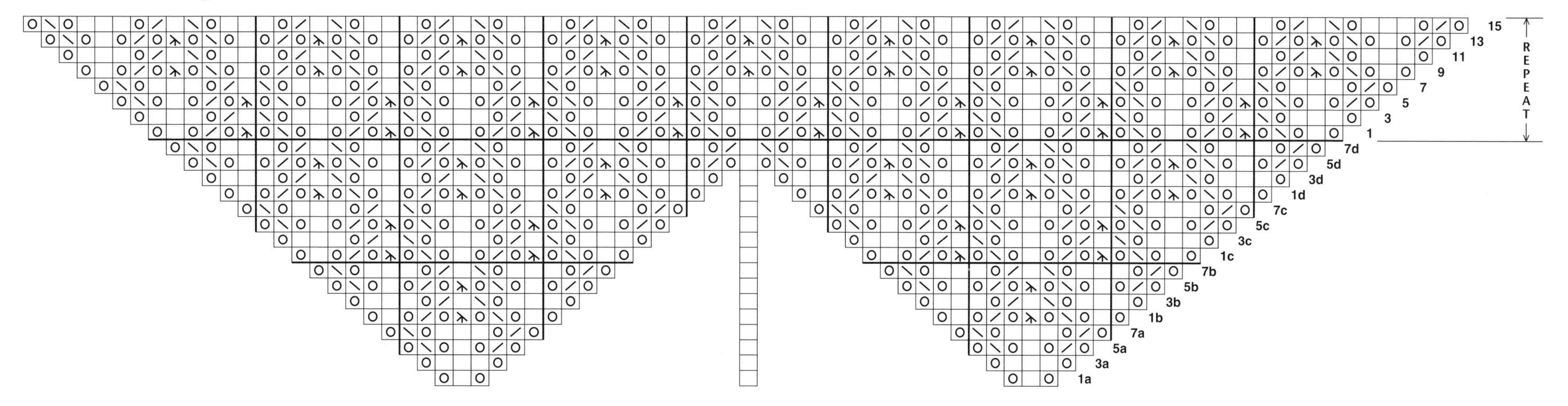

Alberta

Fern lace, a beautiful lace pattern, was selected for this shawl named after our adopted "Grandma Bert" who loved gardening. Unlike many lace patterns, the yarnover increases of fern lace are often not immediately next to the decreases. Angora handspun makes this shawl bloom.

Alberta building block Chart A

O				⋏				O	
O			/		\			O	
O		/				\		O	
O	/						\	O	
			O		O				⋏
\			O		O			/	
	\		O		O		/		
		\	O		O	/			

Ozark Carding Mill
hand spun by Gail White
angora sport weight

The Alberta Seamen's Scarf

Tail #1:

Using a provisional cast-on (page 13), cast on 43 stitches.

Set-up row: K2, pl, kl, pl, kl, place a marker on your needle, purl 31, place a marker on your needle, B6 (page 23).

Using Alberta Chart S, work as many repeats of rows 1-16 as necessary to obtain the length you desire.

Finish tail #1 by working eight rows of seed stitch. Bind off on the ninth row, using the knit-in-pattern bind-off (page 21).

Neckline ribbing:

Remove the provisional cast-on, picking up the 43 stitches.

Set-up row: With the private/wrong side of your scarf facing you, slip the first stitch as if to knit, p3, k4, p4, k4, p4, k3, p4, k4, p4, k4, p3, kl.

Row 1: Slip the first stitch as if to purl, k3, p4, k4, p4, k4, p3, k4, p4, k4, p4, k4.

Row 2: Slip the first stitch as if to purl, p3, k4, p4, k4, p4, k3, p4, k4, p4, k4, p3, kl.

Repeat Rows 1 & 2 until the neckline ribbing measures approximately 70% of the neck measurement of the intended wearer, between 10 inches/25 cm and 12 inches/30 cm. End after working row 1.

Tail #2:

Set-up row: B6, place a marker on your needle, purl 31, place a marker on your needle, B6.

Work the same as for Tail #1, beginning with "Using Alberta Chart S."

Haneke Select
merino/mohair
lace weight

Alberta scarf – Chart S

#		O				⋏				O		O				⋏				O		O				⋏				O		#	15
#		O			/		\			O		O			/		\			O		O			/		\			O		#	13
#		O		/				\		O		O		/				\		O		O		/				\		O		#	11
#		O	/						\	O		O	/						\	O		O	/						\	O		#	9
#	\				O		O				⋏				O		O				⋏				O		O				/	#	7
#		\			O		O			/		\			O		O			/		\			O		O			/		#	5
#			\		O		O		/				\		O		O		/				\		O		O		/			#	3
#				\	O		O	/						\	O		O	/						\	O		O	/				#	1
#		O				⋏				O		O				⋏				O		O				⋏				O		#	15
#		O			/		\			O		O			/		\			O		O			/		\			O		#	13
#		O		/				\		O		O		/				\		O		O		/				\		O		#	11
#		O	/						\	O		O	/						\	O		O	/						\	O		#	9
#	\				O		O				⋏				O		O				⋏				O		O				/	#	7
#		\			O		O			/		\			O		O			/		\			O		O			/		#	5
#			\		O		O		/				\		O		O		/				\		O		O		/			#	3
#				\	O		O	/						\	O		O	/						\	O		O	/				#	1

II I

Alberta Shawl

Using a provisional cast-on (page 13), cast on 7 stitches for seed stitch neck band/front border.

Set-up row: K2, pl, kl, pl, k2. [7 sts]

Rows 2-73: Slip the first stitch as if to purl, kl, pl, kl, pl, k2. [7 sts]

Following the instructions for "Picking up Neck Band Stitches for the Body of Your Shawl" (page 16), pick up 35 stitches.

Pick up the stitches from your provisional cast-on by following the instructions for "Recovering Stitches from the Provisional Cast-On" (page 18). [48 sts]

When working the first row, and only the first row of your shawl, when you have just seven stitches left on your left needle, K2tog, pl, kl, pl, k2. [47 sts]

Using Charts C [side panels] and D [back panel], and following the instructions "Using the Charts for a Faroese-Shaped Shawl" (page 26), begin your shawl.

Row 2a and all even-numbered rows: B6, purl across, B6.

Continue, following the charts in the same sequence. Repeat rows 1-16 as necessary to obtain the length you desire, ending after working row 16.

Knitting on the Lace Border: Go to the instructions on page 27, "The Lace Border." Using Alberta Chart E (page 29), work the lace border.

Or, if you prefer, finish your shawl by working eight rows of seed stitch. Bind off using either the knit-in-pattern bind-off (page 21) or the Icelandic bind-off (page 21) .

Dress your shawl (page 34). Enjoy wearing your beautiful hand knit work of art!

Alberta shawl back panel – Chart D

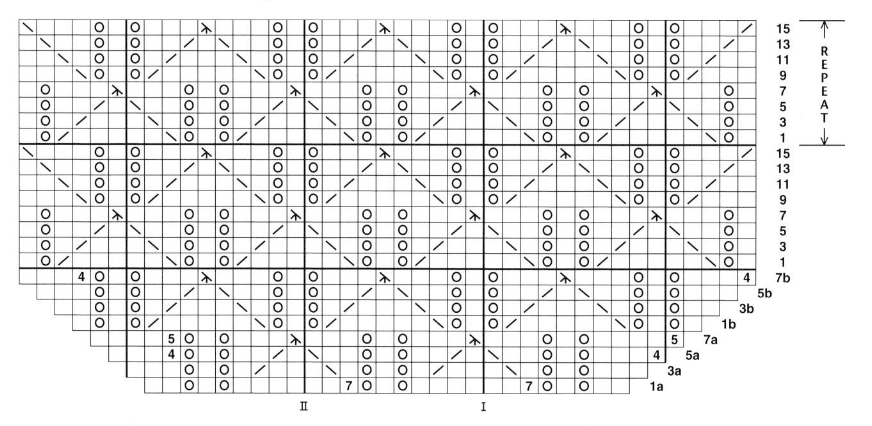

Swatch Chart B rows 1a & 2a in words:

Cast on 15 stitches.

Row 1a: B6, k1, yo, k1, yo, k1, B6; or, in other words:

Slip the first stitch as if to purl, k1, p1, k1, p1, k2, yo, k1, yo, k2, p1, k1, p1, k2.

Row 2a and all even-numbered rows: B6, purl across, B6; or, in other words:

Slip the first stitch as if to purl, k1, p1, k1, p1, k1, purl across to the last six stitches, k1, p1, k1, p1, k2.

Alberta Shawl Charts C & D, row 1a in words:

Work the six border stitches [B6], which are not shown in the chart and which at the beginning of the row are always worked as slip the first stitch as if to purl, k1, p1, k1, p1, k1; place a marker on your needle;

work the first side panel using Chart C, which is k1, yo, k1, yo, k3, yo, k1, yo, k1; place a marker on your needle;

work the back panel using Chart D, which is k2, yo, k1, yo, k7, yo, k1, yo, k7, yo, k1, yo, k2; place a marker on your needle;

work the second side panel, again using Chart C, which is k1, yo, k1, yo, k3, yo, k1, yo, k1; place a marker on your needle;

work the six border stitches [B6], which are not shown on the chart and which at the end of the row are always worked as k1, p1, k1, p1, k2.

Row 2a and all even-numbered rows:

Slip the first stitch as if to purl, k1, p1, k1, p1, k1, purl across to the last marker, k1, p1, k1, p1, k2.

Alberta swatch – Chart B

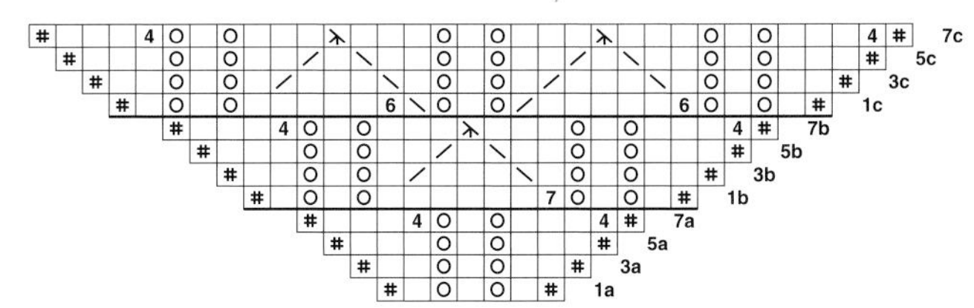

The triangular swatch for this pattern, Alberta Chart B, requires casting on 15 stitches when working with a six-stitch seed stitch border.

Alberta shawl side panel – Chart C

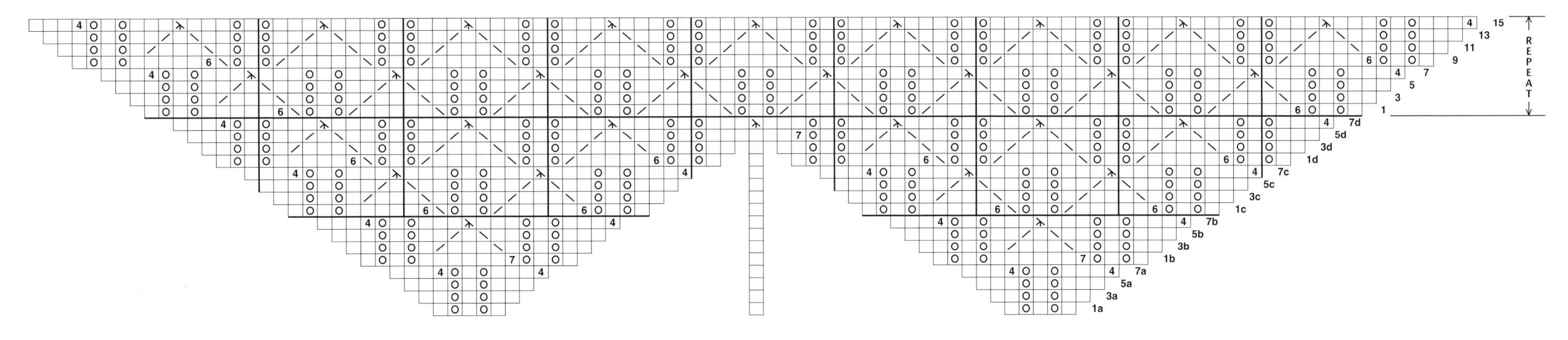

Alka

Named in honor of my Aunt Alice, whose Dutch name is Alka, this lace pattern reminds me of the tulip fields of Holland. The many shawls pictured in the foreground of the cover photo are made from this pattern, as are the shawls in Chapter 8 on "Customizing the Faroese Shawl Patterns."

Alka building block
Chart A

O							7	O	⋏
\	O		O	⋏	O		O	/	
		O	/		\	O			
	O	/				\	O		
O	/					5	\	O	
			O	⋏	O				
O		O	/		\	O		O	⋏
\	O						O	/	
	\	O				O	/		
		\	O		O	/			

Louet Euroflax
linen
4/14 fingering weight

The Alka Seamen's Scarf

Tail #1:

Using a provisional cast-on (page 13), cast on 43 stitches.

Set-up row: K2, p1, k1, p1, k1, place a marker on your needle, purl 31, place a marker on your needle, B6 (page 23).

Using Alka Chart S, work as many repeats of rows 1-20 as necessary to obtain the length you desire.

Finish tail #1 by working eight rows of seed stitch. Bind off on the ninth row, using the knit-in-pattern bind-off (page 21).

Neckline ribbing:

Remove the provisional cast-on, picking up the 43 stitches.

Set-up row: With the private/wrong side of your scarf facing you, slip the first stitch as if to knit, p3, k4, p4, k4, p4, k3, p4, k4, p4, k4, p3, k1.

Row 1: Slip the first stitch as if to purl, k3, p4, k4, p4, k4, p3, k4, p4, k4, p4, k4.

Row 2: Slip the first stitch as if to purl, p3, k4, p4, k4, p4, k3, p4, k4, p4, k4, p3, k1.

Repeat rows 1 & 2 until the neckline ribbing measures approximately 70% of the neck measurement of the intended wearer, between 10 inches/25 cm and 12 inches/30 cm. End after working row 1.

Tail #2:

Set-up row: B6, place a marker on your needle, purl 31, place a marker on your needle, B6.

Work the same as for Tail #1, beginning with "Using Alka Chart S."

Alka scarf – Chart S

#	\	O							7	O	⋏	O							7	O	⋏	O							7	O	/	#	19
#		\	O		O	⋏	O		O	/		\	O		O	⋏	O		O	/		\	O		O	⋏	O		O	/		#	17
#				O	/		\	O					5	O	/		\	O					5	O	/		\	O				#	15
#			O	/				\	O				O	/				\	O				O	/				\	O			#	13
#		O	/					5	\	O		O	/					5	\	O		O	/					5	\	O		#	11
#				4	O	⋏	O							7	O	⋏	O							7	O	⋏	O				4	#	9
#	\	O		O	/		\	O		O	⋏	O		O	/		\	O		O	⋏	O		O	/		\	O		O	/	#	7
#		\	O					5	O	/		\	O					5	O	/		\	O					5	O	/		#	5
#			\	O				O	/				\	O				O	/				\	O				O	/			#	3
#				\	O		O	/					5	\	O		O	/					5	\	O		O	/				#	1
#	\	O							7	O	⋏	O							7	O	⋏	O							7	O	/	#	19
#		\	O		O	⋏	O		O	/		\	O		O	⋏	O		O	/		\	O		O	⋏	O		O	/		#	17
#				O	/		\	O					5	O	/		\	O					5	O	/		\	O				#	15
#			O	/				\	O				O	/				\	O				O	/				\	O			#	13
#		O	/					5	\	O		O	/					5	\	O		O	/					5	\	O		#	11
#				4	O	⋏	O							7	O	⋏	O							7	O	⋏	O				4	#	9
#	\	O		O	/		\	O		O	⋏	O		O	/		\	O		O	⋏	O		O	/		\	O		O	/	#	7
#		\	O					5	O	/		\	O					5	O	/		\	O					5	O	/		#	5
#			\	O				O	/				\	O				O	/				\	O				O	/			#	3
#				\	O		O	/					5	\	O		O	/					5	\	O		O	/				#	1
												II										I											

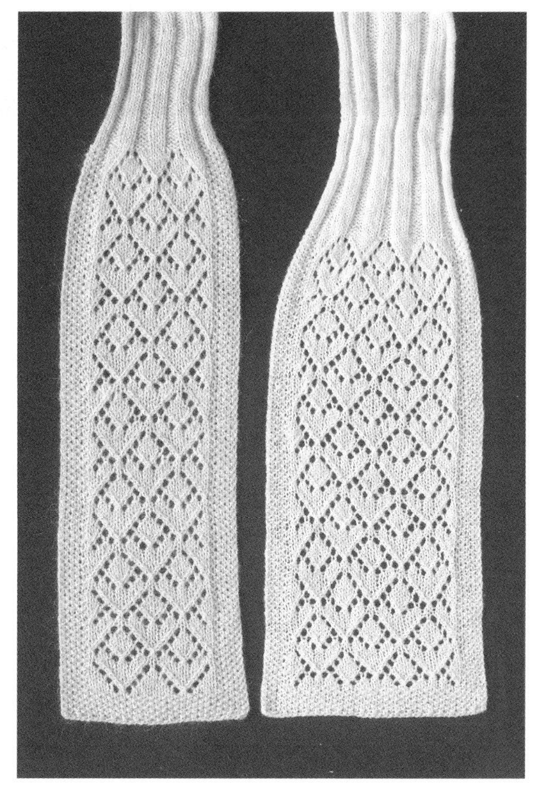

Haneke Select merino/alpaca fingering weight — *Haneke merino lace weight*

Variation: Make a narrower scarf by omitting one pattern repeat.

Cast on 33 stitches and work as above, omitting the stitches between points I and II of Alka Chart S.

For the neckline ribbing: Remove the provisional cast-on and pick up the 33 stitches.

Set-up row: With the private/wrong side of your scarf facing you, slip the first stitch as if to knit, *p3, k4, repeat from *, ending p3, k1.

I have to tell you the Alka shawl is really a pleasure to work on. The pattern is beautiful, and I am absolutely crazy about the Haneke alpaca and silk yarn. I just can't fondle it enough. I've been taking the shawl to work hoping to get time to work on it during lunch hour, and everyone who sees it thinks it's beautiful.

– Evelyn Rude

Alka Shawl

Using a provisional cast-on (page 13), cast on 7 stitches for seed stitch neck band/front border.

Set-up row: K2, pl, kl, pl, k2. [7 sts]

Rows 2-53: Slip the first stitch as if to purl, kl, pl, kl, pl, k2. [7 sts]

Following the instructions for "Picking up Neck Band Stitches for the Body of Your Shawl" (page 16), pick up 25 stitches.

Pick up the stitches from your provisional cast-on by following the instructions for "Recovering Stitches from the Provisional Cast-On" (page 18). [38 sts]

When working the first row, and only the first row of your shawl, when you have just seven stitches left on your left needle, K2tog, pl, kl, pl, k2. [37 sts]

Using Charts C [side panels] and D [back panel], and following the instructions "Using the Charts for a Faroese-Shaped Shawl" (page 26), begin your shawl.

Row 2a and all even-numbered rows: B6, purl across, B6.

Continue, following the charts in the same sequence. Repeat rows 1-20 as necessary to obtain almost the length you desire, ending after working row 20.

Go to Charts CZ and DZ and work rows lz-8z.

Knitting on the Lace Border: Go to the instructions on page 27, "The Lace Border." Using Alka Chart E [page 28], work the lace border.

Or, if you prefer, finish your shawl by working eight rows of seed stitch. Bind off using either the knit-in-pattern bind-off (page 21) or the Icelandic bind-off (page 21) .Dress your shawl (page 34). Enjoy wearing your beautiful hand knit work of art!

Alka shawl back panel – Chart DZ

Use Chart DZ for the final eight rows of the shawl.

Alka shawl back panel – Chart D

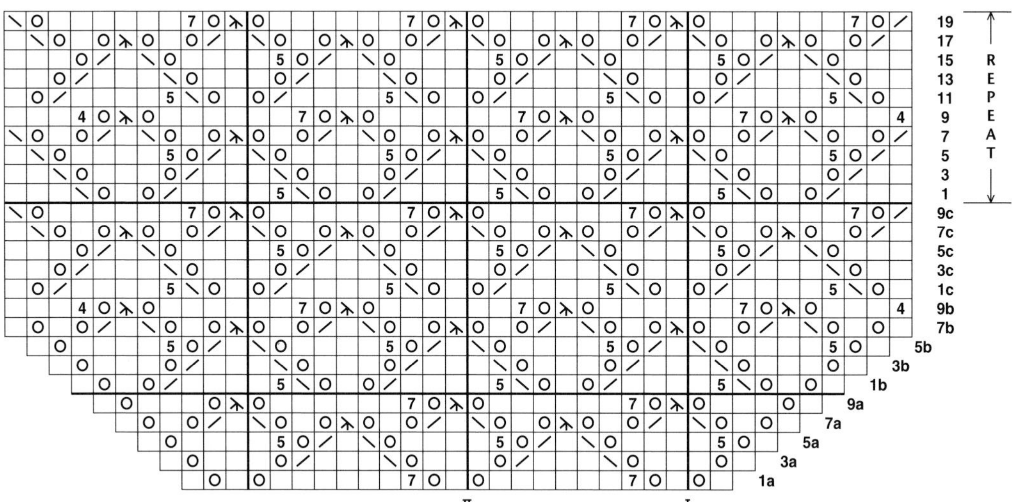

Alka swatch – Chart B

Swatch Chart B:

Cast on 13 stitches.

Row 1: B6, yo, k1, yo, B6; or, in other words:

Slip the first stitch as if to purl, k1, p1, k1, p1, k1, yo, k1, yo, k1, p1, k1, p1, k2.

Row 2 and all even-numbered rows: B6, purl across, B6; or, in other words:

Slip the first stitch as if to purl, k1, p1, k1, p1, k1, purl across to the last six stitches, k1, p1, k1, p1, k2.

Alka Shawl Charts C & D, row 1a in words:

Work the six border stitches [B6], which are not shown in the chart and which at the beginning of the row are always worked as slip the first stitch as if to purl, k1, p1, k1, p1, k1; place a marker on your needle;

work the first side panel using Chart C, which is yo, k1, yo, k1, yo, k1, yo; place a marker on your needle;

work the back panel using Chart D, which is k1, yo, k1, yo, k7, yo, k1, yo, k7, yo, k1, yo, k1; place a marker on your needle;

work the second side panel, again using Chart C, which is yo, k1, yo, k1, yo, k1, yo; place a marker on your needle;

work the six border stitches [B6], which are not shown on the chart and which at the end of the row are always worked as k1, p1, k1, p1, k2.

Row 2a and all even-numbered rows:

Slip the first stitch as if to purl, k1, p1, k1, p1, k1, purl across to the last marker, k1, p1, k1, p1, k2.

Alka shawl side panel – Chart CZ

II ←—— REPEAT ——→ I

Use Chart CZ for the final eight rows of your shawl.

Alka shawl side panel – Chart C

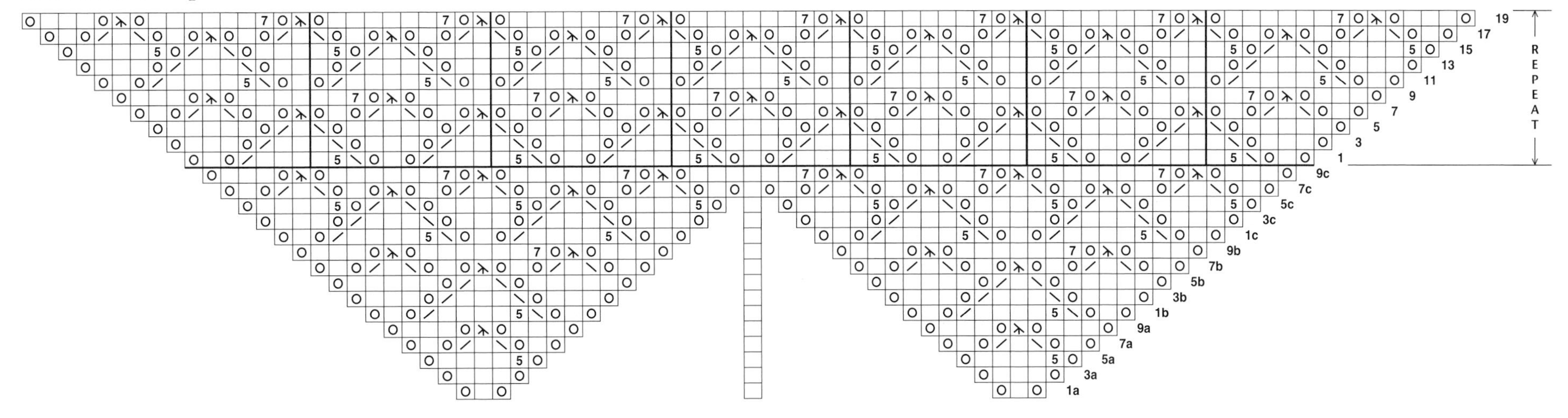

Barbara

No knitter's bookshelf is complete without the works of Barbara G. Walker. This adaptation of "Smiling Diamonds" from *A Treasury of Knitting Stitches* is named for Barbara, who has for years been an inspiration for knitters worldwide.

Barbara building block Chart A

			O	⋏	O				
		O	/		\	O			
	O	/	O	⋏	O	\	O		
O	/	O	/		\	O	\	O	
/	O	/	O		O	\	O	\	
O							7	O	⋏
\	O					5	O	/	
O	\	O				O	/	O	⋏
\	O	\	O		O	/	O	/	
O	\	O	\		/	O	/	O	

Creature Comforts chinchilla/merino/silk fingering weight

The Barbara Seamen's Scarf

Haneke Select merino/alpaca fingering weight

Tail #1:

Using a provisional cast-on (page 13), cast on 43 stitches.

Set-up row: K2, pl, kl, pl, kl, place a marker on your needle, purl 31, place a marker on your needle, B6 (page 23).

Using Barbara Chart S, work as many repeats of rows 1-20 as necessary to obtain the length you desire.

Finish tail #1 by working eight rows of seed stitch. Bind off on the ninth row, using the knit-in-pattern bind-off (page 21).

Neckline ribbing:

Remove the provisional cast-on, picking up the 43 stitches.

Set-up row: With the private side of your scarf facing you, slip the first stitch as if to knit, p3, k4, p4, k4, p4, k3, p4, k4, p4, k4, p3, kl.

Row 1: Slip the first stitch as if to purl, k3, p4, k4, p4, k4, p3, k4, p4, k4, p4, k4.

Row 2: Slip the first stitch as if to purl, p3, k4, p4, k4, p4, k3, p4, k4, p4, k4, p4.

Repeat Rows 1 & 2 until the neckline ribbing measures approximately 70% of the neck measurement of the intended wearer, between 10 inches/25 cm and 12 inches/30 cm. End after working row 1.

Tail #2:

Set-up row: B6, place a marker on your needle, purl 31, place a marker on your needle, B6.

Work the same as for Tail #1, beginning with "Using Barbara Chart S."

Barbara scarf – Chart S

#				4	O	⋏	O							7	O	⋏	O							7	O	⋏	O				4	#	19
#				O	/		\	O					5	O	/		\	O					5	O	/		\	O				#	17
#			O	/	O	⋏	O	\	O				O	/	O	⋏	O	\	O				O	/	O	⋏	O	\	O			#	15
#		O	/	O	/		\	O	\	O		O	/	O	/		\	O	\	O		O	/	O	/		\	O	\	O		#	13
#		/	O	/	O		O	\	O	\		/	O	/	O		O	\	O	\		/	O	/	O		O	\	O	\		#	11
#	\	O							7	O	⋏	O							7	O	⋏	O							7	O	/	#	9
#		\	O					5	O	/		\	O					5	O	/		\	O					5	O	/		#	7
#	\	O	\	O				O	/	O	⋏	O	\	O				O	/	O	⋏	O	\	O				O	/	O	/	#	5
#		\	O	\	O		O	/	O	/		\	O	\	O		O	/	O	/		\	O	\	O		O	/	O	/		#	3
#		O	\	O	\		/	O	/	O		O	\	O	\		/	O	/	O		O	\	O	\		/	O	/	O		#	1
											II										I												

Variation: Make a narrower scarf by omitting one pattern repeat.

Cast on 33 stitches and work as above, omitting the stitches between points I and II of Barbara Chart S.

For the neckline ribbing: Remove the provisional cast-on and pick up the 33 stitches.

Set-up row: With the private side of your scarf facing you, slip the first stitch as if to knit, *p3, k4, repeat from *, ending p3, kl.

Barbara Shawl

My mother-in-law fell in love with the Barbara shawl I proof knit. I am really going to have a difficult time parting with it, but she is really going to be surprised and happy when she opens her Christmas present.
– Connie Spann

Using a provisional cast-on (page 13), cast on 7 stitches for the seed stitch neck band/front border.
Row 1: K2, p1, k1, p1, k2.
Rows 2-41: Slip the first stitch as if to purl, k1, p1, k1, p1, k2. [7 sts]

Following the instruction for "Picking up Neck Band Stitches for the Body of Your Shawl" (page 16), pick up 19 stitches.
Pick up the stitches from your provisional cast-on by following the instructions for "Recovering Stitches from the Provisional Cast-On" (page 18). [32 sts]
When working the first row, and only the first row of your shawl, when you have just seven stitches left on your left needle, K2tog, p1, k1, p1, k2. [31 sts]
Using Charts C [side panels] and D [back panel], and following the instructions "Using the Charts for a Faroese-Shaped Shawl" (page 26), begin your shawl.
Row 2a and all even-numbered rows: B6, purl across, B6.
Continue, following the charts in the same sequence. Repeat rows 1-20 as necessary to obtain the length you desire, ending after working row 20.

Knitting on the Lace Border: Go to the instructions on page 27, "The Lace Border." Using Barbara Chart E (page 29), work the lace border.
Or, if you prefer, finish your shawl by working eight rows of seed stitch. Bind off using the knit-in-pattern bind-off (page 21) or the Icelandic bind-off (page 21).

Dress your shawl (page 34). Enjoy wearing your beautiful hand knit work of art!

Barbara shawl back panel – Chart D

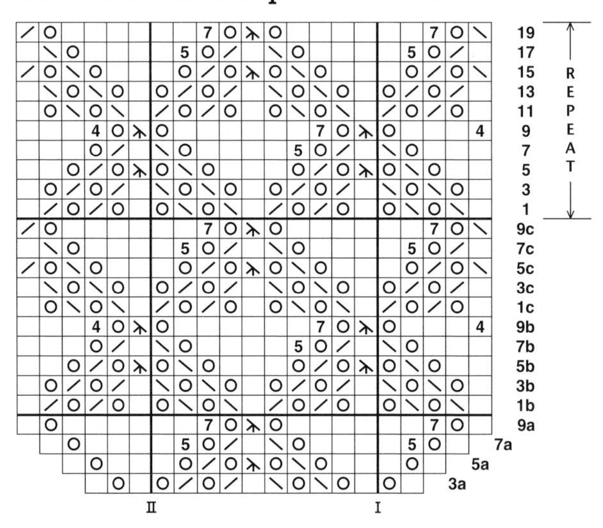

Barbara swatch – Chart B

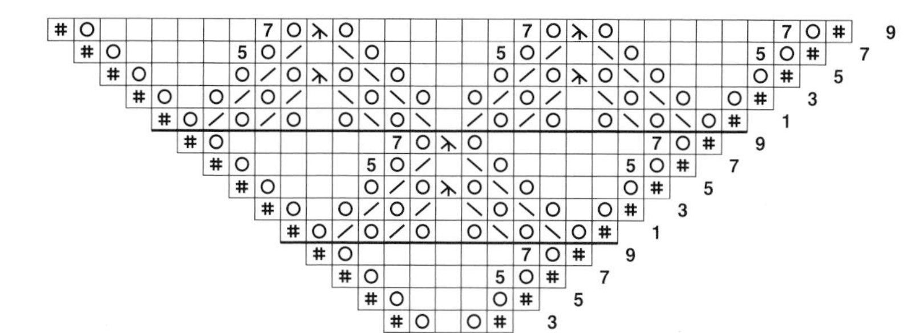

Swatch Chart B rows 3 & 4 in words:

Cast on 13 stitches.

Row 3: B6, yo, kl, yo, B6; or, in other words:

Slip the first stitch as if to purl, kl, pl, kl, pl, kl, yo, kl, yo, kl, pl, kl, pl, k2.

Row 4 and all even-numbered rows: B6, purl across, B6; or, in other words:

Slip the first stitch as if to purl, kl, pl, kl, pl, kl, purl across to the last six stitches, kl, pl, kl, pl, k2.

Barbara Shawl Charts C & D, row 3a in words:

Work the six border stitches [B6], which are not shown in the chart and which at the beginning of the row are always worked as slip the first stitch as if to purl, kl, pl, kl, pl, kl; place a marker on your needle;

work the first side panel using Chart C, which is yo, kl, yo, kl, yo, kl, yo; place a marker on your needle;

work the back panel using Chart D, which is kl, yo, kl, yo, ssk, yo, ssk, kl, k2tog, yo, k2tog, yo, kl, yo, kl; place a marker on your needle;

work the second side panel, again using Chart C, which is yo, kl, yo, kl, yo, kl, yo; place a marker on your needle;

work the six border stitches [B6], which are not shown on the chart and which at the end of the row are always worked as kl, pl, kl, pl, k2.

Row 4a and all even-numbered rows:

Slip the first stitch as if to purl, kl, pl, kl, pl, kl, purl across to the last marker, kl, pl, kl, pl, k2.

The first row of the swatch and the body of the shawl are called row 3 and 3a in keeping with the pattern sequence. You are not missing anything; there is no row 1 or row 2 in the first pattern sequence.

Barbara shawl side panel – Chart C

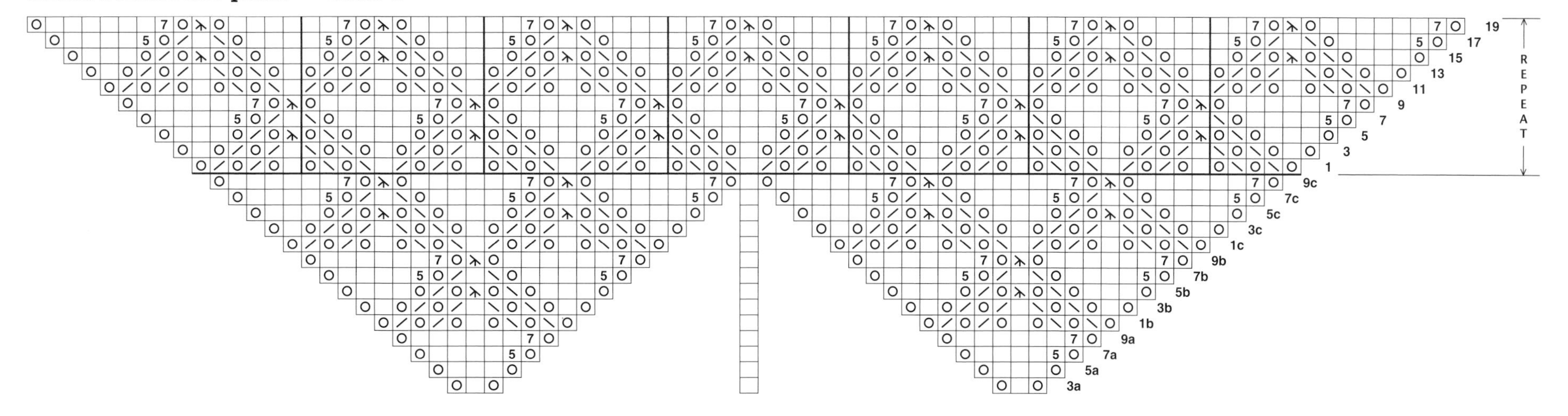

Susan

The beautifully simple diamond, formed when 3-to-1 decreases in a vertical column are diagonally bordered with yarnovers, creates Susan, named for the many Susans who have influenced my life.

Susan building block Chart A

			O	↑	O				
		O		↑		O			
	O			↑			O		
O				↑				O	
O							7	O	↑
	O					5	O		↑
		O				O			↑
			O		O				↑

Haneke Melange
alpaca
fingering weight

The Susan Seamen's Scarf

Haneke Heaven Sent alpaca/merino fingering weight

Tail #1:

Using a provisional cast-on (page 13), cast on 43 stitches.

Set-up row: K2, pl, kl, pl, kl, place a marker on your needle, purl 31, place a marker on your needle, B6 (page 23).

Using Susan Chart S, work as many repeats of rows 1-16 as necessary to obtain the length you desire.

Finish tail #1 by working eight rows of seed stitch. Bind off on the ninth row, using the knit-in-pattern bind-off (page 21).

Neckline ribbing:

Remove the provisional cast-on, picking up the 43 stitches.

Set-up row: With the private/wrong side of your scarf facing you, slip the first stitch as if to knit, p3, k4, p4, k4, p4, k3, p4, k4, p4, k4, p3, kl.

Row 1: Slip the first stitch as if to purl, k3, p4, k4, p4, k4, p3, k4, p4, k4, p4, k4.

Row 2: Slip the first stitch as if to purl, p3, k4, p4, k4, p4, k3, p4, k4, p4, k4, p3, kl.

Repeat Rows 1 & 2 until the neckline ribbing measures approximately 70% of the neck measurement of the intended wearer, between 10 inches/25 cm and 12 inches/30 cm. End after working row 1.

Tail #2:

Set-up row: B6, place a marker on your needle, purl 31, place a marker on your needle, B6.

Work the same as for Tail #1, beginning with "Using Susan Chart S."

Susan scarf – Chart S

#				4	O	↑	O							7	O	↑	O							7	O	↑	O				4	#	15
#				O		↑		O					5	O		↑		O					5	O		↑		O				#	13
#			O			↑			O				O			↑			O				O			↑			O			#	11
#		O				↑				O		O				↑				O		O				↑				O		#	9
#	/	O							7	O	↑	O							7	O	↑	O							7	O	\	#	7
#	/		O					5	O		↑		O					5	O		↑		O					5	O		\	#	5
#	/			O				O			↑			O				O			↑			O				O			\	#	3
#	/				O		O				↑				O		O				↑				O		O				\	#	1
#				4	O	↑	O							7	O	↑	O							7	O	↑	O				4	#	15
#				O		↑		O					5	O		↑		O					5	O		↑		O				#	13
#			O			↑			O				O			↑			O				O			↑			O			#	11
#		O				↑				O		O				↑				O		O				↑				O		#	9
#	/	O							7	O	↑	O							7	O	↑	O							7	O	\	#	7
#	/		O					5	O		↑		O					5	O		↑		O					5	O		\	#	5
#	/			O				O			↑			O				O			↑			O				O			\	#	3
#	/				O		O				↑				O		O				↑				O		O				\	#	1
											II										I												

Variation: Make a narrower scarf by omitting one pattern repeat.

Cast on 33 stitches and work as above, omitting the stitches between points I and II of Susan Chart S.

For the neckline ribbing: Remove the provisional cast-on and pick up the 33 stitches.

Set-up row: With the private side of your scarf facing you, slip the first stitch as if to knit, *p3, k4, repeat from *, ending p3, kl.

I'm about 12 rows into the lace pattern of my Susan shawl, and I am having a wonderful time. It's very relaxing.
– Susan Lewis

Susan Shawl

Using a provisional cast-on (page 13), cast on 7 stitches for seed stitch neck band/front border.
Set-up row: K2, pl, kl, pl, k2. [7 sts]
Rows 2-53: Slip the first stitch as if to purl, kl, pl, kl, pl, k2. [7 sts]

Following the instructions for "Picking up Neck Band Stitches for the Body of Your Shawl" (page 16), pick up 25 stitches.
Pick up the stitches from your provisional cast-on by following the instructions for "Recovering Stitches from the Provisional Cast-On" (page 18). [38 sts]
When working the first row, and only the first row of your shawl, when you have just seven stitches left on your left needle, K2tog, pl, kl, pl, k2. [37 sts]
Using Charts C [side panels] and D [back panel], and following the instructions "Using the Charts for a Farorse-Shaped Shawl" (page 26), begin your shawl.
Row 2a and all even-numbered rows: B6, purl across, B6.
Continue, following the charts in the same sequence. Repeat rows 1-16 as necessary to obtain the length you desire, ending after working row 8.

Knitting on the Lace Border: Go to the instructions on page 27, "The Lace Border." Using Susan Chart E [page 29], work the lace border.
Or, if you prefer, finish your shawl by working eight rows of seed stitch. Bind off using either the knit-in-pattern bind-off (page 21) or the Icelandic bind-off (page 21) .

Dress your shawl (page 34). Enjoy wearing your beautiful hand knit work of art!

Use rows 1z - 8z for the final eight rows of your shawl.

Susan shawl back panel – Chart D

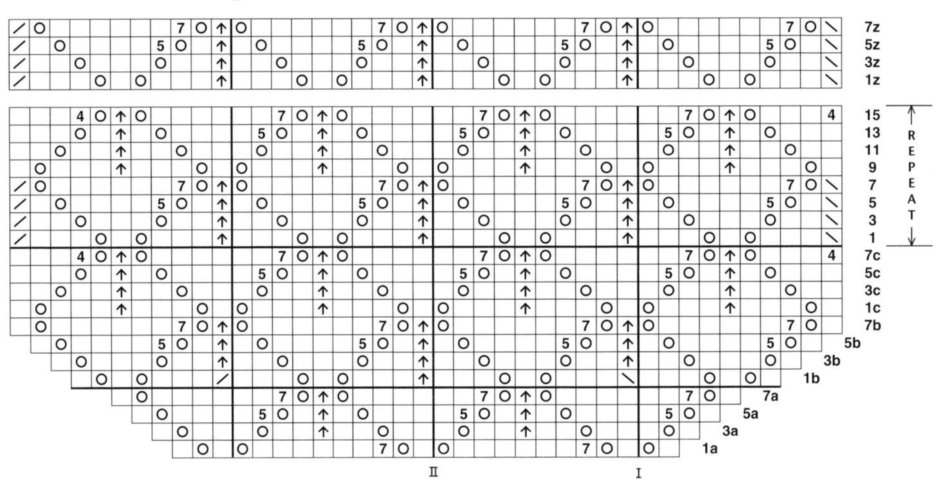

Susan swatch – Chart B

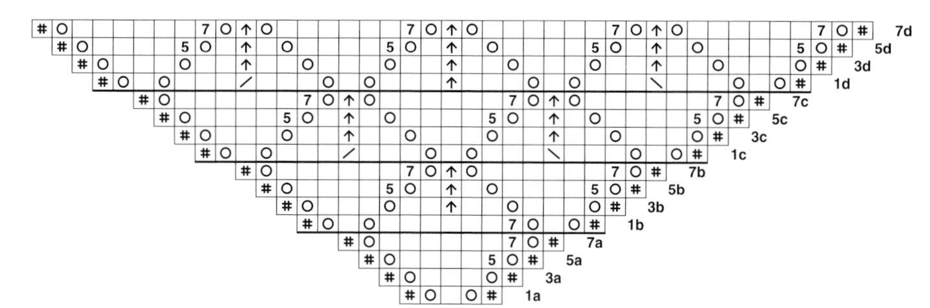

Swatch Chart B rows 1a & 2a in words:

Cast on 13 stitches.

Row 1a: B6, yo, k1, yo, B6; or, in other words:

Slip the first stitch as if to purl, k1, p1, k1, p1, k1, yo, k1, yo, k1, p1, k1, p1, k2.

Row 2a and all even-numbered rows: B6, purl across, B6; or, in other words:

Slip the first stitch as if to purl, k1, p1, k1, p1, k1, purl across to the last six stitches, k1, p1, k1, p1, k2.

Susan Shawl Charts C & D, row 1a in words:

Work the six border stitches [B6], which are not shown in the chart and which at the beginning of the row are always worked as slip the first stitch as if to purl, k1, p1, k1, p1, k1; place a marker on your needle;

work the first side panel using Chart C, which is yo, k1, yo, k1, yo, k1, yo; place a marker on your needle;

work the back panel using Chart D, which is k1, yo, k1, yo, k7, yo, k1, yo, k7, yo, k1, yo, k1; place a marker on your needle;

work the second side panel, again using Chart C, which is yo, k1, yo, k1, yo, k1, yo; place a marker on your needle;

work the six border stitches [B6], which are not shown on the chart and which at the end of the row are always worked as k1, p1, k1, p1, k2.

Row 2a and all even-numbered rows:

Slip the first stitch as if to purl, k1, p1, k1, p1, k1, purl across to the last marker, k1, p1, k1, p1, k2.

Use rows 1z - 8z for the final eight rows of your shawl.

Susan shawl side panel – Chart C

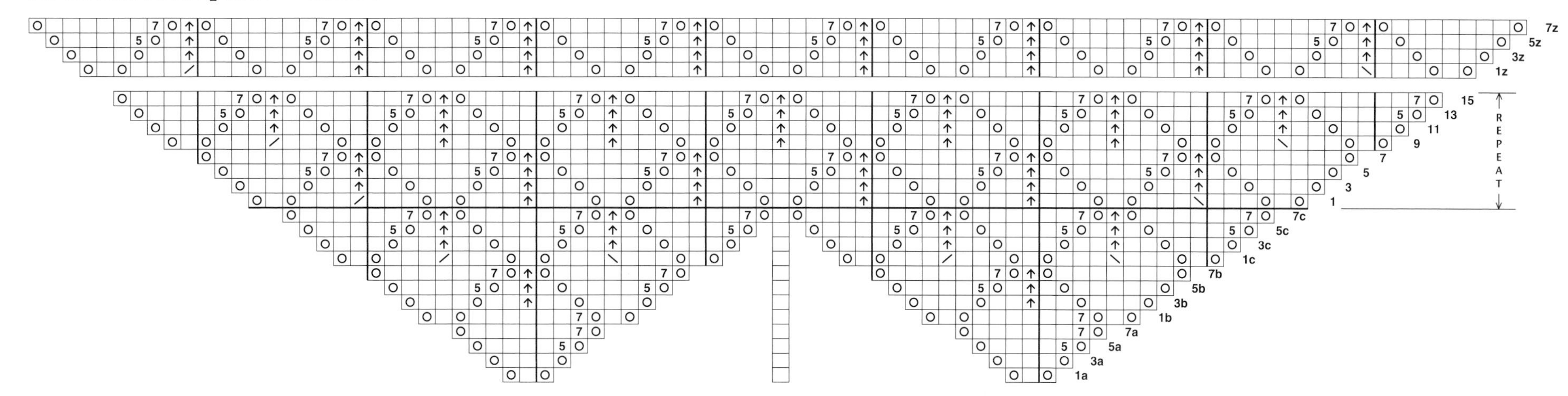

Gracie

Elves are magical creatures who can do great things. This shawl using the elfin lace pattern is named after Gracie Larsen, founder of the Lacy Knitters Guild, who has helped make magic in the lives of many lacy knitters.

Gracie building block
Chart A

O					5	O	⋏
	O	/		\	O		
O	/				\	O	
					6	\	O
		O	⋏	O			
\	O				O	/	
	\	O		O	/		
		\	O				

Haneke Select
merino/alpaca
fingering weight

The Gracie Seamen's Scarf

Tail #1:

Using a provisional cast-on (page 13), cast on 37 stitches.

Set-up row: K2, pl, kl, pl, kl, place a marker on your needle, purl 25, place a marker on your needle, B6 (page 23).

Using Gracie Chart S, work as many repeats of rows 1-16 as necessary to obtain the length you desire.

Finish tail #1 by working eight rows of seed stitch. Bind off on the ninth row, using the knit-in-pattern bind-off (page 21).

Neckline ribbing:

Remove the provisional cast-on, picking up the 37 stitches.

Set-up row: With the private/wrong side of your scarf facing you, slip the first stitch as if to knit, p4, k4, p4, k4, p3, k4, p4, k4, ending p4, kl.

Row 1: Slip the first stitch as if to purl, k4, p4, k4, p4, k3, p4, k4, p4, k5.

Row 2: Slip the first stitch as if to purl, p4, k4, p4, k4, p3, k4, p4, k4, ending p4, kl.

Repeat Rows 1 & 2 until the neckline ribbing measures approximately 70% of the neck measurement of the intended wearer, between 10 inches/25 cm and 12 inches/30 cm. End after working row 1.

Tail #2:

Set-up row: B6, place a marker on your needle, purl 25, place a marker on your needle, B6.

Work the same as for Tail #1, beginning with "Using Gracie Chart S."

Haneke merino fingering weight

Gracie scarf – Chart S

#				O	⋏	O					5	O	⋏	O					5	O	⋏	O				#	15
#		\	O				O	/		\	O				O	/		\	O				O	/		#	13
#			\	O		O	/				\	O		O	/				\	O		O	/			#	11
#				\	O						6	\	O						6	\	O				4	#	9
#	\	O					5	O	⋏	O					5	O	⋏	O					5	O	/	#	7
#			O	/		\	O				O	/		\	O				O	/		\	O			#	5
#		O	/				\	O		O	/				\	O		O	/				\	O		#	3
#							7	\	O						6	\	O								8	#	1
#				O	⋏	O					5	O	⋏	O					5	O	⋏	O				#	15
#		\	O				O	/		\	O				O	/		\	O				O	/		#	13
#			\	O		O	/				\	O		O	/				\	O		O	/			#	11
#				\	O						6	\	O						6	\	O				4	#	9
#	\	O					5	O	⋏	O					5	O	⋏	O					5	O	/	#	7
#			O	/		\	O				O	/		\	O				O	/		\	O			#	5
#		O	/				\	O		O	/				\	O		O	/				\	O		#	3
#							7	\	O						6	\	O								8	#	1

II I

Variation: Make a wider scarf by adding one pattern repeat. Using a provisional cast-on, cast on 45 stitches and work as above, repeating once between points I and II of Gracie Chart S.

For the neckline ribbing: Remove the provisional cast-on and pick up the 45 stitches.

Set-up row: With the private side of your scarf facing you, slip the first stitch as if to knit, p4, k4, p4, k4, p4, k3, p4, k4, p4, k4, p4, kl.

Instructions are provided for a seed stitch neck band/front border. The Gracie shawl is pictured with a mock ribbing neck band/front border. For instructions on making a mock ribbing neck band/front border see page 15.

Gracie Shawl

Using a provisional cast-on (page 13), cast on 7 stitches for seed stitch neck band/front border.

Set-up row: K2, pl, kl, pl, k2. [7 sts]

Rows 2-45: Slip the first stitch as if to purl, kl, pl, kl, pl, k2. [7 sts]

Following the instructions for "Picking up Neck Band Stitches for the Body of Your Shawl" (page 16), pick up 21 stitches.

Pick up the stitches from your provisional cast-on by following the instructions for "Recovering Stitches from the Provisional Cast-On" (page 18). [34 sts]

When working the first row, and only the first row of your shawl, when you have just seven stitches left on your left needle, K2tog, pl, kl, pl, k2. [33 sts]

Using Charts C [side panels] and D [back panel], and following the instructions "Using the Charts for a Faroese-Shaped Shawl" (page 26), begin your shawl. Note that this pattern begins with what is labeled as row 3a; this is done to keep the pattern sequence. You haven't missed anything; just begin with row 3a.

Row 4a and all even-numbered rows: B6, purl across, B6.

Continue, following the charts in the same sequence. Repeat rows 1-16 as necessary to obtain the length you desire, ending after working row 16.

Knitting on the Lace Border: Go to the instructions on page 27, "The Lace Border." Using Gracie Chart E (page 28), work the lace border.

Or, if you prefer, finish your shawl by working eight rows of seed stitch. Bind off using either the knit-in-pattern bind-off (page 21) or the Icelandic bind-off (page 21) .

Dress your shawl (page 34). Enjoy wearing your beautiful hand knit work of art!

Gracie shawl back panel – Chart D

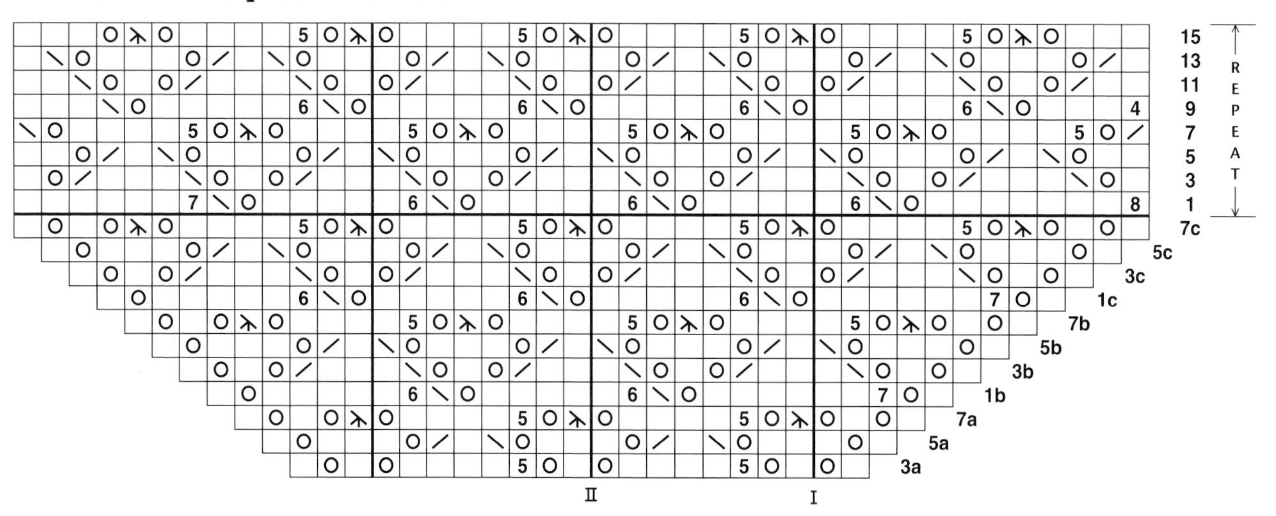

Gracie swatch – Chart B

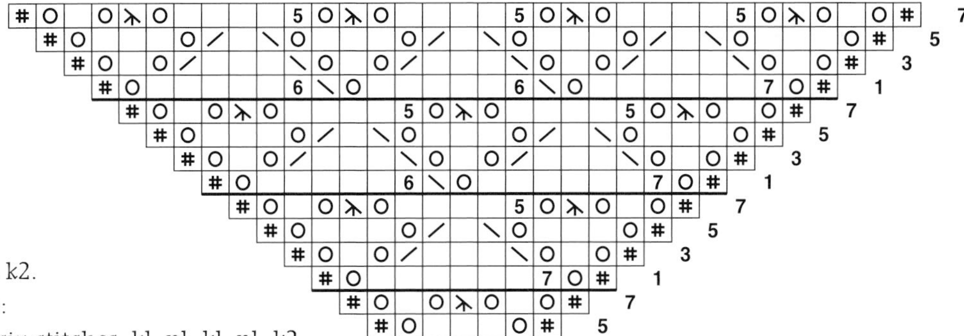

Swatch Chart B rows 3 & 4 in words:

Cast on 13 stitches.

Row 3: B6, yo, k1, yo, B6; or, in other words:

Slip the first stitch as if to purl, k1, p1, k1, p1, k1, yo, k1, yo, k1, p1, k1, p1, k2.

Row 4 and all even-numbered rows: B6, purl across, B6; or, in other words:

Slip the first stitch as if to purl, k1, p1, k1, p1, k1, purl across to the last six stitches, k1, p1, k1, p1, k2.

Gracie Shawl Charts C & D, row 3a in words:

Work the six border stitches [B6], which are not shown in the chart and which at the beginning of the row are always worked as slip the first stitch as if to purl, k1, p1, k1, p1, k1; place a marker on your needle;

work the first side panel using Chart C, which is yo, k1, yo, k1, yo, k1, yo; place a marker on your needle;

work the back panel using Chart D, which is k1, yo, k1, yo, k5, yo, k1, yo, k5, yo, k1, yo, k1; place a marker on your needle;

work the second side panel, again using Chart C, which is yo, k1, yo, k1, yo, k1, yo; place a marker on your needle;

work the six border stitches [B6], which are not shown on the chart and which at the end of the row are always worked as k1, p1, k1, p1, k2.

Row 4a and all even-numbered rows:

Slip the first stitch as if to purl, k1, p1, k1, p1, k1, purl across to the last marker, k1, p1, k1, p1, k2.

The first rows of the swatch and the body of the shawl are called rows 3 and 3a in keeping with the pattern sequence. You are not missing anything; there is no row 1 or row 2 in the first pattern sequence.

Gracie shawl side panel – Chart C

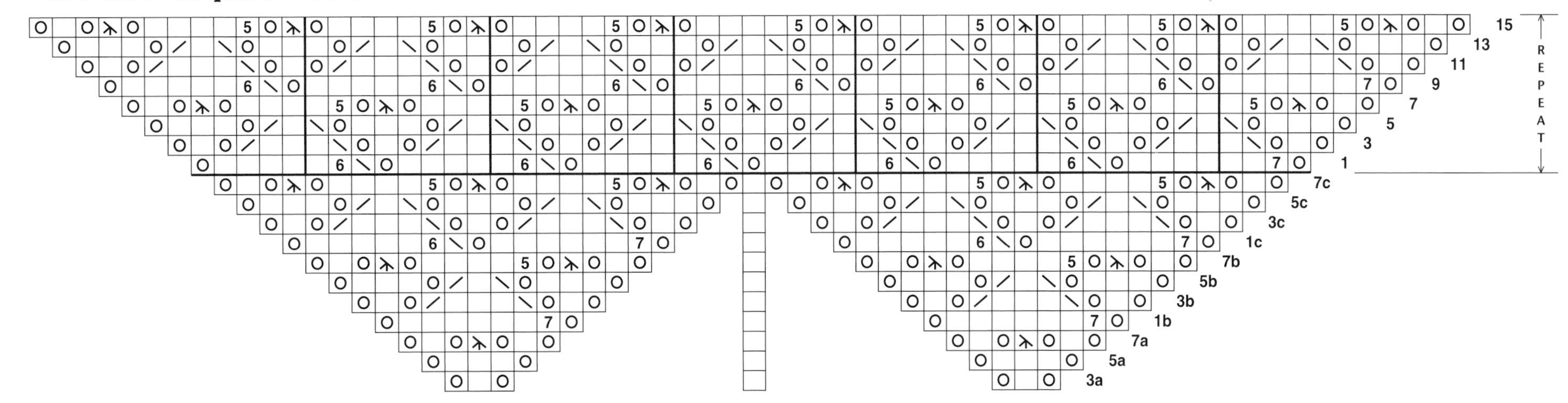

Anne

This very lacy shawl is named in part after my Aunt Annie, a fabulous lace crocheter who played a major role in my learning to knit. Having a very wide back panel, this shawl compliments the amply endowed lover of shawls or drapes beautifully on a smaller frame.

Anne building block Chart A

O	ℓ	ℓ	O	⋏	O	ℓ	ℓ	O	⋏
O	/	O	/		\	O	\	O	
	O	/	O	⋏	O	\	O		
O	/	ℓ	O	⋏	O	ℓ	\	O	
O	ℓ	ℓ	O	⋏	O	ℓ	ℓ	O	⋏
\	O	\	O		O	/	O	/	
O	\	O				O	/	O	⋏
O	ℓ	\	O		O	/	ℓ	O	⋏

Haneke merino singles

The Anne Seamen's Scarf

Tail #1:

Using a provisional cast-on (page 13), cast on 43 stitches.

Set-up row: K2, p1, k1, p1, k1, place a marker on your needle, purl 31, place a marker on your needle, B6 (page 23).

Using Anne Chart S, work as many repeats of rows 1-16 as necessary to obtain the length you desire.

Finish tail #1 by working eight rows of seed stitch. Bind off on the ninth row, using the knit-in-pattern bind-off (page 21).

Neckline ribbing:

Remove the provisional cast-on, picking up the 43 stitches.

Set-up row: With the private/wrong side facing you, slip the first stitch as if to knit, p3, k4, p4, k4, p4, k3, p4, k4, p4, k4, p3, k1

Row 1: Slip the first stitch as if to purl, k3, p4, k4, p4, k4, p3, k4, p4, k4, p4, k4.

Row 2: Slip the first stitch as if to purl, p3, k4, p4, k4, p4, k3, p4, k4, p4, k4, p3, k1.

Repeat Rows 1 & 2 until the neckline ribbing measures approximately 70% of the neck measurement of the intended wearer, between 10 inches/25 cm and 12 inches/30 cm. End after working row 1.

Tail #2:

Set-up row: B6, place a marker on your needle, purl 31, place a marker on your needle, B6.

Work the same as for Tail #1, beginning with "Using Anne Chart S."

Haneke merino lace weight

Anne scarf – Chart S

#	\	O	ℓ	ℓ	O	⋏	O	ℓ	ℓ	O	⋏	O	ℓ	ℓ	O	⋏	O	ℓ	ℓ	O	⋏	O	ℓ	ℓ	O	⋏	O	ℓ	ℓ	O	/	#	15
#		O	/	O	/		\	O	\	O		O	/	O	/		\	O	\	O		O	/	O	/		\	O	\	O		#	13
#			O	/	O	⋏	O	\	O				O	/	O	⋏	O	\	O				O	/	O	⋏	O	\	O			#	11
#		O	/	ℓ	O	⋏	O	ℓ	\	O		O	/	ℓ	O	⋏	O	ℓ	\	O		O	/	ℓ	O	⋏	O	ℓ	\	O		#	9
#	\	O	ℓ	ℓ	O	⋏	O	ℓ	ℓ	O	⋏	O	ℓ	ℓ	O	⋏	O	ℓ	ℓ	O	⋏	O	ℓ	ℓ	O	⋏	O	ℓ	ℓ	O	/	#	7
#		\	O	\	O		O	/	O	/		\	O	\	O		O	/	O	/		\	O	\	O		O	/	O	/		#	5
#	\	O	\	O				O	/	O	⋏	O	\	O				O	/	O	⋏	O	\	O				O	/	O	/	#	3
#	\	O	ℓ	\	O		O	/	ℓ	O	⋏	O	ℓ	\	O		O	/	ℓ	O	⋏	O	ℓ	\	O		O	/	ℓ	O	/	#	1
#	\	O	ℓ	ℓ	O	⋏	O	ℓ	ℓ	O	⋏	O	ℓ	ℓ	O	⋏	O	ℓ	ℓ	O	⋏	O	ℓ	ℓ	O	⋏	O	ℓ	ℓ	O	/	#	15
#		O	/	O	/		\	O	\	O		O	/	O	/		\	O	\	O		O	/	O	/		\	O	\	O		#	13
#			O	/	O	⋏	O	\	O				O	/	O	⋏	O	\	O				O	/	O	⋏	O	\	O			#	11
#		O	/	ℓ	O	⋏	O	ℓ	\	O		O	/	ℓ	O	⋏	O	ℓ	\	O		O	/	ℓ	O	⋏	O	ℓ	\	O		#	9
#	\	O	ℓ	ℓ	O	⋏	O	ℓ	ℓ	O	⋏	O	ℓ	ℓ	O	⋏	O	ℓ	ℓ	O	⋏	O	ℓ	ℓ	O	⋏	O	ℓ	ℓ	O	/	#	7
#		\	O	\	O		O	/	O	/		\	O	\	O		O	/	O	/		\	O	\	O		O	/	O	/		#	5
#	\	O	\	O				O	/	O	⋏	O	\	O				O	/	O	⋏	O	\	O				O	/	O	/	#	3
#	\	O	ℓ	\	O		O	/	ℓ	O	⋏	O	ℓ	\	O		O	/	ℓ	O	⋏	O	ℓ	\	O		O	/	ℓ	O	/	#	1
											II										I												

Anne Shawl

Using a provisional cast-on (page 13), cast on 7 stitches for seed stitch neck band/front border.
Set-up row: K2, pl, kl, pl, k2.
Rows 2-57: Slip the first stitch as if to purl, kl, pl, kl, pl, k2. [7 sts]

Following the instructions for "Picking up Neck Band Stitches for the Body of Your Shawl" (page 16), pick up 27 stitches.
Pick up the stitches from your provisional cast-on by following the instructions for "Recovering Stitches from the Provisional Cast-On" (page 18). [40 sts]
When working the first row, and only the first row of your shawl, when you have just seven stitches left on your left needle, K2tog, pl, kl, pl, k2. [39 sts]
Using Charts C [side panels] and D [back panel], and following the instructions "Using the Charts for a Faroese-Shaped Shawl" (page 26), begin your shawl.
Row 2a and all even-numbered rows: B6, purl across, B6.
Continue, following the charts in the same sequence. Repeat rows 1-16 as necessary to obtain the length you desire, ending after working row 8.

Knitting on the Lace Border: Go to the instructions on page 27, "The Lace Border." Using Anne Chart E (page 29), work the lace border.
Or, if you prefer, finish your shawl by working eight rows of seed stitch. Bind off using either the knit-in-pattern bind-off (page 21) or the Icelandic bind-off (page 21) .

Dress your shawl (page 34). Enjoy wearing your beautiful hand knit work of art!

Anne shawl back panel – Chart D

7z
5z
3z
1z

15
13
11
9
7
5
3
1
REPEAT

7d
5d
3d
1d
7c
5c
3c
1c
7b
5b
3b
1b
7a
5a
3a
1a

II
I

Anne shawl side panel – Chart C

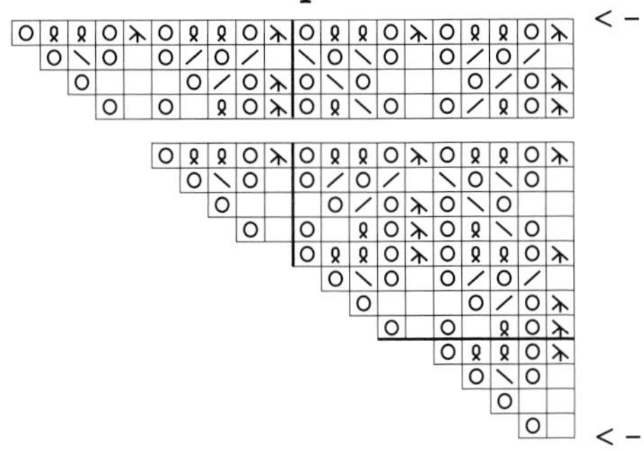

Anne swatch – Chart B

Swatch Chart B:

Cast on 13 stitches.

Row 1: B6, yo, k1, yo, B6; or, in other words:

Slip the first stitch as if to purl, k1, p1, k1, p1, k1, yo, k1, yo, k1, p1, k1, p1, k2.

Row 2 and all even-numbered rows: B6, purl across, B6; or, in other words:

Slip the first stitch as if to purl, k1, p1, k1, p1, k1, purl across to the last six stitches, k1, p1, k1, p1, k2.

Anne Shawl Charts C & D row 1a in words:

Work the six border stitches [B6], which are not shown in the chart and which at the beginning of the row are always worked as slip the first stitch as if to purl, k1, p1, k1, p1, k1; place a marker on your needle;

work the first side panel using Chart C, which is yo, k1, yo, k1, yo, k1, yo; place a marker on your needle;

work the back panel using Chart D, which is (k1, yo, k1, yo, k1, k1 into the back, yo, k1, yo, k1 into the back) three times, k1, yo, k1, yo, k1; place a marker on your needle;

work the second side panel, again using Chart C, which is yo, k1, yo, k1, yo, k1, yo; place a marker on your needle;

work the six border stitches [B6], which are not shown on the chart and which at the end of the row are always worked as k1, p1, k1, p1, k2.

Row 2a and all even-numbered rows:

Slip the first stitch as if to purl, k1, p1, k1, p1, k1, purl across to the last marker, k1, p1, k1, p1, k2.

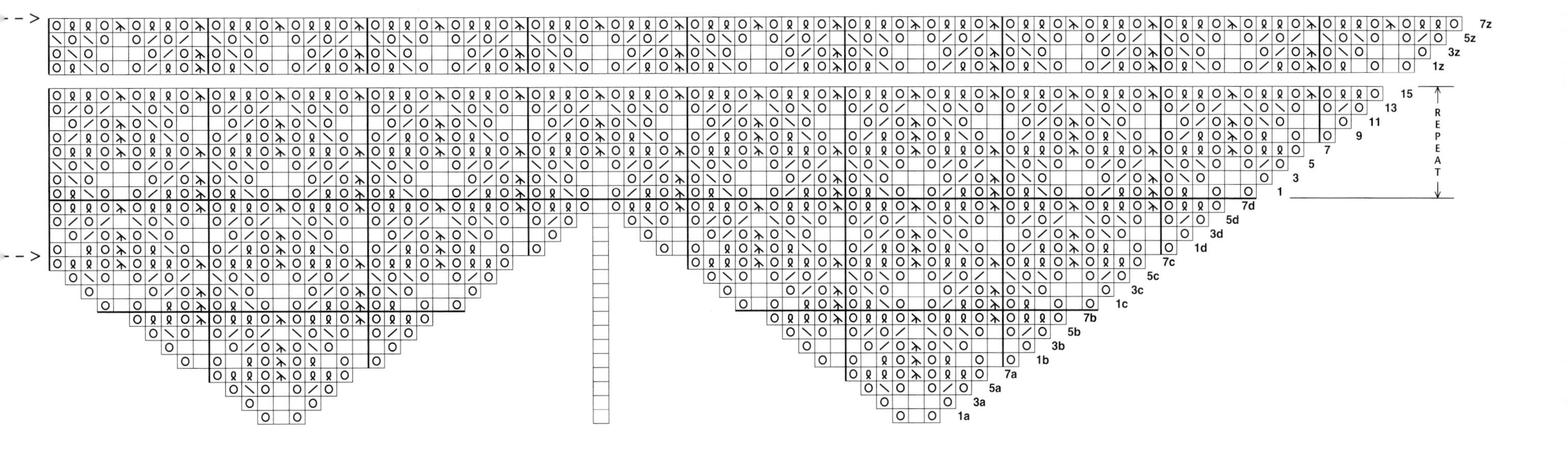

Frances

My mind immediately turned to Auntie Frances, a great teacher of the mathematical sciences, when I saw the geometrics of this pattern. The challenges of this beautiful pattern are as much fun as the challenges faced when discovering the mysteries of mathematics.

Frances building block Chart A

\	O	\	O			O	⋏	O		\	O	\	O		
	\	O			O	/		\	O		\	O			
			4	O	/	\	O		\	O				\	O
O			O	/	\	O	\	O		\	O		\	O	\
		O	/			\	O				\	O		\	O
	O	/	\	O				4	\	O		\	O		
O		\	O	\	O			\	O	\	O			O	⋏
\	O		\	O				4	\	O			O	/	
	\	O				\	O				4	O	/	\	O
O		\	O		\	O	\	O			O	/	\	O	\
			\	O		\	O			O	/			\	O
	\	O		\	O				O	/	\	O			

Haneke Select merino/alpaca fingering weight

The Frances Seamen's Scarf

Haneke Select
merino/kid mohair
lace weight

Tail #1:

Using a provisional cast-on (page 13), cast on 45 stitches.

Set-up row: K2, pl, kl, pl, kl, place a marker on your needle, purl 33, place a marker on your needle, B6 (page 23).

Using Frances Chart S, work as many repeats of rows 1-24 as necessary to obtain the length you desire.

Finish tail #1 by working eight rows of seed stitch. Bind off on the ninth row, using the knit-in-pattern bind-off (page 21).

Neckline ribbing:

Remove the provisional cast-on, picking up the 45 stitches.

Set-up row: With the private/wrong side of your scarf facing you, slip the first stitch as if to knit, p4, k4, p4, k4, p4, k3, p4, k4, p4, k4, p4, kl.

Row 1: Slip the first stitch as if to purl, k4, p4, k4, p4, k4, p3, k4, p4, k4, p4, k5.

Row 2: Slip the first stitch as if to purl, p4, k4, p4, k4, p4, k3, p4, k4, p4, k4, p4, kl.

Repeat Rows 1 & 2 until the neckline ribbing measures approximately 70% of the neck measurement of the intended wearer, between 10 inches/25 cm and 12 inches/30 cm. End after working row 1.

Tail #2:

Set-up row: B6, place a marker on your needle, purl 33, place a marker on your needle, B6.

Work the same as for Tail #1, beginning with "Using Frances Chart S."

Frances scarf – Chart S

#		\	O	\	O			O	⋏	O		\	O	\	O			\	O	\	O			O	⋏	O		\	O	\	O			#	23
#			\	O			O	/		\	O		\	O				4	\	O			O	/		\	O		\	O				#	21
#					5	O	/	\	O		\	O				\	O				4	O	/	\	O		\	O					5	#	19
#	\	O			O	/	\	O	\	O		\	O		\	O	\	O			O	/	\	O	\	O		\	O		\	O		#	17
#				O	/			\	O				\	O		\	O			O	/			\	O				\	O				#	15
#			O	/	\	O				4	\	O		\	O				O	/	\	O				4	\	O		\	O			#	13
#	\	O		\	O	\	O			\	O	\	O			O	⋏	O		\	O	\	O			\	O	\	O			O	/	#	11
#		\	O		\	O				4	\	O			O	/		\	O		\	O				4	\	O			O	/		#	9
#			\	O				\	O				4	O	/	\	O		\	O				\	O				4	O	/			#	7
#	\	O		\	O		\	O	\	O			O	/	\	O	\	O		\	O		\	O	\	O			O	/	\	O		#	5
#				4	\	O		\	O			O	/			\	O				\	O		\	O			O	/				4	#	3
#			\	O		\	O				O	/	\	O				4	\	O		\	O				O	/	\	O				#	1
#		\	O	\	O			O	⋏	O		\	O	\	O			\	O	\	O			O	⋏	O		\	O	\	O			#	23
#			\	O			O	/		\	O		\	O				4	\	O			O	/		\	O		\	O				#	21
#					5	O	/	\	O		\	O				\	O				4	O	/	\	O		\	O					5	#	19
#	\	O			O	/	\	O	\	O		\	O		\	O	\	O			O	/	\	O	\	O		\	O		\	O		#	17
#				O	/			\	O				\	O		\	O			O	/			\	O				\	O				#	15
#			O	/	\	O				4	\	O		\	O				O	/	\	O				4	\	O		\	O			#	13
#	\	O		\	O	\	O			\	O	\	O			O	⋏	O		\	O	\	O			\	O	\	O			O	/	#	11
#		\	O		\	O				4	\	O			O	/		\	O		\	O				4	\	O			O	/		#	9
#			\	O				\	O				4	O	/	\	O		\	O				\	O				4	O	/			#	7
#	\	O		\	O		\	O	\	O			O	/	\	O	\	O		\	O		\	O	\	O			O	/	\	O		#	5
#				4	\	O		\	O			O	/			\	O				\	O		\	O			O	/				4	#	3
#			\	O		\	O				O	/	\	O				4	\	O		\	O				O	/	\	O				#	1
									II																I										

While working the first few rows of the Frances shawl, I was continuing to make a mistake. I soon realized I was going by feel and not by sight when I reached the far left side of the chart. I was working an ssk instead of just knitting the one stitch as is required for the shaping.

After I completed the first three rows of the second pattern repeat, it went s-o-o-o-o easily. I now have "the rhythm" you talked about, and it is wonderful. Now my eyes have the pattern down, and my fingers almost know what they are supposed to be doing.

– Polly Garvey

Frances Shawl

Using a provisional cast-on (page 13), cast on 7 stitches for seed stitch neck band/front border.

Set-up row: K2, pl, kl, pl, k2. [7 sts]

Rows 2-65: Slip the first stitch as if to purl, kl, pl, kl, pl, k2. [7 sts]

Following the instructions for "Picking up Neck Band Stitches for the Body of Your Shawl" (page 16), pick up 31 stitches.

Pick up the stitches from your provisional cast-on by following the instructions for "Recovering Stitches from the Provisional Cast-On" (page 18). [44 sts]

When working the first row, and only the first row of your shawl, when you have just seven stitches left on your left needle, K2tog, pl, kl, pl, k2. [43 sts]

Using Charts C [side panels] and D [back panel], and following the instructions "Using the Charts for a Faroese-Shaped Shawl" (page 26), begin your shawl.

Row 2a and all even-numbered rows: B6, purl across, B6.

Continue, following the charts in the same sequence. Repeat rows 1-24 as necessary to obtain the length you desire, ending after working row 12. Note: When working the final repeat work row llz.

Knitting on the Lace Border: Go to the instructions on page 27, "The Lace Border." Using Frances Chart E (page 30), work the lace border.

Or, if you prefer, finish your shawl by working eight rows of seed stitch. Bind off using either the knit-in-pattern bind-off (page 21) or the Icelandic bind-off (page 21) .

Dress your shawl (page 34). Enjoy wearing your beautiful hand knit work of art!

Frances shawl back panel – Chart D

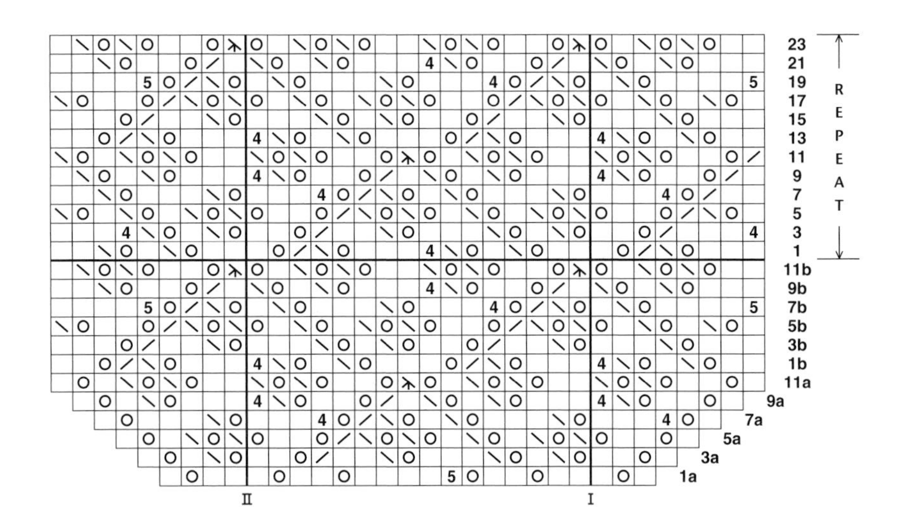

Frances shawl side panel – Chart C

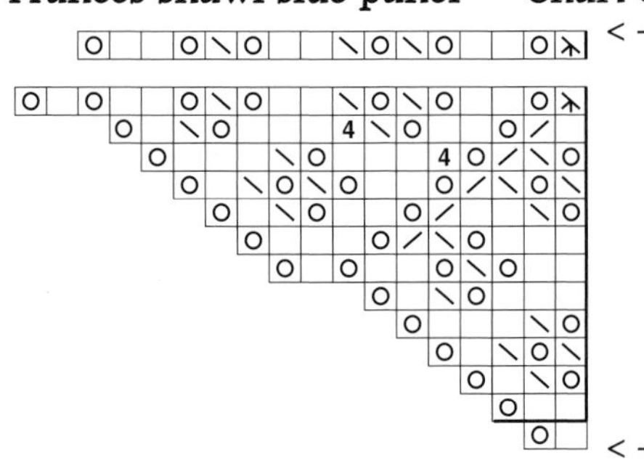

Frances swatch – Chart B

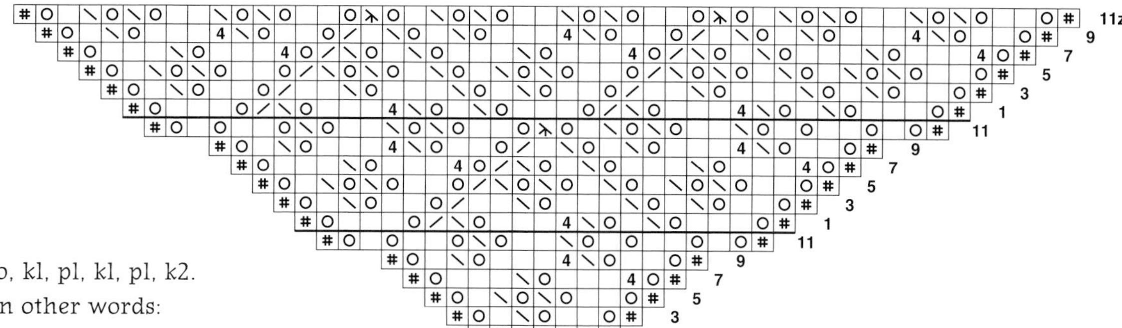

Swatch Chart B rows 1 & 2 in words:

Cast on 15 stitches.

Row 1: B6, yo, k3, yo, B6; or, in other words:

Slip the first stitch as if to purl, kl, pl, kl, pl, kl, yo, k3, yo, kl, pl, kl, pl, k2.

Row 2 and all even-numbered rows: B6, purl across, B6; or, in other words:

Slip the first stitch as if to purl, kl, pl, kl, pl, kl, purl across to the last six stitches, kl, pl, kl, pl, k2.

Frances Shawl Charts C & D, row la in words:

Work the six border stitches [B6], which are not shown in the chart and which at the beginning of the row are always worked as slip the first stitch as if to purl, kl, pl, kl, pl, kl; place a marker on your needle;

work the first side panel using Chart C, which is yo, k3, yo, kl, yo, k3, yo; place a marker on your needle;

work the back panel using Chart D, which is kl, yo, k3, yo, k2, yo, k5, yo, k2, yo, k3, yo, kl; place a marker on your needle;

work the second side panel, again using Chart C, which is yo, k3, yo, kl, yo, k3, yo; place a marker on your needle;

work the six border stitches [B6], which are not shown on the chart and which at the end of the row are always worked as kl, pl, kl, pl, k2.

Row 2a and all even-numbered rows:

Slip the first stitch as if to purl, kl, pl, kl, pl, kl, purl across to the last marker, kl, pl, kl, pl, k2.

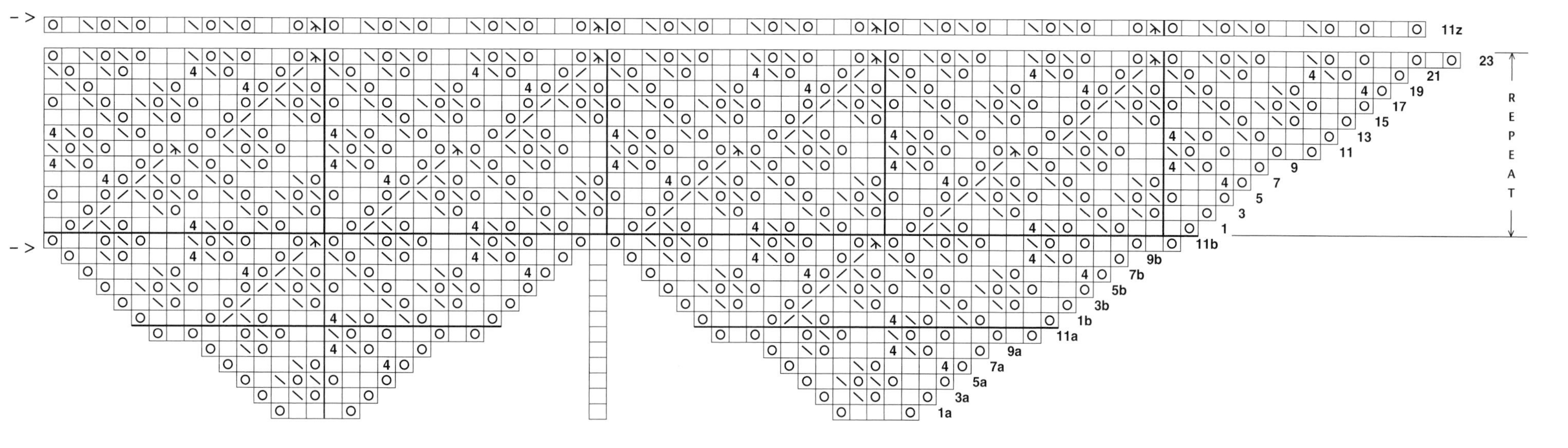

Elizabeth

Baskets of flowers are formed by this adaptation of a German lace design which incorporates all the usual lace stitches plus twisted stitches. To the many Elizabeths who have been, and continue to be, important to so many aspects of my life, I dedicate this shawl.

Elizabeth building block Chart A

	O	⋏	O				O	⋏	O				O	⋏	O		
O				O	/	O	/	−	\	O	\	O				O	⋏
	O	⋏	O		O	/	−	−	−	\	O		O	⋏	O		
O				O	/	−	−	ℓ	−	−	\	O				O	⋏
	O	/	O	/	−	−	ℓ	ℓ	ℓ	−	−	\	O	\	O		
O		O	/	−	−	ℓ	ℓ	−	ℓ	ℓ	−	−	\	O		O	⋏
	O	/	−	−	ℓ	ℓ	−	−	−	ℓ	ℓ	−	−	\	O		
O	/	−	−	ℓ	ℓ	−	−	−	−	−	ℓ	ℓ	−	−	\	O	
O				O	⋏	O				O	⋏	O				O	⋏
\	O	\	O				O	⋏	O				O	/	O	/	−
−	\	O		O	⋏	O				O	⋏	O		O	/	−	−
−	−	\	O				O	⋏	O				O	/	−	−	ℓ
ℓ	−	−	\	O	\	O				O	/	O	/	−	−	ℓ	ℓ
ℓ	ℓ	−	−	\	O		O	⋏	O		O	/	−	−	ℓ	ℓ	−
−	ℓ	ℓ	−	−	\	O				O	/	−	−	ℓ	ℓ	−	−
−	−	ℓ	ℓ	−	−	\	O		O	/	−	−	ℓ	ℓ	−	−	−

Hunt Valley Cashmere fingering weight

The Elizabeth Seamen's Scarf

Tail #1:

Using a provisional cast-on (page 13), cast on 49 stitches.

Set-up row: K2, pl, kl, pl, kl, place a marker on your needle, purl 37, place a marker on your needle, B6 (page 23).

Using Elizabeth Chart S, work as many repeats of rows 1-32 as necessary to obtain the length you desire. You may stop after working row 16 or row 32.

Finish tail #1 by working eight rows of seed stitch. Bind off on the ninth row, using the knit-in-pattern bind-off (page 21).

Neckline ribbing:

Remove the provisional cast-on, picking up the 49 stitches.

Set-up row: With the private/wrong side of your scarf facing you, slip the first stitch as if to knit, p5, k4, p4, k4, p4, k5, p4, k4, p4, k4, p5, kl.

Row 1: Slip the first stitch as if to purl, k5, p4, k4, p4, k4, p5, k4, p4, k4, p4, k6.

Row 2: Slip the first stitch as if to purl, p5, k4, p4, k4, p4, k5, p4, k4, p4, k4, p5, kl.

Repeat Rows 1 & 2 until the neckline ribbing measures approximately 70% of the neck measurement of the intended wearer, generally between 10 inches/25 cm and 12 inches/30 cm. End after working row 1.

Tail #2:

Set-up row: B6, place a marker on your needle, purl 31, place a marker on your needle, B6.

Work the same as for Tail #1, beginning with "Using Elizabeth Chart S."

Haneke Heaven Sent alpaca/merino fingering weight

Elizabeth scarf – Chart S

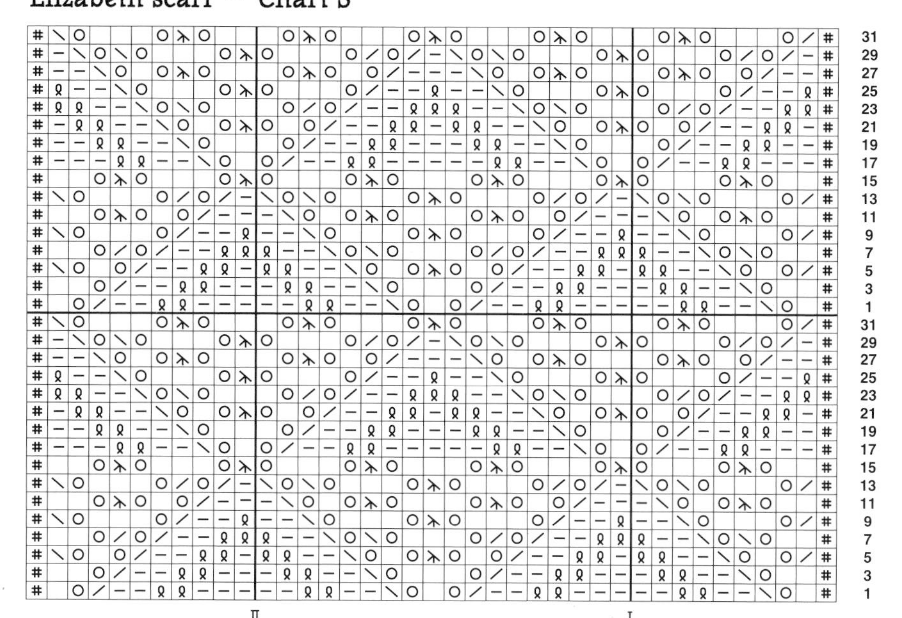

Elizabeth Shawl

Using a provisional cast-on (page 13), cast on 7 stitches for seed stitch neck band/front border.

Set-up row: K2, pl, kl, pl, k2. [7 sts]

Rows 2-57: Slip the first stitch as if to purl, kl, pl, kl, pl, k2. [7 sts]

Following the instructions for "Picking up Neck Band Stitches for the Body of Your Shawl" (page 16), pick up 27 stitches.

Pick up the stitches from your provisional cast-on by following the instructions for "Recovering Stitches from the Provisional Cast-On" (page 18). [40 sts]

When working the first row, and only the first row of your shawl, when you have just seven stitches left on your left needle, K2tog, pl, kl, pl, k2. [39 sts]

Using Charts C [side panels] and D [back panel], and following the instructions "Using the Charts for a Faroese-Shaped Shawl" (page 26), begin your shawl.

Continue, following the charts in the same sequence. Repeat rows 1-32 as necessary to obtain the length you desire, ending after working row 32.

Knitting on the Lace Border: Go to the instructions on page 27, "The Lace Border." Using Elizabeth Chart E (page 30), work the lace border.

Or, if you prefer, finish your shawl by working eight rows of seed stitch. Bind off using either the knit-in-pattern bind-off (page 21) or the Icelandic bind-off (page 21) .

Dress your shawl (page 34). Enjoy wearing your beautiful hand knit work of art!

Elizabeth shawl back panel – Chart D

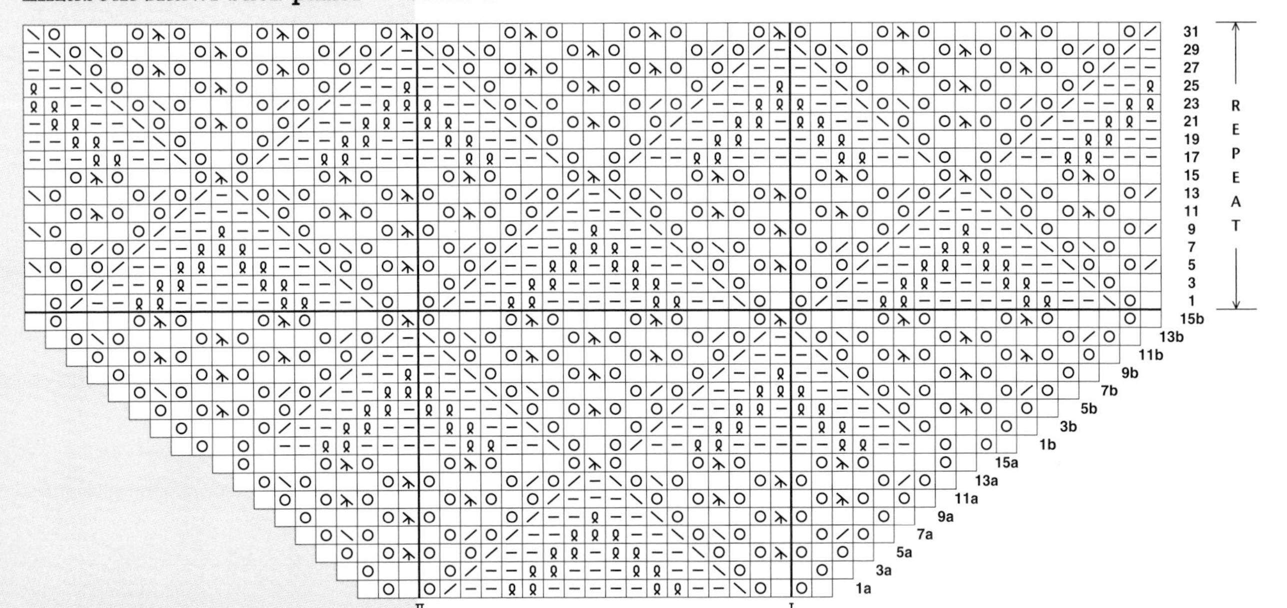

Elizabeth shawl side panel – Chart C

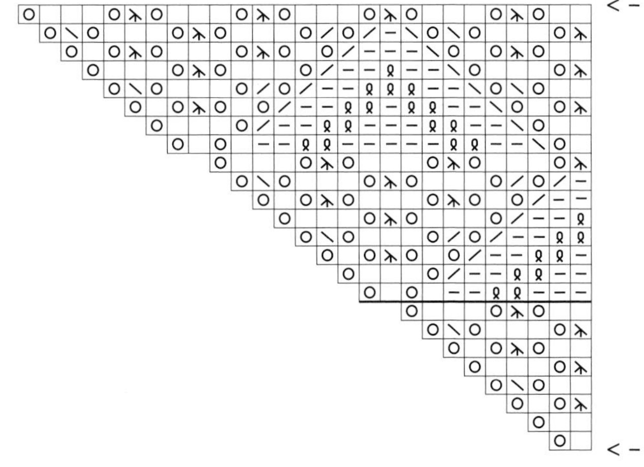

Elizabeth swatch – Chart B

Swatch Chart B rows 1 & 2 in words:

Cast on 13 stitches.

Row 1: B6, yo, k1, yo, B6; or, in other words:

Slip the first stitch as if to purl, k1, p1, k1, p1, k1, yo, k1, yo, k1, p1, k1, p1, k2.

Row 2 and all even-numbered rows: B6, purl across, B6; or, in other words:

Slip the first stitch as if to purl, k1, p1, k1, p1, k1, purl across to the last six stitches, k1, p1, k1, p1, k2.

Elizabeth Shawl Charts C & D, row 1a in words:

Work the six border stitches [B6], which are not shown in the chart and which at the beginning of the row are always worked as slip the first stitch as if to purl, k1, p1, k1, p1, k1; place a marker on your needle;

work the first side panel using Chart C, which is yo, k1, yo, k1, yo, k1, yo; place a marker on your needle;

work the back panel using Chart D, which is k1, yo, k1, yo, ssk, p2, (k into the back) twice, p5, (k into the back) twice, p2, k2tog, yo, k1, yo, k1; place a marker on your needle;

work the second side panel, again using Chart C, which is yo, k1, yo, k1, yo, k1, yo; place a marker on your needle;

work the six border stitches [B6], which are not shown on the chart and which at the end of the row are always worked as k1, p1, k1, p1, k2.

Row 2a and all even-numbered rows:

Slip the first stitch as if to purl, k1, p1, k1, p1, k1, purl across to the last marker, k1, p1, k1, p1, k2.

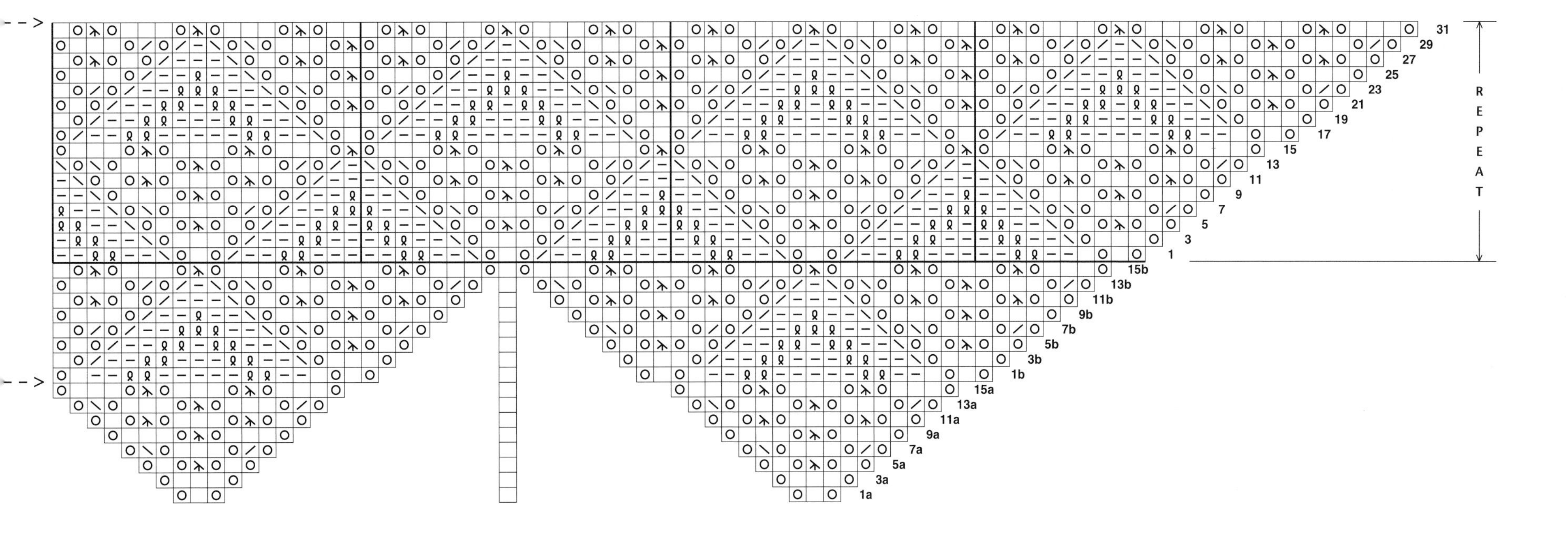

Josephine

Vortex, from Barbara G. Walker's *Charted Knitting Designs*, is symbolic of the whirlwind that so many women face while balancing home, family and a career. This beautiful shawl is named in honor of a dear friend and sister attorney who has conquered more challenges than any one person should have to face in an entire lifetime.

Josephine building block Chart A

O	/						6	O	⋏	O	\	O	\	O	\	O	\	O	
	O	/				4	O	/		\	O	\	O	\	O	\	O		
O	/	O	/			O	/	O	\		\	O	\	O	\	O			
	O	/	O	/	O	/	O	/				\	O	\	O				
O	/	O	/	O	/	O	/	O	\				\	O					5
	O	/	O	/	O	/	O	/				\	O	\	O				
O	/	O	/			O	/	O	\		\	O	\	O	\	O			
	O	/				4	O	/		\	O	\	O	\	O	\	O		
O	/						6	O	⋏	O	\	O	\	O	\	O	\	O	
O	\	O	\	O	\	O	\	O		O	/						6	O	⋏
\	O	\	O	\	O	\	O				O	/				4	O	/	
	\	O	\	O	\	O				O	/	O	/			O	/	O	\
		\	O	\	O					5	O	/	O	/	O	/	O	/	
			\	O					5	O	/	O	/	O	/	O	/	O	\
		\	O	\	O					5	O	/	O	/	O	/	O	/	
	\	O	\	O	\	O				O	/	O	/			O	/	O	\
\	O	\	O	\	O	\	O				O	/				4	O	/	
O	\	O	\	O	\	O	\	O		O	/						6	O	⋏

Haneke Exotics
super fine alpaca /tencel
fingering weight

The Josephine Seamen's Scarf

Tail #1:

Using a provisional cast-on (page 13), cast on 42 stitches.

Set-up row: K2, pl, kl, pl, kl, place a marker on your needle, purl 30, place a marker on your needle, B6 (page 23).

Using Josephine Chart S, work as many repeats of rows 1-36 as necessary to obtain the length you desire.

Seed stitch border: Row 1: Slip the first stitch as if to purl, (kl, pl) 9 times, kl, p2tog, (kl, pl) 9 times, k2.

Rows 2-8: Work in seed stitch. Bind off on the ninth row, using the knit-in-pattern bind-off (page 21).

Neckline ribbing:

Remove the provisional cast-on, picking up the 42 stitches.

Set-up row: With the private/wrong side of your scarf facing you, slip the first stitch as if to knit, p3, k4, p3, k4, p4, k4,p4, k4, p3, k4, p3, kl.

Row 1: Slip the first stitch as if to purl, k3, p4, k3, p4, k4, p4, k4, p4, k3, p4, k4.

Row 2: Slip the first stitch as if to purl, p3, k4, p3, k4, p4, k4, p4, k4, p3, k4, p3, kl.

Repeat Rows 1 & 2 until the neckline ribbing measures approximately 70% of the neck measurement of the intended wearer, between 10 inches/25 cm and 12 inches/30 cm. End after working row 1.

Tail #2:

Set-up row: B6, place a marker on your needle, purl 30, place a marker on your needle, B6.

Using Josephine Chart S, beginning with row 19, work as many repeats of rows 19-18 as necessary to obtain the length you desire.

Seed stitch border: Row 1: Slip the first stitch as if to purl, (kl, pl) 9 times, kl, p2tog, (kl, pl) 9 times, k2.

Rows 2-8: Work in seed stitch. Bind off on the ninth row, using the knit-in-pattern bind-off (page 21).

MOCO Yarns
qiviut
lace weight

Josephine scarf – Chart S

#	O	/						6	O	⋏	O	\	O	\	O	\	O	\	O		O	/						6	O	/	#	35
#		O	/				4	O	/		\	O	\	O	\	O	\	O				O	/				4	O	/		#	33
#	O	/	O	/			O	/	O	\		\	O	\	O	\	O				O	/	O	/			O	/	O	\	#	31
#		O	/	O	/	O	/	O	/				\	O	\	O					5	O	/	O	/	O	/	O	/		#	29
#	O	/	O	/	O	/	O	/	O	\				\	O					5	O	/	O	/	O	/	O	/	O	\	#	27
#		O	/	O	/	O	/	O	/				\	O	\	O					5	O	/	O	/	O	/	O	/		#	25
#	O	/	O	/			O	/	O	\		\	O	\	O	\	O				O	/	O	/			O	/	O	\	#	23
#		O	/				4	O	/		\	O	\	O	\	O	\	O				O	/				4	O	/		#	21
#	O	/						6	O	⋏	O	\	O	\	O	\	O	\	O		O	/						6	O	\	#	19
#		\	O	\	O	\	O	\	O		O	/						6	O	⋏	O	\	O	\	O	\	O	\	O		#	17
#	\	O	\	O	\	O	\	O				O	/				4	O	/		\	O	\	O	\	O	\	O			#	15
#		\	O	\	O	\	O				O	/	O	/			O	/	O	\		\	O	\	O	\	O				#	13
#			\	O	\	O					5	O	/	O	/	O	/	O	/				\	O	\	O				4	#	11
#				\	O					5	O	/	O	/	O	/	O	/	O	\				\	O					5	#	9
#			\	O	\	O					5	O	/	O	/	O	/	O	/				\	O	\	O				4	#	7
#		\	O	\	O	\	O				O	/	O	/			O	/	O	\		\	O	\	O	\	O				#	5
#	\	O	\	O	\	O	\	O				O	/				4	O	/		\	O	\	O	\	O	\	O			#	3
#		\	O	\	O	\	O	\	O		O	/						6	O	⋏	O	\	O	\	O	\	O	\	O		#	1

I am intrigued with the lace pattern in my Josephine shawl. It looks big and complicated but has a very nice rhythm. When I get an hour or two to myself, the shawl just seems to grow under my fingers. The swatch was grabbed by a friend who repairs and restores dolls. Some dolly is going to be very warm and very fashionable indeed.
– Anya Konzi-Ashburn

Josephine Shawl

Using a provisional cast-on (page 13), cast on 7 stitches for seed stitch neck band/front border. Set-up row: K2, pl, kl, pl, k2.
Rows 2-47: Slip the first stitch as if to purl, kl, pl, kl, pl, k2. [7 sts]

Following the instructions for "Picking up Neck Band Stitches for the Body of Your Shawl" (page 16), pick up 22 stitches.
Pick up the stitches from your provisional cast-on by following the instructions for "Recovering Stitches from the Provisional Cast-On" (page 18). [35 sts]
When working the first row, and only the first row of your shawl, when you have just seven stitches left on your left needle, K2tog, pl, kl, pl, k2. [34 sts]
Using Charts C [side panels] and D [back panel], and following the instructions "Using the Charts for a Faroese-Shaped Shawl" (page 26), begin your shawl.
Row 2a and all even-numbered rows: B6, purl across, B6.
Continue, following the charts in the same sequence. Repeat rows 1-36 as necessary to obtain the length you desire, ending after working row 36.

Knitting on the Lace Border: Go to the instructions on page 27, "The Lace Border." Using Josephine Chart E (page 30), work the lace border.
Or, if you prefer, finish your shawl by working eight rows of seed stitch. Bind off using either the knit-in-pattern bind-off (page 21) or the Icelandic bind-off (page 21) .

Dress your shawl (page 34). Enjoy wearing your beautiful hand knit work of art!

Josephine shawl back panel – Chart D

Josephine shawl side panel – Chart C

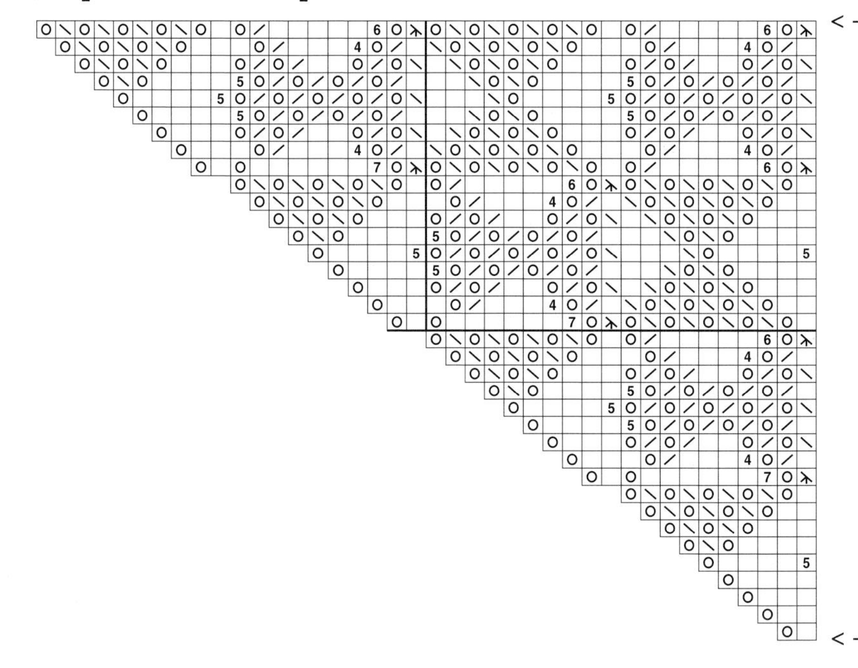

Josephine swatch – Chart B

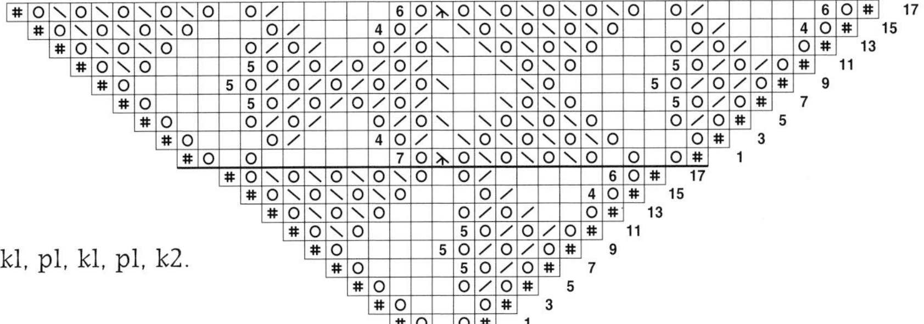

Swatch Chart B rows 1 & 2 in words:

Cast on 13 stitches.

Row 1: B6, yo, k1, yo, B6; or, in other words:

Slip the first stitch as if to purl, k1, p1, k1, p1, k1, yo, k1, yo, k1, p1, k1, p1, k2.

Row 2 and all even-numbered rows: B6, purl across, B6; or, in other words:

Slip the first stitch as if to purl, k1, p1, k1, p1, k1, purl across to the last six stitches, k1, p1, k1, p1, k2.

Josephine Shawl Charts C & D, row 1a in words:

Work the six border stitches [B6], which are not shown in the chart and which at the beginning of the row are always worked as slip the first stitch as if to purl, k1, p1, k1, p1, k1; place a marker on your needle;

work the first side panel using Chart C, which is yo, k1, yo, k1, yo, k1, yo; place a marker on your needle;

work the back panel using Chart D, which is (k1, yo) seven times, k7, yo, k1, yo, k1; place a marker on your needle;

work the second side panel, again using Chart C, which is yo, k1, yo, k1, yo, k1, yo; place a marker on your needle;

work the six border stitches [B6], which are not shown on the chart and which at the end of the row are always worked as k1, p1, k1, p1, k2.

Row 2a and all even-numbered rows:

Slip the first stitch as if to purl, k1, p1, k1, p1, k1, purl across to the last marker, k1, p1, k1, p1, k2.

REPEAT

Part III

Seamen's Scarves

Chapter 1: The Construction of Seamen's Scarves

Much of the information in Part I is applicable to the knitting of a Seamen's scarf. Do familiarize yourself with that information before beginning your first Seamen's scarf. I recommend knitting a Seamen's scarf using the pattern stitch you have selected for knitting a lace Faroese-shaped shawl. It is a wonderful way to try out the stitch pattern, the yarn and the needles you selected for your shawl.

Because of the adaptability of these scarf patterns, I do not instruct you on the yarn or size needle to use, but do provide information on the fiber used. See the Robert Seamen's scarves knit from 100% angora cob web weight and also knit from 100% merino three-ply bulky, page 7. Enjoy using your creative abilities in selecting the fiber and needle size for your scarves.

> *I did the Berdien's Boxes with Haneke's Heaven Sent 100% alpaca. It took one skein exactly. I love working with that yarn – love it, love it, love it – it is absolutely the best to fondle. My mom visited me last month and promptly "stole" that scarf from me. Fortunately I have more and will knit that scarf again!!!*
>
> *– Evelyn Rude*

The scarf patterns included in this book provide a vast array of stitch patterns. Some stitch patterns are simple enough for the beginning knitter, whereas others may challenge the experienced knitter. Some stitch patterns are very masculine; many are very feminine. For some patterns, instructions are provided only in words. Most are provided in chart form, and many are both in words and in chart form. Several patterns work well when using the traditional end-to-end construction, but the majority work best with the Stahman method of construction.

Knitting a Seamen's Scarf in the Traditional Fashion – From End-to-End

The traditional garter stitch Seamen's scarf is worked from end-to-end. It is begun by using your favorite cast-on for the bottom of tail #1 and working in garter stitch for 14 inches, working the neckline ribbing in four-by-four ribbing for 18 inches, followed by working 14 inches of garter stitch for tail #2. This method of construction works well for the traditional garter stitch scarf.

Marilyn (page 113), Walter (page 116), Jerrold's Basket Weave (page 122), Charles' Diamonds (page 123), Jeffrey (page 124) and Matt (page 131) are appropriate patterns for knitting from end-to-end. To knit these scarves from end-to-end, cast on the number of stitches required; work eight rows of seed stitch; work tail #1 following the chart or the written instructions; work the neckline ribbing as instructed; work tail #2; work eight rows of seed stitch; bind off.

The I.J. (page 104) and Robert (page 106) scarves include specific instructions for knitting from end-to-end.

The Stahman Method of Constructing a Seamen's Scarf

Many stitch patterns have a definite directional design, and knitting from end-to-end results in the pattern appearing upside-down on one end of the scarf. To avoid this look, I developed the "Stahman method" of construction for Seamen's scarves.

Using a provisional cast-on (page 13) and leaving about an 18-inch tail of yarn, cast on the number of stitches required for the scarf. Go to the written instructions or the chart and begin working the first tail. Work two to three inches in pattern to ensure you are pleased with the pattern stitch, the yarn and the needle size you have selected. Complete the first tail of your scarf, or follow "Myrna's Knitting Sequence" (page 102).

Remove the provisional cast-on and pick up each stitch as it is released from the provisional cast-on (page 18). You will pick up the same number of stitches as you cast on. One end stitch will look "different," and the stitches will be one-half stitch off because you are now knitting in the opposite direction. Begin by using the 18-inch tail which you left when you did your provisional cast-on. When you have approximately six inches remaining of that tail, splice your fiber (page 20). Work the neck ribbing for the desired length. Work the second tail of your scarf.

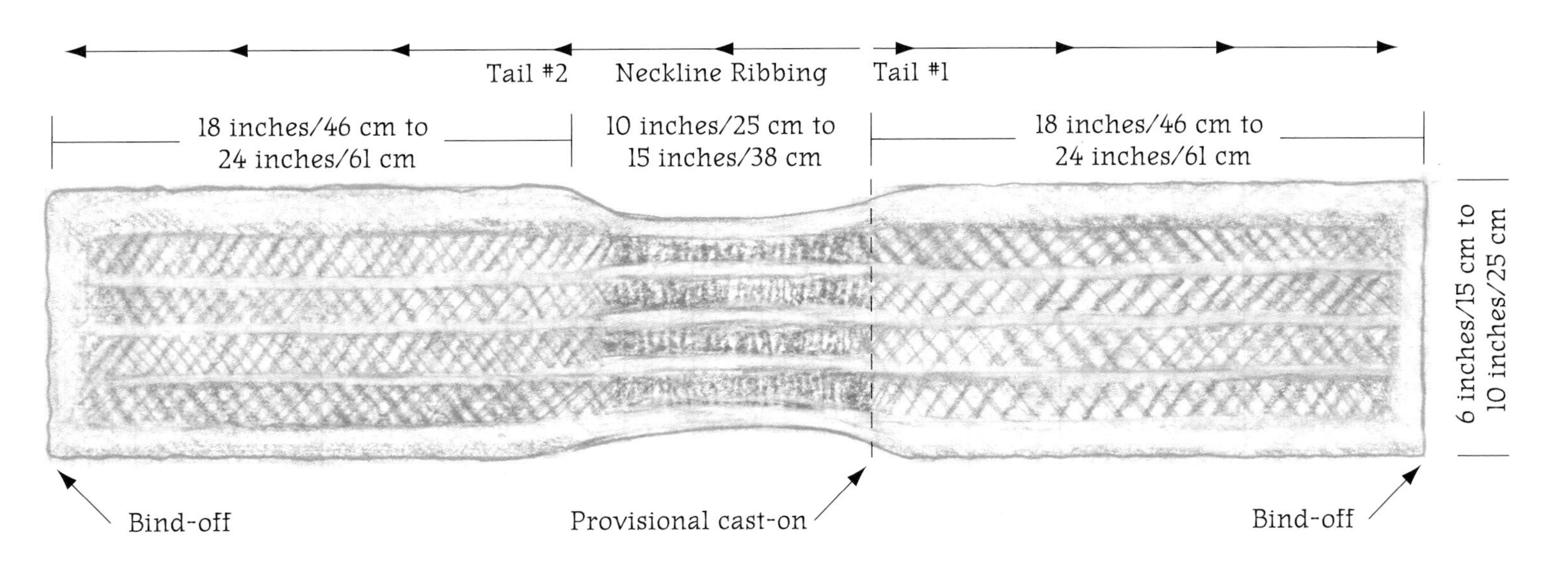

Illustration 25: Schematic of the Stahman adaptation of the traditional Seamen's scarf.

Myrna's Knitting Sequence

After knitting two or three inches on the first tail of my scarf, I remove the provisional cast-on and use the other end of my circular needle to pick up the live stitches.

Using the 18-inch tail left when I did my provisional cast-on, I begin the neckline ribbing, splicing in a second ball of wool. I then work the neckline ribbing section.

When I have completed the neckline ribbing section, I work the pattern in rows equal to the number I had worked in the first tail.

When both tails are an equal length, I work on both tails at the same time until they are the desired length. Although it is best to use two balls of yarn, I will often use both ends of a center-pull ball when using a luxury yarn. I am then provided with the challenge of keeping my yarn untangled.

Working both tails at the same time helps me in two ways. My tension varies from day to day, depending upon how relaxed or stressed I am at the time. Working both tails at the same time ensures my tension is the same at equal points for both tails. I find it easiest to keep track of my pattern when I work both tails at the same time. Best of all, if I fail to follow the pattern correctly I have the same "design feature" in both tails at the same point. If you look carefully, you will discover several special "design features" in one Seamen's scarf pictured in this book.

Working from Written Instructions vs. Working from a Chart

If you are not accustomed to knitting from a chart, you will be happy to know that many of the Seamen's scarf patterns in this section include written instructions. If you have not previously knit from a chart, I urge you to try it; feel free to enlarge the chart for your personal use. Knitting from a chart will help you learn to "read" your knitting. If you make a mistake, you often can compare your work to the chart and discover what went wrong. I hope you will soon enjoy knitting from charts as much as I do.

Chapter 2: The Seamen's Scarf Patterns

The Traditional Seamen's Scarf

The beginning of a new millennium is a great time to join a service project which began over a century ago. The Seamen's Church Institute invites you to participate in the Christmas-at-Sea program by knitting a Seamen's scarf and a matching watch cap using the pattern in Appendix F. The pattern for the original garter stitch Seamen's Church Institute Seamen's scarf and two variations on that pattern follow.

Seamen's Scarves Using the Lace Patterns of the Faroese-Shaped Shawls

Each lace Faroese-shaped shawl pattern includes instructions for knitting a Seamen's scarf using the same lace pattern. See pages 37-97. You may wish to try out a Seamen's scarf using your favorite lace pattern prior to beginning your shawl.

More Seamen's Scarves

I had so much fun using pattern stitches in knitting Seamen's Scarves that I could hardly stop designing and knitting. Patterns for 28 more Seamen's scarves are provided.

"Let's Make the World a Better Place for All" Seamen's Scarves

A gift made by the giver is one of the nicest gifts to receive. What better way to relax and share your love of knitting than knitting a scarf and giving it to someone you don't know. Included are the two Seamen's scarf patterns designed in memory of Matthew Shepard and three scarves in memory of the teacher and students who died in the Columbine High School tragedy. Please use these patterns to knit scarves and give to someone you don't know. Copy these five patterns and share them with your knitting friends so they too can share their love of knitting by giving Seamen's scarves.

Design Your Own Seamen's Scarves

You too can design an original Seamen's scarf. Chapter 3 provides information on designing your own Seamen's scarf.

> *I like the fact that a Seamen's Scarf is like a map, and we will be able to experiment with our own designs if we like. It will be a fun way to try out patterns we have wanted to experiment with.*
>
> *– Polly Garvey*

The Seamen's Church Institute's Christmas-at-Sea Seamen's Scarf

MATERIALS: 4-ply washable wool or synthetic in a bright or dark color; one scarf takes 4 1/2 ounces
NEEDLES: Pair No. 6 needles; wool needle for joining yarn & finishing garment
GAUGE: 5 sts = 1" 7 rows = 1" (Garter Stitch) IMPORTANT: CHECK GAUGE
DIRECTIONS: Cast on 32 sts with medium tension. Knit even for 14 inches. K4, P4 for 18 inches. K even for 14 inches. Bind off with medium tension.
NOTE: Measurement of completed scarf: Approx. Width 6-1/2"; Length 46"
PLEASE DO NOT BLOCK SCARF

The I.J. Seamen's Scarf

Haneke Select
merino/alpaca
medium weight

This scarf may be made as wide as you wish. Using "Neckline Ribbing" (pages 135-136), select the neckline ribbing sequence for the number of stitches you have selected to make the scarf the width you desire.

The Traditional End-to-End Method of Construction

Using your favorite cast-on, cast on any multiple of 8, plus 6 stitches; the most usual numbers are 30, 38 or 46.

Tail #1: Always slipping the first stitch as if to purl, knit across. Knit until piece measures approximately 16 inches/41 cm.

Neckline ribbing:

Row 1: Slip the first stitch as if to purl, *k4, p4, repeat from *, ending k5.

Row 2: Slip the first stitch as if to purl, *p4, k4, repeat from *, ending p4, k1.

Repeat rows 1 & 2 above until ribbing portion of scarf equals approximately the neck measurement of the intended wearer, between 14 inches/35.5 cm and 17 inches/43 cm.

Tail #2: Always slipping the first stitch as if to purl, knit across. Knit the same number of rows as knit for Tail #1.

Bind off using either the knit-in-pattern bind-off (page 21) or the Icelandic bind-off (page 26).

The Stahman Method of Construction

Using a provisional cast-on (page 13), cast on any multiple of 8, plus 6 stitches; the most usual numbers are 30, 38 or 46.

Neckline ribbing:

Set-up row: K1, *p4, k4, repeat from * ending p4, k1.

Row 1: Slip the first stitch as if to purl, *k4, p4, repeat from *, ending k5.

Row 2: Slip the first stitch as if to purl, *p4, k4, repeat from *, ending p4, k1.

Repeat rows 1 & 2 above until ribbing portion of scarf equals the neck measurement of the intended wearer.

Tail #1 and tail #2: Remove the provisional cast-on (page 18). Using two balls of yarn, or each end of a center-pull ball, work both tails at the same time in garter stitch, always slipping the first stitch as if to purl. Knit until the scarf is the length you desire. Bind off, using either the knit-in-pattern bind-off (page 21) or the Icelandic bind-off (page 21).

A version of this pattern first appeared in "The Elegant Seamen's Scarf," *Interweave Knits*, Fall 1998.

The Fenna Seamen's Scarf

The Stahman Method of Construction

Using a provisional cast-on (page 13), cast on any multiple of 8, plus 6 stitches, the most usual numbers are 30, 38 or 46.

Neckline ribbing:
Set-up row: Kl, *p4, k4, repeat from *, ending p4, kl.
Row l: Slip the first stitch as if to purl, *k4, p4, repeat from *, ending k5.
Row 2: Slip the first stitch as if to purl, *p4, k4, repeat from *, ending p4, kl.
Repeat rows l & 2 above until ribbing portion of scarf equals approximately the neck measurement of the intended wearer, between 14 inches/35.5 cm and 17 inches/43 cm.

Tail #1 and tail #2: Remove the provisional cast-on (page 18). Using two balls of yarn, or each end of a center-pull ball, work both tails at the same time in garter stitch, always slipping the first stitch as if to purl. Knit until the scarf is approximately four or five inches shorter than the length you desire.

Decrease shaping:

Variation I:
Place a marker on your needle with one-half of the stitches on each side of the marker.
Row l: Work to within two stitches of the marker, k2tog, slip marker, ssk, work to the end.
Row 2: Work across.
Repeat rows l and 2 until you have only two stitches left; k2tog.

Variation II:
Row l: Slip the first stitch as if to purl, k2tog, work to the last three stitches, ssk, kl.
Row 2: Work across.
Repeat rows l and 2 until you have four stitches left. Slip the first as if to purl, sll-k2tog-psso, pass the first stitch over; cut your yarn and pull through.

Haneke Select
merino/alpaca
medium weight

This scarf may be made as wide as you wish. Using "Neckline Ribbing" (pages 135-136), select the neckline ribbing sequence for the number of stitches you need to make the scarf the width you desire. This is a great scarf knit from sport or medium weight wool. The finer the wool, the more stitches you will cast on.

Haneke Select merino bulky weight

This lace pattern, consisting of just two pattern rows with a purl row separating each pattern row, is an excellent means for practicing your lace knitting techniques. Robert is beautiful worked in any weight yarn, from cobweb to bulky.

Instructions are provided for three different widths.

The Robert Seamen's Scarves

The Stahman Method of Construction

Tail #1: Using a provisional cast-on (page 13), cast on [31] [41] [51] stitches.

Set-up row: K2, p1, k1, p1, k1, place a marker on your needle, purl [19] [29] [39], place a marker on your needle, B6 (page 23).

Using Robert Chart S1 or S2, knitter's choice, work as many repeats of rows 1-4 as necessary to obtain the length you desire.

Finish tail #1 by working eight rows of seed stitch. Bind off on the ninth row, using the knit-in-pattern bind-off (page 21).

Neckline ribbing:

Remove the provisional cast-on, picking up the [31] [41] [51] stitches.

Set-up row: With the private side of your scarf facing you, slip the first stitch as if to knit, [p4, *k3, p3, repeat from *, ending p4, k1] [p3, k4, p3, k4, p3, k5, p3, k4, p3, k4, p3, k1] [p5, k4, p4, k4, p5, k5, p5, k4, p4, k4, p5, k1].

Row 1: Slip the first stitch as if to purl, [k4, *p3, k3, repeat from *, ending k5] [k3, p4, k3, p4, k3, p5, k3, p4, k3, p4, k4] [k5, p4, k4, p4, k5, p5, k5, p4, k4, p4, k6].

Row 2: Slip the first stitch as if to purl, [p4, *k3, p3, repeat from *, ending p4, k1] [p3, k4, p3, k4, p3, k5, p3, k4, p3, k4, p3, k1] [p5, k4, p4, k4, p5, k5, p5, k4, p4, k4, p5, k1].

Repeat Rows 1 & 2 until the neckline ribbing measures approximately 70% of the neck measurement of the intended wearer, between 10 inches/25 cm and 12 inches/30 cm. End after working row 1.

Tail #2:

Set-up row: B6. place a marker on your needle, purl [19] [29] [39], place a marker on your needle, B6.

Work the same as for tail #1, beginning with "Using Robert Chart S1 or S2." Use the same chart used for tail #1.

Worked From End-to-End

Tail #1: Using your favorite cast-on, cast on [31] [41] [51] stitches. Work eight rows of seed stitch.

Using Robert Chart S1 and Method (b) for doing the 3-to-1 decrease, work as many repeats of the pattern as necessary to make Tail #1 the length you desire, ending after working row 4.

Neckline ribbing: Follow the instructions for Rows 1 & 2.

Tail #2: Using Robert Chart S2 and Method (b) for doing the 3-to-1 decrease, work as many rows as worked for Tail #1, ending with eight rows of seed stitch and your favorite bind-off.

The ⋏ (3-to-1) may be done in either of two ways:

(a) slip the first stitch, knit two together, pass the slipped stitch over [s-k2tog-psso]; or

(b) slip the first two stitches together as if to knit, knit one, pass the slipped stitches over.

Method (a) crosses the stitches, breaking up the vertical line of the pattern, and appears somewhat like "chicken feet." Method (b) gives a very vertical line to the pattern. When knitting from end-to-end, you must use Method (b) to get mirror-image tails.

Charts S1 and S2 show three pattern repeats.

For a scarf worked on 31 stitches and two pattern repeats, simply omit the stitches between I and II.

For a scarf worked on 41 stitches and three pattern repeats, follow the chart as written.

For a scarf worked on 51 stitches and four pattern repeats, work the stitches between I and II twice.

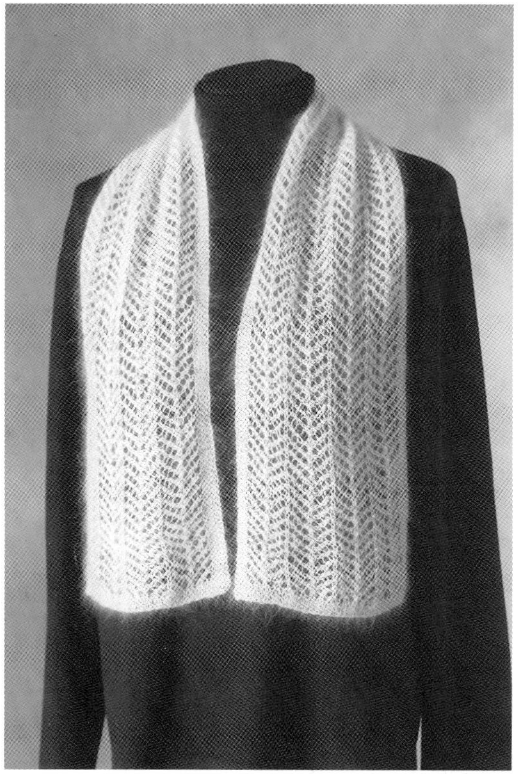

Hand spun by Susan Emerson
angora
cobweb weight

Robert Scarf – Chart S2

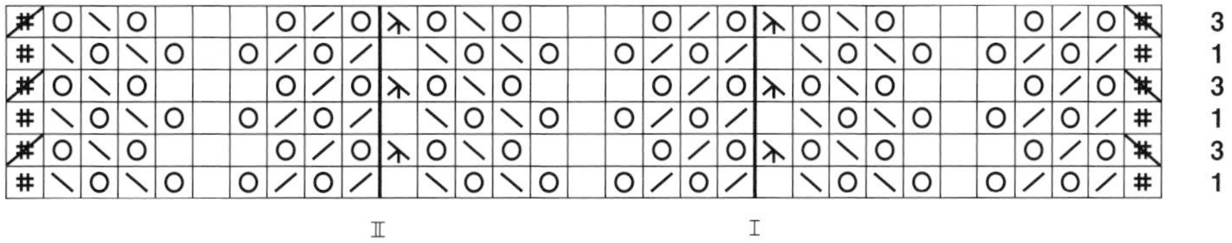

Row 1: B6, which at the beginning of the row is slip the first stitch as if to purl, k1, p1, k1, p1, k1 [(k2tog, yo) twice, k1, (yo, ssk) twice, k1] three times ending the last repeat ssk, [B6, which at the end of the row is k1, p1, k1, p1, k2].

Rows 2 & 4: B6, p 31, B6.

Row 3: Slip the first stitch as if to purl, k1, p1, k1, p1, ssk, (yo, k2tog, yo, k3, yo, ssk, yo, 3-to-1) three times ending last repeat k2tog rather than 3-to-1, then p1, k1, p1, k2.

Robert Scarf – Chart S1

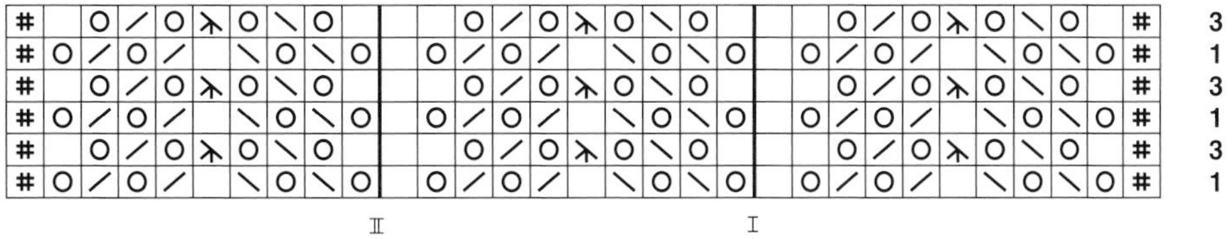

Row 1: B6, [(yo, ssk) twice, k1, (k2tog, yo) twice, k1] three times, ending last repeat after the yo, B6.

Rows 2 & 4: B6, p 31, B6.

Row 3: B6, (k1, yo, ssk, yo, 3-to-1, yo, k2tog, yo, k2) three times, ending last repeat k1 rather than k2, B6.

= Slip the first stitch as if to purl, k1, p1, k1, p1, ssk

= k2tog, p1, k1, p1, k2

Windsor Farms Rabbitry
Hand spun by Gail Smith
angora/merino/silk
sport weight

Variation: Make a wider scarf by casting on 51 stitches and repeating once between points I and II of Chart S. For the neckline ribbing: Remove the provisional cast-on and pick up the 51 stitches. Set-up row: With the private side of your scarf facing you, slip the first stitch as if to knit, p5, k4, p4, k4, p5, k5, p5, k4, p4, k4, p5, k1.

The Anastasia Seamen's Scarf

Tail #1:

Using a provisional cast-on (page 13), cast on 38 stitches.

Set-up row: K2, p1, k1, p1, k1, place a marker on your needle, purl 26, place a marker on your needle, B6 (page 23).

Using Anastasia Chart S, work as many repeats of rows 1-6 as necessary to obtain the length you desire; on final pattern repeat work row 5z, instead of row 5. End after working row 6.

Finish Tail #1 as follows:

Row 1: Slip the first stitch as if to purl, (k1, p1) eight times, k1, p2tog, (k1, p1) eight times, k2. [37 sts]

Rows 2-8: Slip the first stitch as if to purl, *k1, p1, repeat from *, ending k2.

Bind off on the next row, using the knit-in-pattern bind-off (page 21).

Neckline ribbing:

Remove the provisional cast-on, picking up the 38 stitches.

Set-up row: With the private/wrong side of your scarf facing you, slip the first stitch as if to knit, p4, k4, p4, k4, p4, k4, p4, k4, ending p4, k1.

Row 1: Slip the first stitch as if to purl, k4, p4, k4, p4, k4, p4, k4, p4, k5.

Row 2: Slip the first stitch as if to purl, p4, k4, p4, k4, p4, k4, p4, k4, ending p4, k1.

Repeat Rows 1 & 2 until the neckline ribbing measures approximately 70% of the neck measurement of the intended wearer, between 10 inches/25 cm and 12 inches/30 cm. End after working row 1.

Tail #2:

Set-up row: B6, place a marker on your needle, purl 26, place a marker on your needle, B6.

Work the same as for Tail #1, beginning with "Using Anastasia Chart S."

Anastasia Scarf – Chart S

																												Row
#	—				O	/	—	\	O				—	—				O	/	—	\	O				—	#	5z
#	—	O	/		O	/	—	\	O		\	O	—	—	O	/		O	/	—	\	O		\	O	—	#	5
#	—			O	/		—		\	O			—	—			O	/		—		\	O			—	#	3
#	—		O	/			—			\	O		—	—		O	/			—			\	O		—	#	1
II														I														

Pattern in words:

Row 1: [B6, which at the beginning of the row is slip the first stitch as if to purl, k1, p1, k1, p1, k1] [(p1, k1, yo, ssk, k2, p1, k2, k2tog, yo, k1, p1) twice] [B6, which at the end of the row is k1, p1, k1, p1, k2].

Row 2 and all even-numbered rows: B6, p 26, B6.

Row 3: B6, (p1, k2, yo, ssk, k1, p1, k1, k2tog, yo, k2, p1) twice, B6.

Row 5: B6, (p1, yo, ssk, k1, yo, ssk, p1, k2tog, yo, k1, k2tog, yo, p1) twice, B6.

The Joan Seamen's Scarf

Tail #1:

Using a provisional cast-on (page 13), cast on 43 stitches.

Set-up row: K2, p1, k1, p1, k1, place a marker on your needle, purl 31, place a marker on your needle, B6 (page 23).

Using Joan Chart S, work as many repeats of rows 1-10 as necessary to obtain the length you desire, ending the last repeat after working row 8.

Finish tail #1 by working eight rows of seed stitch. Bind off on the ninth row, using the knit-in-pattern bind-off (page 21).

Neckline ribbing:

Remove the provisional cast-on, picking up the 43 stitches.

Set-up row: With the private/wrong side of your scarf facing you, slip the first stitch as if to knit, p3, k4, p4, k4, p4, k3, p4, k4, p4, k4, p3, k1

Row 1: Slip the first stitch as if to purl, k3, p4, k4, p4, k4, p3, k4, p4, k4, p4, k4.

Row 2: Slip the first stitch as if to purl, p3, k4, p4, k4, p4, k3, p4, k4, p4, k4, p3, k1.

Repeat Rows 1 & 2 until the neckline ribbing measures approximately 70% of the neck measurement of the intended wearer, between 10 inches/25 cm and 12 inches/30 cm. End after working row 1.

Tail #2:

Set-up row: B6, place a marker on your needle, purl 31, place a marker on your needle, B6.

Work the same as for Tail #1, beginning with "Using Joan Chart S."

Creature Comforts
chinchilla/merino/silk
fingering weight

Joan Scarf – Chart S

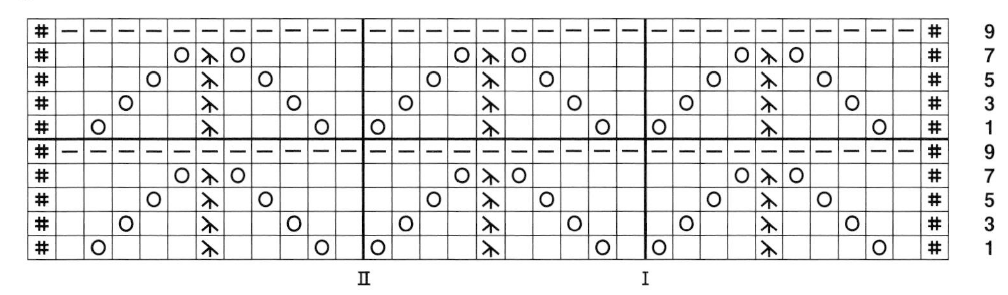

Variation: Make a wider scarf by casting on 53 stitches and repeating once between points I and II of Chart S. Make a narrower scarf by casting on 33 stitches and deleting the stitches between points I and II of Chart S. Using "Neckline Ribbing" (pages 136-137), select the neckline ribbing sequence for the number of stitches you have selected to make your scarf.

Pattern in words:

Row 1: [B6, which at the beginning of the row is slip the first stitch as if to purl, k1, p1, k1, p1, k1] [(k1, yo, k3, sl1-k2tog-psso, k3, yo) three times, k1)] [B6, which at the end of the row is k1, p1, k1, p1, k2].

Row 2 and all even-numbered rows: B6, p 31, B6.

Row 3: B6, (k2, yo, k2, sl1-k2tog-psso, k2, yo, k1) three times, k1, B6.

Row 5: B6, (k3, yo, k1, sl1-k2tog-psso, k1, yo, k2) three times, k1, B6.

Row 7: B6, (k4, yo, sl1-k2tog-psso, yo, k3) three times, k1, B6.

Row 9: B6, p 31, B6.

Merino/possum
fingering weight

Peter Chart S shows only the odd-numbered rows. For the even-numbered rows work the seed stitch borders in pattern, work the five border cable stitches as presented, and purl across the 16 center stitches.

The Peter Seamen's Scarf

Tail #1:

Using a provisional cast-on (page 13), cast on 38 stitches.

Set-up row: K2, pl, kl, pl, kl, place a marker on your needle, purl 26, place a marker on your needle, B6 (page 23).

Using Peter Chart S, work as many repeats of rows 1-8 as necessary to obtain the length you desire.

Finish tail #1 as follows:

Row 1: Slip the first stitch as if to purl, (kl, pl) eight times, kl, p2tog, (kl, pl) eight times, ending k2. [37 sts]

Rows 2-8: Slip the first stitch as if to purl, *kl, pl, repeat from *, ending k2.

Bind off on the next row, using the knit-in-pattern bind-off (page 21).

Neckline ribbing:

Remove the provisional cast-on, picking up the 38 stitches.

Set-up row 1: With the private/wrong side of your scarf facing you, slip the first stitch as if to knit, p4, k4, p4, k4, p4, k4, p4, k4, ending p4, kl.

Row 1: Slip the first stitch as if to purl, k4, p4, k4, p4, k4, p4, k4, p4, k5.

Row 2: Slip the first stitch as if to purl, p4, k4, p4, k4, p4, k4, p4, k4, ending p4, kl.

Repeat Rows 1 & 2 until the neckline ribbing measures approximately 70% of the neck measurement of the intended wearer, between 10 inches/25 cm and 12 inches/30 cm. End after working row 1.

Tail #2:

Set-up row: B6, place a marker on your needle, purl 26, place a marker on your needle, B6.

Work the same as for Tail #1, beginning with "Using Peter Chart S."

Peter Scarf – Chart S

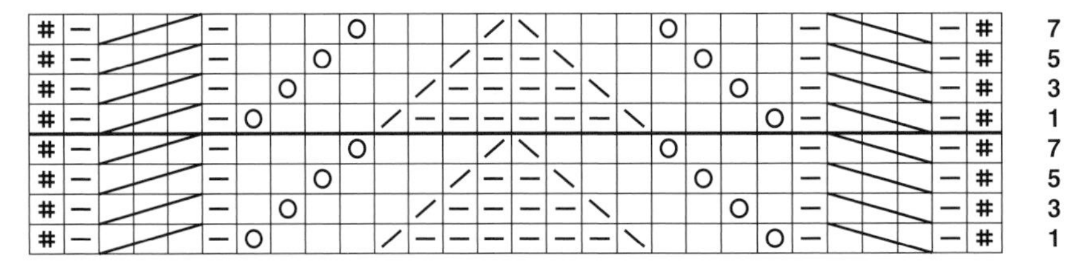

Row 1: [B6, which at the beginning of the row is slip the first stitch as if to purl, kl, pl, kl, pl, kl] [pl, (CF, which is slip the first stitch onto a cable needle and hold in front, knit the next two stitches, knit the stitch from the cable needle), pl, yo, k3, ssk, p6, k2tog, k3, yo, pl, (CB, which is put two stitches on a cable needle and hold in back, knit the next stitch, knit the two stitches from the cable needle), pl] [B6, which at the end of the row is kl, pl, kl, pl, k2].

Row 2 and all even-numbered rows: B6, kl, p3, kl, p 16, kl, p3, kl, B6.

Row 3: B6, pl, CF, pl, kl, yo, k3, ssk, p4, k2tog, k3, yo, kl, pl, CB, pl, B6.

Row 5: B6, pl, CF, pl, k2, yo, k3, ssk, p2, k2tog, k3, yo, k2, pl, CB, pl, B6.

Row 7: B6, pl, CF, pl, k3, yo, k3, ssk, k2tog, k3, yo, k3, pl, CB, pl, B6.

Beth's Candy Canes Seamen's Scarf

Tail #1:

Using a provisional cast-on (page 13), cast on 37 stitches.

Set-up row 1: K2, p1, k1, p1, k1, place a marker on your needle, purl 25, place a marker on your needle, B6 (page 23).

Set-up rows 2 & 4: B6, knit 25, B6.

Set-up rows 3 & 5: B6, purl 25, B6.

Using Beth's Candy Canes Chart S1, work as many repeats of rows 1-14 as necessary to obtain the length you desire.

Finish tail #1 by working eight rows of seed stitch. Bind off on the ninth row, using the knit-in-pattern bind-off (page 21).

Neckline ribbing:

Remove the provisional cast-on, picking up the 37 stitches.

Set-up row: With the private side of your scarf facing you, slip the first stitch as if to knit, p4, k4, p4, k4, p3, k4, p4, k4, ending p4, k1.

Row 1: Slip the first stitch as if to purl, k4, p4, k4, p4, k3, p4, k4, p4, k5.

Row 2: Slip the first stitch as if to purl, p4, k4, p4, k4, p3, k4, p4, k4, ending p4, k1.

Repeat Rows 1 & 2 until the neckline ribbing measures approximately 70% of the neck measurement of the intended wearer, between 10 inches/25 cm and 12 inches/30 cm. End after working row 1.

Tail #2:

Set-up row 1: B6, place a marker on your needle, purl 25, place a marker on your needle, B6.

Go to the instructions for tail #1, and work set-up rows 2-5.

Using Beth's Candy Canes Chart S2, work as many pattern repeats as worked for tail #1.

Finish tail #2 by working eight rows of seed stitch. Bind off on the ninth row, using the knit-in-pattern bind-off (page 21).

Haneke Exotics
merino/angora
sport weight

Beth's Candy Cane Scarf – Chart S1

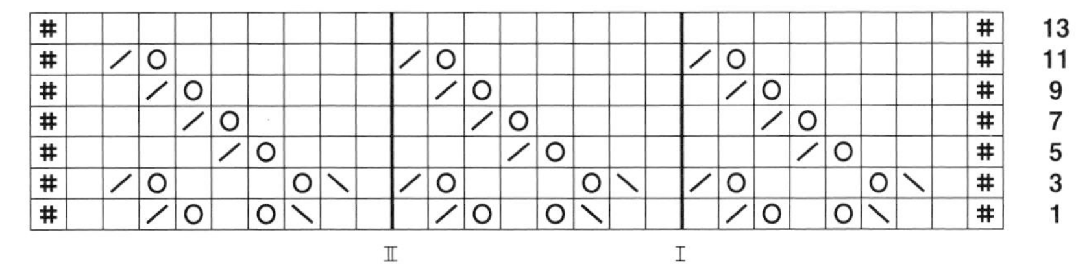

Beth's Candy Cane Scarf – Chart S2

#																									#	13
#							O	\							O	\							O	\		#	11
#						O	\							O	\							O	\			#	9
#					O	\							O	\							O	\				#	7
#				O	\							O	\							O	\					#	5
#		/	O				O	\		/	O				O	\		/	O				O	\		#	3
#			/	O		O	\				/	O		O	\				/	O		O	\			#	1

II I

Even-numbered rows are worked as B6, purl across, B6.

Many different variations of this pattern may be worked. To make the scarf wider, just add another pattern repeat. To add variety, stagger the candy canes; or alternate the direction in which they face. Be creative and have fun. If you change the number of stitches cast on, go to "Neckline Ribbing" (pages 135-136) to select the neckline ribbing sequence for the number of stitches you have selected.

Creature Comforts
chinchilla/merino/silk
fingering weight

Variation: Make a narrower scarf by deleting one pattern repeat. Using a provisional cast-on, cast on 37 stitches and work as above, omitting the stitches between points I and II of Chart S. For the neckline ribbing: Remove the provisional cast-on and pick up the 37 stitches. Set-up row: With the private side of your scarf facing you, slip the first stitch as if to knit, p4, k4, p4, k4, p3, k4, p4, k4, ending p4, k1.

Carolyn's Rosebuds and Hearts Seamen's Scarf

Tail #1:

Using a provisional cast-on (page 13), cast on 49 stitches.

Set-up row: K2, p1, k1, p1, k1, place a marker on your needle, purl 37, place a marker on your needle, B6 (page 23).

Using Carolyn's Rosebuds and Hearts Chart S, work as many repeats of rows 1-14 as necessary to obtain the length you desire.

Finish tail #1 by working eight rows of seed stitch. Bind off on the ninth row, using the knit-in-pattern bind-off (page 21).

Neckline ribbing:

Set-up row: With the private/wrong side of your scarf facing you, slip the first stitch as if to knit, p5, k4, p4, k4, p4, k5, p4, k4, p4, k4, p5, k1.

Row 1: Slip the first stitch as if to purl, k5, p4, k4, p4, k4, p5, k4, p4, k4, p4, k6.

Row 2: Slip the first stitch as if to purl, p5, k4, p4, k4, p4, k5, p4, k4, p4, k4, p5, k1.

Repeat Rows 1 & 2 until the neckline ribbing measures approximately 70% of the neck measurement of the intended wearer, between 10 inches/25 cm and 12 inches/30 cm. End after working row 1.

Tail #2:

Set-up row: B6, place a marker on your needle, purl 37, place a marker on your needle, B6.

Work the same as for Tail #1, beginning with "Using Carolyn's Rosebuds and Hearts Chart S."

Carolyn's Rosebuds and Hearts Scarf – Chart S

13
11
9
7
5
3
1

II I

Row 1: [B6, which at the beginning of the row is slip the first stitch as if to purl, k1, p1, k1, p1, k1] [k1, (k3, k2tog, yo, k1, yo, ssk, k4) three times] [B6, which at the end of the row is k1, p1, k1, p1, k2].

Row 2 and all even-numbered rows: B6, p 37, B6.

Row 3: B6, k1, (k2, k2tog, yo, k3, yo, ssk, k3) three times, B6.

Row 5: B6, k1, (k1, k2tog, yo, k2tog, yo, k1, yo, ssk, yo, ssk, k2) three times, B6.

Row 7: B6, k1, (k2tog, yo, k2tog, yo, k3, yo, ssk, yo, ssk, k1) three times, B6.

Row 9: B6, k2tog, (yo, k2tog, yo, k5, yo, ssk, yo, sl1-k2tog-psso) three times, ending last repeat ssk, B6.

Row 11: B6, k1, (k2tog, yo, k1, yo, ssk, k1, k2tog, yo, k1, yo, ssk, k1) three times, B6.

Row 13: B6, k2tog, (yo, k3, yo, sl1-k2tog-psso, yo, k3, yo, sl1-k2tog-psso) three times, ending the last repeat ssk, B6.

The Marilyn Seamen's Scarf

Tail #1:

Using a provisional cast-on (page 13), cast on 41 stitches.

Set-up row: K2, pl, kl, pl, kl, place a marker on your needle, purl 29, place a marker on your needle, B6 (page 23).

Using Marilyn Chart S, work as many repeats of rows 1-24 as necessary to obtain the length you desire.

Finish tail #1 by working eight rows of seed stitch. Bind off on the ninth row, using the knit-in-pattern bind-off (page 21).

Neckline ribbing:

Remove the provisional cast-on, picking up the 41 stitches.

Set-up row: With the private/wrong side of your scarf facing you, slip the first stitch as if to knit, p3, k4, p3, k4, p3, k5, p3, k4, p3, k4, p3, kl.

Row 1: Slip the first stitch as if to purl, k3, p4, k3, p4, k3, p5, k3, p4, k3, p4, k4.

Row 2: Slip the first stitch as if to purl, p3, k4, p3, k4, p3, k5, p3, k4, p3, k4, p3, kl.

Repeat Rows 1 & 2 until the neckline ribbing measures approximately 70% of the neck measurement of the intended wearer, between 10 inches/25 cm and 12 inches/30 cm. End after working row 1.

Tail #2:

Set-up row: B6, place a marker on your needle, purl 29, place a marker on your needle, B6.

Work the same as for Tail #1, beginning with "Using Marilyn Chart S."

Haneke Select
merino/kid mohair
lace weight

This pattern is appropriate for knitting from end-to-end; see "Knitting a Seamen's Scarf in the Traditional Fashion – From End-to-End" (page 100).

Marilyn Scarf – Chart S

#	\	O		\	O					5	O	/		O	⋏	O		\	O					5	O	/		O	/	#	23
#		\	O		\	O				O	/		O	/		\	O		\	O				O	/		O	/		#	21
#			\	O		\	O		O	/		O	/				\	O		\	O		O	/		O	/			#	19
#	\	O		\	O					5	O	/		O	⋏	O		\	O					5	O	/		O	/	#	17
#		\	O		\	O				O	/		O	/		\	O		\	O				O	/		O	/		#	15
#			\	O		\	O		O	/		O	/				\	O		\	O		O	/		O	/			#	13
#				O	/		O	⋏	O		\	O					5	O	/		O	⋏	O		\	O				#	11
#			O	/		O	/		\	O		\	O				O	/		O	/		\	O		\	O			#	9
#		O	/		O	/				\	O		\	O		O	/		O	/				\	O		\	O		#	7
#				O	/		O	⋏	O		\	O					5	O	/		O	⋏	O		\	O				#	5
#			O	/		O	/		\	O		\	O				O	/		O	/		\	O		\	O			#	3
#		O	/		O	/				\	O		\	O		O	/		O	/				\	O		\	O		#	1

Rows 1 & 7: [B6, which at the beginning of the row is slip the first stitch as if to purl, kl, pl, kl, pl, kl] [(kl, yo, ssk, kl, yo, ssk, k3, k2tog, yo, kl, k2tog, yo) twice, kl] [B6, which at the end of the row is kl, pl, kl, pl, k2].

Row 2 and all even-numbered rows: B6, p 29, B6.

Rows 3 & 9: B6, (k2, yo, ssk, kl, yo, ssk, kl, k2tog, yo, kl, k2tog, yo, k2) twice, kl, B6.

Rows 5 & 11: B6, (k3, yo, ssk, kl, yo, sll-k2tog-psso, yo, kl, k2tog, yo, k2) twice, kl, B6.

Rows 13 & 19: B6, (k2, k2tog, yo, kl, k2tog, yo, kl, yo, ssk, kl, yo, ssk, kl) twice, kl, B6.

Rows 15 & 21: B6, (kl, k2tog, yo, kl, k2tog, yo, k3, yo, ssk, kl, yo, ssk) twice, kl, B6.

Rows 17 & 23: B6, k2tog, yo, kl, k2tog, yo, k5, yo, ssk, kl, yo, sll-k2tog-psso, yo, kl, k2tog, yo, k5, yo, ssk, kl, yo, ssk, B6.

Creature Comforts chinchilla/merino/silk medium weight

Creature Comforts chinchilla/merino/silk fingering weight

Variation: The side and bottom borders of the scarf may be worked in mock ribbing. Odd/public side rows: Slip the first stitch as if to purl, k1, p1, k1, p1, k2, work across in pattern to the last six stitches, k1, p1, k1, p1, k2. Even/private side rows: Slip the first stitch as if to purl, purl across to the last stitch of the row, k1.

Berdien's Boxes Seamen's Scarf

Tail #1:

Using a provisional cast-on (page 13), cast on 37 stitches.

Set-up row: K2, p1, k1, p1, k1, place a marker on your needle, purl 25, place a marker on your needle, B6.

Using Berdien's Boxes Chart S, work as many repeats of rows 1-32 as necessary to obtain the length you desire. The scarf pictured has three and one-half pattern repeats, ending after row 16.

Finish tail #1 by working eight rows of seed stitch. Bind off on the ninth row, using the knit-in-pattern bind-off (page 21).

Neckline ribbing:

Remove the provisional cast-on, picking up the 37 stitches.

Set-up row: With the private/wrong side of your scarf facing you, slip the first stitch as if to knit, p4, k4, p4, k4, p3, k4, p4, k4, ending p4, k1.

Row 1: Slip the first stitch as if to purl, k4, p4, k4, p4, k3, p4, k4, p4, k5.

Row 2: Slip the first stitch as if to purl, p4, k4, p4, k4, p3, k4, p4, k4, ending p4, k1.

Repeat Rows 1 & 2 until the neckline ribbing measures approximately 70% of the neck measurement of the intended wearer, generally between 10 inches/25 cm and 12 inches/30 cm. End after working row 1.

Tail #2:

Set-up row: B6, place a marker on your needle, purl 25, place a marker on your needle, B6.

Work the same as for Tail #1, beginning with "Using Berdien's Boxes Chart S."

Berdien's Boxes Scarf – Chart S

#	/	O	–	–	–	–	–	–	–	–	–	O	↑	O	–	–	–	–	–	–	–	–	–	O	\	#	31
#	/		O	–	–	–	–	–	–	–	O		↑		O	–	–	–	–	–	–	–	O		\	#	29
#	/			O	–	–	–	–	–	O			↑			O	–	–	–	–	–	O			\	#	27
#	/				O	–	–	–	O				↑				O	–	–	–	O				\	#	25
#	–	\				O	–	O				/	–	\				O	–	O				/	–	#	23
#	–	–	\			O		O			/	–	–	–	\			O		O			/	–	–	#	21
#	–	–	–	\		O		O		/	–	–	–	–	–	\		O		O		/	–	–	–	#	19
#	–	–	–	–	\	O		O	/	–	–	–	–	–	–	–	\	O		O	/	–	–	–	–	#	17
#	–	–	–	–	–	O	↑	O	–	–	–	–	–	–	–	–	–	O	↑	O	–	–	–	–	–	#	15
#	–	–	–	–	O		↑		O	–	–	–	–	–	–	–	O		↑		O	–	–	–	–	#	13
#	–	–	–	O			↑			O	–	–	–	–	–	O			↑			O	–	–	–	#	11
#	–	–	O				↑				O	–	–	–	O				↑				O	–	–	#	9
#	–	O				/	–	\				O	–	O				/	–	\				O	–	#	7
#		O			/	–	–	–	\			O		O			/	–	–	–	\			O		#	5
#		O		/	–	–	–	–	–	\		O		O		/	–	–	–	–	–	\		O		#	3
#		O	/	–	–	–	–	–	–	–	\	O		O	/	–	–	–	–	–	–	–	\	O		#	1

Even-numbered rows are worked as B6, purl across, B6.

Irling's Half Diamond Seamen's Scarf

Tail #1:

Using a provisional cast-on (page 13), cast on 37 stitches.

Set-up row: K2, pl, kl, pl, kl, place a marker on your needle, purl 25, place a marker on your needle, B6 (page 23).

Using Irling's Half Diamond Chart S, work as many repeats of rows 1-24 as necessary to make the scarf the length you desire.

Finish tail #1 by working eight rows of seed stitch. Bind off on the ninth row, using the knit-in-pattern bind-off (page 21).

Neckline ribbing:

Remove the provisional cast-on, picking up the 37 stitches.

Set-up row: With the private/wrong side of your scarf facing you, slip the first stitch as if to knit, p4, k4, p4, k4, p3, k4, p4, k4, ending p4, kl.

Row 1: Slip the first stitch as if to purl, k4, p4, k4, p4, k3, p4, k4, p4, k5.

Row 2: Slip the first stitch as if to purl, p4, k4, p4, k4, p3, k4, p4, k4, ending p4, kl.

Repeat rows 1 & 2 above until ribbing portion of scarf equals approximately the neck measurement of the intended wearer, between 14 inches/35.5 cm and 17 inches/43 cm. End after working row 1.

Tail #2:

Set-up row: B6, place a marker on your needle, purl 25 , place a marker on your needle, B6.

Work the same as for Tail #1, beginning with "Using Irling's Half Diamond Chart S."

Irling's Half Diamond Scarf – Chart S

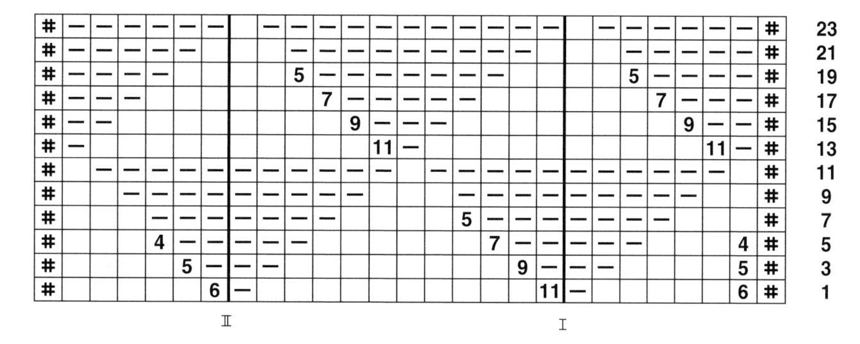

Row 1: [B6, which at the beginning of the row is slip the first stitch as if to purl, kl, pl, kl, pl, kl] [k6, pl, k ll, pl, k6] [B6, which at the end of the row is kl, pl, kl, pl, k2].

Row 2: B6, p6, kl, p ll, kl, p6, B6.

Row 3: B6, k5, p3, k9, p3, k5, B6.

Row 4: B6, p5, k3, p9, k3, p5, B6.

Row 5: B6, k4, p5, k7, p5, k4, B6.

Row 6: B6, p4, k5, p7, k5, p4, B6.

Row 7: B6, k3, p7, k5, p7, k3, B6.

Row 8: B6, p3, k7, p5, k7, p3, B6.

Row 9: B6, k2, p9, k3, p9, k2, B6.

Row 10: B6, p2, k9, p3, k9, p2, B6.

Row ll: B6, kl, p ll, kl, p ll, kl, B6.

Row 12: B6, pl, k ll, pl, k ll, pl, B6.

Row 13: B6, pl, k ll, pl, k ll, pl, B6.

Row 14: B6, kl, p ll, kl, p ll, kl, B6.

Row 15: B6, p2, k9, p3, k9, p2, B6.

Row 16: B6, k2, p9, k3, p9, k2, B6.

Row 17: B6, p3, k7, p5, k7, p3, B6.

Row 18: B6, k3, p7, k5, p7, k3, B6.

Row 19: B6, p4, k5, p7, k5, p4, B6.

Row 20: B6, k4, p5, k7, p5, k4, B6.

Row 21: B6, p5, k3, p9, k3, p5, B6.

Row 22: B6, k5, p3, k9, p3, k5, B6.

Row 23: B6, p6, kl, p ll, kl, p6, B6.

Row 24: B6, k6, pl, k ll, pl, k6, B6.

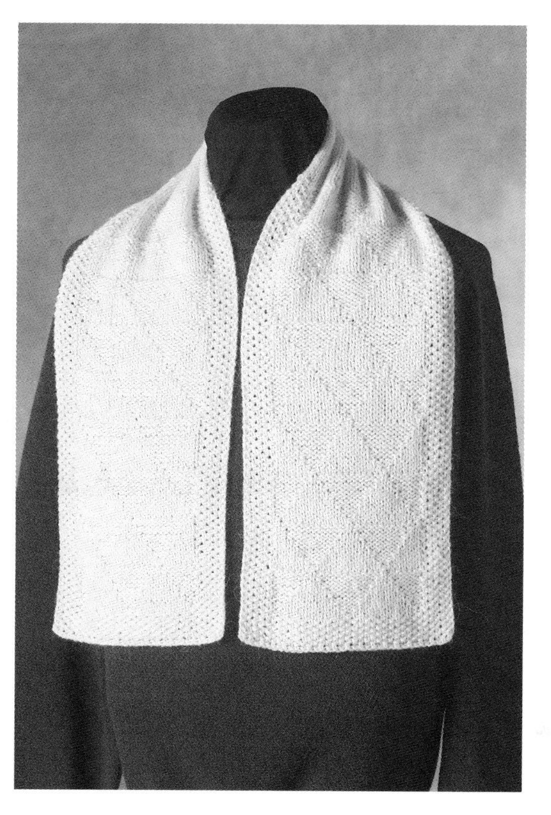

Haneke Select
merino/alpaca
sport weight

The chart shows the odd-numbered rows only. Work the stitches in the even-numbered rows as the stitches present themselves. In other words, when looking at the scarf, row 2 will look exactly like row l; row 4 will look exactly like row 3, etc.

Haneke Select
merino/alpaca
medium weight

Use stitch markers between the seed stitch border and each pattern segment.

The chart shows the odd-numbered rows only. Work the even-numbered rows as the stitches present themselves.

This pattern is appropriate for knitting from end-to-end as explained in "Knitting a Seamen's Scarf in the Traditional Fashion – From End-to-End" (page 100).

The Walter Seamen's Scarf

Tail #1:

Using a provisional cast-on (page 13), cast on 38 stitches.

Using Walter Chart S and working a 4 stitch I-cord border on each side, work as many repeats of rows 1-28 as necessary to obtain the length you desire.

Finish tail #1 by working an I-cord bind-off (page 21).

Neckline ribbing:

Remove the provisional cast-on, picking up the 38 stitches.

Set-up row 1: With the public/right side of your scarf facing you, slip the first stitch as if to knit, k4, p4, k4, p4, k4, p4, k4, p4, k5.

Set-up row 2: Slip the first stitch as if to purl, p4, k4, p4, k4, p4, k4, p4, k4, ending p4, k1.

Row 1: Slip the first stitch as if to purl, k4, p4, k4, p4, k4, p4, k4, p4, k5.

Row 2: Slip the first stitch as if to purl, p4, k4, p4, k4, p4, k4, p4, k4, ending p4, k1.

Repeat Rows 1 & 2 until the neckline ribbing measures approximately the neck measurement of the intended wearer, between 14 inches/35.5 cm and 17 inches/43 cm. End after working row 2.

Tail #2:

Work the same as for Tail #1, beginning with "Using Walter Chart S."

Walter Scarf – Chart S

#			—	—			—	—			—	—			—	—			—	—			—	—			—	—			#	27
#	—	—			—	—			—	—	—	—			—	—			—	—	—	—			—	—			—	—	#	25
#			—	—			—	—			—	—			—	—			—	—			—	—			—	—			#	23
#	—	—			—	—			—	—	—	—			—	—			—	—	—	—			—	—			—	—	#	21
#			—	—			—	—			—	—			—	—			—	—			—	—			—	—			#	19
#	—	—			—	—			—	—	—	—			—	—			—	—	—	—			—	—			—	—	#	17
#			—	—			—	—			—	—			—	—			—	—			—	—			—	—			#	15
#	—	—			—	—			—	—			—	—			—	—			—	—			—	—			—	—	#	13
#	—	—			—	—			—	—	—	—			—	—			—	—	—	—			—	—			—	—	#	11
#	—	—			—	—			—	—			—	—			—	—			—	—			—	—			—	—	#	9
#	—	—			—	—			—	—	—	—			—	—			—	—	—	—			—	—			—	—	#	7
#	—	—			—	—			—	—			—	—			—	—			—	—			—	—			—	—	#	5
#	—	—			—	—			—	—	—	—			—	—			—	—	—	—			—	—			—	—	#	3
#	—	—			—	—			—	—			—	—			—	—			—	—			—	—			—	—	#	1

Rows 1, 5, 9, & 13: K4, (p2, k2) across, ending p2, S4, which is slip the last four stitches.

Rows 2, 6, 10 & 14: P4, (k2, p2) across, ending k2, S4.

Rows 3, 7 & 11: K4, (p2, k2) twice, p2, (p2, k2) twice, p2, (p2, k2) twice, p2, S4.

Rows 4, 8 & 12: P4, (k2, p2) twice, k2, (k2, p2) twice, k2, (k2, p2) twice, k2, S4.

Rows 15, 19, 23 & 27: K4, (k2, p2) across ending k2, S4.

Rows 16, 20, 24 & 28: P4, (p2, k2) across ending p2, S4.

Rows 17, 21 & 25: K4, (p2, k2) twice, p2, (p2, k2) twice, p2, (p2, k2) twice, p2, S4.

Rows 18, 22, & 26: P4, (k2, p2) twice, k2, (k2, p2) twice, k2, (k2, p2) twice, k2, S4.

The Patricia Seamen's Scarf

Haneke Heaven Sent
baby alpaca/merino
fingering weight

Tail #1:

Using a provisional cast-on (page 13), cast on 45 stitches.

Set-up row 1: K2, p1, k1, p1, k1, place a marker on your needle, purl 33, place a marker on your needle, B6 (page 23).

Set-up row 2: B6, k 33, B6.

Set-up row 3: B6, p 33, B6.

Using Patricia Chart S, work as many repeats of rows 1-32, plus one repeat of rows 1-16, as necessary to obtain the length you desire.

Next row: B6, k 33, B6.

Next row: B6, p 33, B6.

Next row: B6, k 33, B6.

Finish tail #1 by working eight rows of seed stitch. Bind off on the ninth row, using the knit-in-pattern bind-off (page 21).

Neckline ribbing:

Remove the provisional cast-on, picking up the 45 stitches.

Set-up row: With the private/wrong side of your scarf facing you, slip the first stitch as if to knit, p4, k4, p4, k4, p4, k3, p4, k4, p4, k4, p4, k1.

Row 1: Slip the first stitch as if to purl, k4, p4, k4, p4, k4, p3, k4, p4, k4, p4, k5.

Row 2: Slip the first stitch as if to purl, p4, k4, p4, k4, p4, k3, p4, k4, p4, k4, p4, k1.

Repeat Rows 1 & 2 until the neckline ribbing measures approximately 70% of the neck measurement of the intended wearer, between 10 inches/25 cm and 12 inches/30 cm. End after working row 1.

Tail #2:

Set-up row 1: B6, purl 33, B6.

Work the same as for Tail #1, beginning with "Set-up row 2."

Patricia Scarf – Chart S

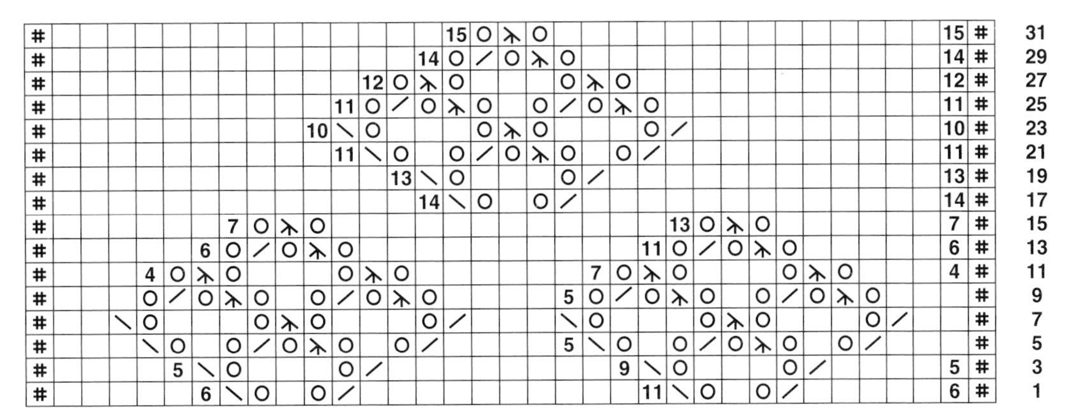

Even-numbered rows are worked as B6, purl across, B6.

Artisan NZ
merino
lace weight

Even-numbered rows are worked as B6, purl across, B6.

The Margaret Seamen's Scarf

Tail #1:

Using a provisional cast-on (page 13), cast on 49 stitches.

Set-up row: K2, pl, kl, pl, kl, place a marker on your needle, purl 37, place a marker on your needle, B6 (page 23).

Using Margaret Chart S, work as many repeats of rows 1-32 as necessary to obtain the length you desire.

Finish tail #1 by working eight rows of seed stitch. Bind off on the ninth row, using the knit-in-pattern bind-off (page 21).

Neckline ribbing:

Remove the provisional cast-on and pick up the 49 stitches.

Set-up row: With the private/wrong side of your scarf facing you, slip the first stitch as if to knit, p5, k4, p4, k4, p4, k5, p4, k4, p4, k4, p5, kl.

Row l: Slip the first stitch as if to purl, k5, p4, k4, p4, k4, p5, k4, p4, k4, p4, k6.

Row 2: Slip the first stitch as if to purl, p5, k4, p4, k4, p4, k5, p4, k4, p4, k4, p5, kl.

Repeat Rows l & 2 until the neckline ribbing measures approximately 70% of the neck measurement of the intended wearer, between 10 inches/25 cm and 12 inches/30 cm. End after working row l.

Tail #2:

Set-up row: B6, place a marker on your needle, purl 37, place a marker on your needle, B6.

Work the same as for Tail #1, beginning with "Using Margaret Chart S."

Margaret Scarf – Chart S

#			O	/		O	/		O	⋏	O		\	O		\	O				O	/		O	/		O	⋏	O		\	O		\	O			#	31
#		O	/		O	/		O	/	ℓ	\	O		\	O		\	O		O	/		O	/		O	/	ℓ	\	O		\	O		\	O		#	29
#				O	/		O	/	—	ℓ	—	\	O		\	O						O	/		O	/	—	ℓ	—	\	O		\	O				#	27
#			O	/		O	/	—	—	ℓ	—	—	\	O		\	O				O	/		O	/	—	—	ℓ	—	—	\	O		\	O			#	25
#		O	/		O	/	ℓ	—	—	ℓ	—	—	ℓ	\	O		\	O		O	/		O	/	ℓ	—	—	ℓ	—	—	ℓ	\	O		\	O		#	23
#				O	/	—	ℓ	—	—	ℓ	—	—	ℓ	—	\	O						O	/	—	ℓ	—	—	ℓ	—	—	ℓ	—	\	O				#	21
#			O	/	—	—	ℓ	—	—	ℓ	—	—	ℓ	—	—	\	O				O	/	—	—	ℓ	—	—	ℓ	—	—	ℓ	—	—	\	O			#	19
#		O	/	ℓ	—	—	ℓ	—	—	ℓ	—	—	ℓ	—	—	ℓ	\	O		O	/	ℓ	—	—	ℓ	—	—	ℓ	—	—	ℓ	—	—	ℓ	\	O		#	17
#	\	O		\	O		\	O				O	/		O	/		O	⋏	O		\	O		\	O				O	/		O	/		O	/	#	15
#	ℓ	\	O		\	O		\	O		O	/		O	/		O	/	ℓ	\	O		\	O		\	O		O	/		O	/		O	/	ℓ	#	13
#	ℓ	—	\	O		\	O						O	/		O	/	—	ℓ	—	\	O		\	O						O	/		O	/	—	ℓ	#	11
#	ℓ	—	—	\	O		\	O				O	/		O	/	—	—	ℓ	—	—	\	O		\	O				O	/		O	/	—	—	ℓ	#	9
#	ℓ	—	—	ℓ	\	O		\	O		O	/		O	/	ℓ	—	—	ℓ	—	—	ℓ	\	O		\	O		O	/		O	/	ℓ	—	—	ℓ	#	7
#	ℓ	—	—	ℓ	—	\	O						O	/	—	ℓ	—	—	ℓ	—	—	ℓ	—	\	O						O	/	—	ℓ	—	—	ℓ	#	5
#	ℓ	—	—	ℓ	—	—	\	O				O	/	—	—	ℓ	—	—	ℓ	—	—	ℓ	—	—	\	O				O	/	—	—	ℓ	—	—	ℓ	#	3
#	ℓ	—	—	ℓ	—	—	ℓ	\	O		O	/	ℓ	—	—	ℓ	—	—	ℓ	—	—	ℓ	—	—	ℓ	\	O		O	/	ℓ	—	—	ℓ	—	—	ℓ	#	1

The Catharina Seamen's Scarf

Tail #1:

Using a provisional cast-on (page 13), cast on 49 stitches.

Set-up row: K2, pl, kl, pl, kl, place a marker on your needle, purl 37, place a marker on your needle, B6 (page 23).

Using Catharina Chart S, work as many repeats of rows 1-36 as necessary to obtain the length you desire.

Finish tail #1 by working eight rows of seed stitch.

Bind off on the ninth row, using the knit-in-pattern bind-off (page 21).

Neckline ribbing:

Remove the provisional cast-on, picking up the 49 stitches.

Set-up row: With the private/wrong side of your scarf facing you, slip the first stitch as if to knit, p5, k4, p4, k4, p4, k5, p4, k4, p4, k4, p5, kl.

Row 1: Slip the first stitch as if to purl, k5, p4, k4, p4, k4, p5, k4, p4, k4, p4, k6.

Row 2: Slip the first stitch as if to purl, p5, k4, p4, k4, p4, k5, p4, k4, p4, k4, p5, kl.

Repeat rows 1 & 2 until the neckline ribbing measures approximately 70% of the neck measurement of the intended wearer, between 10 inches/25 cm and 12 inches/30 cm. End after working row 1.

Tail #2:

Set-up row: B6, place a marker on your needle, purl 37, place a marker on your needle, B6.

Work the same as for Tail #1, beginning with "Using Catharina Chart S."

MOCO Yarns
qiviut
lace weight

Catharina Scarf – Chart S

																																							Row
#	\	O															15	O	⋏	O															15	O	/	#	35
#		\	O													13	O	/		\	O													13	O	/		#	33
#	\	O	\	O											11	O	/	O	⋏	O	\	O											11	O	/	O	/	#	31
#		\	O	\	O									9	O	/	O	/		\	O	\	O									9	O	/	O	/		#	29
#	\	O	\	O	\	O							7	O	/	O	/	O	⋏	O	\	O	\	O							7	O	/	O	/	O	/	#	27
#		\	O	\	O	\	O					5	O	/	O	/	O	/		\	O	\	O	\	O					5	O	/	O	/	O	/		#	25
#	\	O	\	O	\	O	\	O				O	/	O	/	O	/	O	⋏	O	\	O	\	O	\	O				O	/	O	/	O	/	O	/	#	23
#		\	O	\	O	\	O	\	O		O	/	O	/	O	/	O	/		\	O	\	O	\	O	\	O		O	/	O	/	O	/	O	/		#	21
#			\	O	\	O	\	O				O	/	O	/	O	/				\	O	\	O	\	O				O	/	O	/	O	/			#	19
#								8	O	⋏	O															15	O	⋏	O								8	#	17
#							7	O	/		\	O													13	O	/		\	O							7	#	15
#						6	O	/	O	⋏	O	\	O											11	O	/	O	⋏	O	\	O						6	#	13
#					5	O	/	O	/		\	O	\	O									9	O	/	O	/		\	O	\	O					5	#	11
#				4	O	/	O	/	O	⋏	O	\	O	\	O							7	O	/	O	/	O	⋏	O	\	O	\	O				4	#	9
#				O	/	O	/	O	/		\	O	\	O	\	O					5	O	/	O	/	O	/		\	O	\	O	\	O				#	7
#			O	/	O	/	O	/	O	⋏	O	\	O	\	O	\	O				O	/	O	/	O	/	O	⋏	O	\	O	\	O	\	O			#	5
#		O	/	O	/	O	/	O	/		\	O	\	O	\	O	\	O		O	/	O	/	O	/	O	/		\	O	\	O	\	O	\	O		#	3
#			O	/	O	/	O	/				\	O	\	O	\	O				O	/	O	/	O	/				\	O	\	O	\	O			#	1
										II																		I											

Even-numbered rows are worked as B6, purl across, B6.

MOCO Yarns
qiviut
lace weight

Even-numbered rows are worked as B6, purl across, B6.

The Nancy Seamen's Scarf

Tail #1:
Using a provisional cast-on (page 13), cast on 41 stitches.
Set-up row: K2, p1, k1, p1, k1, place a marker on your needle, purl 29, place a marker on your needle, B6 (page 23).
Using Nancy Chart S, work as many repeats of rows 1-36 as necessary to obtain the length you desire.
Finish tail #1 by working eight rows of seed stitch. Bind off on the ninth row, using the knit-in-pattern bind-off (page 21).

Neckline ribbing:
Remove the provisional cast-on and pick up the 41 stitches.
Set-up row: With the private/wrong side of your scarf facing you, slip the first stitch as if to knit, p3, k4, p3, k4, p3, k5, p3, k4, p3, k4, p3, k1.
Row 1: Slip the first stitch as if to purl, k3, p4, k3, p4, k3, p5, k3, p4, k3, p4, k4.
Row 2: Slip the first stitch as if to purl, p3, k4, p3, k4, p3, k5, p3, k4, p3, k4, p3, k1.
Repeat Rows 1 & 2 until the neckline ribbing measures approximately 70% of the neck measurement of the intended wearer, between 10 inches/25 cm and 12 inches/30 cm. End after working row 1.

Tail #2:
Set-up row: B6, place a marker on your needle, purl 29, place a marker on your needle, B6.
Work the same as for Tail #1, beginning with "Using Nancy Chart S."

Nancy Scarf – Chart S

#	\	O											11	O	↑	O											11	O	/	#	35
#		\	O				O	↑	O				O	/		\	O				O	↑	O				O	/		#	33
#	\	O	\	O		O	/		\	O		O	/	O	↑	O	\	O		O	/		\	O		O	/	O	/	#	31
#		\	O	\	O					5	O	/	O	/		\	O	\	O					5	O	/	O	/		#	29
#	\	O	\	O	\	O				O	/	O	/	O	↑	O	\	O	\	O				O	/	O	/	O	/	#	27
#		\	O	\	O	\	O		O	/	O	/	O	/		\	O	\	O	\	O		O	/	O	/	O	/		#	25
#			\	O	\	O				O	/	O	/				\	O	\	O				O	/	O	/			#	23
#			O	↑	O	\	O		O	/	O	↑	O				O	↑	O	\	O		O	/	O	↑	O			#	21
#		O	/		\	O				O	/		\	O		O	/		\	O				O	/		\	O		#	19
#						6	O	↑	O											11	O	↑	O						6	#	17
#	\	O				O	/		\	O				O	↑	O				O	/		\	O				O	/	#	15
#		\	O		O	/	O	↑	O	\	O		O	/		\	O		O	/	O	↑	O	\	O		O	/		#	13
#				O	/	O	/		\	O	\	O					5	O	/	O	/		\	O	\	O				#	11
#			O	/	O	/	O	↑	O	\	O	\	O				O	/	O	/	O	↑	O	\	O	\	O			#	9
#		O	/	O	/	O	/		\	O	\	O	\	O		O	/	O	/	O	/		\	O	\	O	\	O		#	7
#			O	/	O	/				\	O	\	O				O	/	O	/				\	O	\	O			#	5
#		O	/	O	↑	O				O	↑	O	\	O		O	/	O	↑	O				O	↑	O	\	O		#	3
#			O	/		\	O		O	/		\	O				O	/		\	O		O	/		\	O			#	1

The Lace Christmas Tree Seamen's Scarf

Tail #1:

Using a provisional cast-on (page 13), cast on 41 stitches.

Set-up row: K2, p1, k1, p1, k1, place a marker on your needle, purl 29, place a marker on your needle, B6 (page 23).

Using Lace Christmas Tree Chart S, work as many repeats of rows 1-60 as necessary to obtain the length you desire ending after row 32.

Finish tail #1 by working eight rows of seed stitch. Bind off on the ninth row, using the knit-in-pattern bind-off (page 21).

Neckline ribbing:

Remove the provisional cast-on, picking up the 41 stitches.

Set-up row: With the private/wrong side of your scarf facing you, slip the first stitch as if to knit, p3, k4, p3, k4, p3, k5, p3, k4, p3, k4, p3, k1.

Row 1: Slip the first stitch as if to purl, k3, p4, k3, p4, k3, p5, k3, p4, k3, p4, k4.

Row 2: Slip the first stitch as if to purl, p3, k4, p3, k4, p3, k5, p3, k4, p3, k4, p3, k1.

Repeat Rows 1 & 2 until the neckline ribbing measures approximately 90% of the neck measurement of the intended wearer, between 12 inches/30 cm and 14 inches/35.5 cm. End after working row 1.

Tail #2:

Set-up row: B6, place a marker on your needle, purl 29, place a marker on your needle, B6.

Work the same as for Tail #1, beginning with "Using Lace Christmas Tree Chart S."

Haneke Melange alpaca fingering weight

Lace Christmas Tree Scarf – Chart S

#													13	O	⋏	O													13	#	59
#												12	O	/		|O												12	#	57
#											11	O	/	O	⋏	O	|O											11	#	55
#										10	O	/	O	/		|O	|O										10	#	53
#									9	O	/	O	/	O	⋏	O	|O	|O									9	#	51
#										10	O	/	O	/		|O	|O										10	#	49
#											11	O	/	O	⋏	O	|O											11	#	47
#												12	O	/		|O												12	#	45
#											11	O	/	O	⋏	O	|O											11	#	43
#										10	O	/	O	/		|O	|O										10	#	41
#											11	O	/	O	⋏	O	|O											11	#	39
#												12	O	/		|O												12	#	37
#													13	O	⋏	O													13	#	35
#													13	/	O														14	#	33
#																														#	31
#						6	O	⋏	O											11	O	⋏	O						6	#	29
#					5	O	/		|O									9	O	/		|O					5	#	27
#				4	O	/	O	⋏	O	|O							7	O	/	O	⋏	O	|O				4	#	25
#				O	/	O	/		|O	|O					5	O	/	O	/		|O	|O				#	23
#			O	/	O	/	O	⋏	O	|O	|O				O	/	O	/	O	⋏	O	|O	|O			#	21
#				O	/	O	/		|O	|O					5	O	/	O	/		|O	|O				#	19
#				4	O	/	O	⋏	O	|O							7	O	/	O	⋏	O	|O				4	#	17
#					5	O	/		|O									9	O	/		|O					5	#	15
#				4	O	/	O	⋏	O	|O							7	O	/	O	⋏	O	|O				4	#	13
#				O	/	O	/		|O	|O					5	O	/	O	/		|O	|O				#	11
#				4	O	/	O	⋏	O	|O							7	O	/	O	⋏	O	|O				4	#	9
#					5	O	/		|O									9	O	/		|O					5	#	7
#						6	O	⋏	O											11	O	⋏	O						6	#	5
#						6	/	O												12	/	O							7	#	3
#																														#	1
#																														#	1a

Even-numbered rows are worked as B6, purl across, B6.

Haneke Select
merino/alpaca
sport weight

Use stitch markers between the seed stitch border and each pattern segment.

The chart shows every row of the pattern as viewed from the right/public side of the scarf. For even-numbered rows, work the stitches the opposite of what is shown on the chart.

This pattern is appropriate for knitting from end-to-end as explained in "Knitting a Seamen's Scarf in the Traditional Fashion – From End-to-end" (page 100).

This pattern may be worked on any multiple of seven stitches, plus the 12 border stitches.

Jerrold's Basket Weave Seamen's Scarf

Tail #1:

Using a provisional cast-on (page 13), cast on 33 stitches.

Set-up row: K2, p1, k1, p1, k1, place a marker on your needle, purl 21, place a marker on your needle, B6 (page 23).

Using Jerrold Chart S, work as many repeats of rows 1-22 as necessary to obtain the length you desire.

Finish tail #1 by working eight rows of seed stitch. Bind off on the ninth row, using the knit-in-pattern bind-off (page 21).

Neckline ribbing:

Remove the provisional cast-on, picking up the 33 stitches.

Set-up row: With the private/wrong side of your scarf facing you, slip the first stitch as if to knit, *p3, k4, repeat from *, ending p3, k1.

Row 1: Slip the first stitch as if to purl, k3, *p4, k3, repeat from *, ending k4.

Row 2: Slip the first stitch as if to purl, *p3, k4, repeat from *, ending p3, k1.

Repeat Rows 1 & 2 until the neckline ribbing measures approximately the neck measurement of the intended wearer, between 14 inches/35.5 cm and 17 inches/43 cm. End after working row 1.

Tail #2:

Set-up row: B6, place a marker on your needle, purl 21, place a marker on your needle, B6.

Work the same as for Tail #1, beginning with "Using Jerrold's Basket Weave Chart S."

Jerrold's Basket Weave Scarf – Chart S

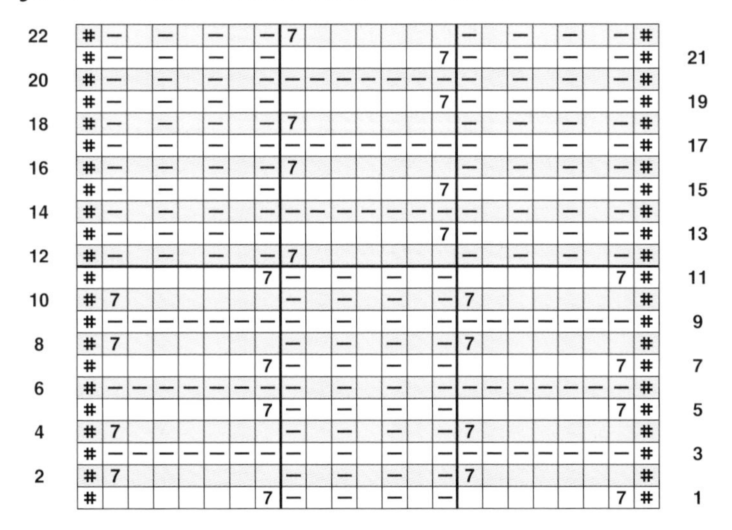

Rows 1, 5, 7, & 11: B6, k7, (p1, k1) 3 times, p1, k7, B6.

Rows 2, 4, 8 & 10: B6, p7, (k1, p1) 3 times, k1, p7, B6.

Row 3 & 9: B6, p8, (k1, p1) 3 times, p7, B6.

Row 6: B6, k8, (p1, k1) 3 times, k7, B6.

Rows 12, 16, 18 & 22: B6, (k1, p1) 4 times, p5, (p1, k1) 4 times, B6.

Rows 13, 15, 19 & 21: B6, (p1, k1) 4 times, k5, (k1, p1) 4 times, B6.

Rows 14 & 20: B6, (k1, p1) 3 times, k9, (p1, k1) 3 times, B6.

Row 17: B6, (p1, k1) 3 times, p9, (k1, p1) 3 times, B6.

Charles' Diamonds Seamen's Scarf

Tail #1:

Using a provisional cast-on (page 13), cast on 49 stitches.

Set-up row: K2, p1, k1, p1, k1, place a marker on your needle, purl 37, place a marker on your needle, B6 (page 23).

Using Charles Chart S, work as many repeats of rows 1-12 as necessary to obtain the length you desire.

Finish tail #1 by working eight rows of seed stitch. Bind off on the ninth row, using the knit-in-pattern bind-off (page 21).

Neckline ribbing:

Remove the provisional cast-on, picking up the 49 stitches.

Set-up row: With the private/wrong side of your scarf facing you, slip the first stitch as if to knit, p5, k4, p4, k4, p4, k5, p4, k4, p4, k4, p5, k1.

Row 1: Slip the first stitch as if to purl, k5, p4, k4, p4, k4, p5, k4, p4, k4, p4, k6.

Row 2: Slip the first stitch as if to purl, p5, k4, p4, k4, p4, k5, p4, k4, p4, k4, p5, k1.

Repeat Rows 1 & 2 until the neckline ribbing measures approximately the neck measurement of the intended wearer, between 14 inches/35.5 cm and 17 inches/43 cm. End after working row 1.

Tail #2:

Set-up row: B6, place a marker on your needle, purl 37, place a marker on your needle, B6.

Work the same as for Tail #1, beginning with "Using Charles Chart S."

Haneke Select merino/alpaca fingering weight

Charles' Diamonds Scarf – Chart S

12	#	—		—	7							—		—		—	7							—		—		—	7							—		—	#	
	#		—		—					5	—		—		—		—					5	—		—		—		—					5	—		—		#	11
10	#			—		—				—		—				—		—				—		—				—		—				—		—			#	
	#				—		—		—		—					5	—		—		—		—					5	—		—		—		—				#	9
8	#	4				—		—		—	7							—		—		—	7							—		—		—	4				#	
	#					5	—		—									9	—		—									9	—		—					5	#	7
6	#	4				—		—		—	7							—		—		—	7							—		—		—	4				#	
	#				—		—		—		—					5	—		—		—		—					5	—		—		—		—				#	5
4	#			—		—				—		—				—		—				—		—				—		—				—		—			#	
	#		—		—					5	—		—		—		—					5	—		—		—		—					5	—		—		#	3
2	#	—		—	7							—		—		—	7							—		—		—	7							—		—	#	
	#		—									9	—		—									9	—		—									9	—		#	1
														II												I														

Row 1: [B6, which at the beginning of the row is slip the first stitch as if to purl, k1, p1, k1, p1, k1] [(K1, p1, k9, p1) three times, k1] [B6, which at the end of the row is k1, p1, k1, p1, k2].

Rows 2 & 12: B6, k1, (p1, k1, p7, k1, p1, k1) three times, B6.

Rows 3 & 11: B6, (k1, p1, k1, p1, k5, p1, k1, p1) three times, K1, B6.

Rows 4 & 10: B6, p1, (p1, k1, p1, k1, p3, p1, k1, p1, p2) three times, B6.

Rows 5 & 9: B6, (k3, p1, k1, p1, k1, p1, k1, p1, k2) three times, k1, B6.

Rows 6 & 8: B6, p1, (p3, k1, p1, k1, p1, k1, p3) three times, B6.

Row 7: B6, k5, p1, k1, p1, k4) three times, k1, B6.

Use stitch markers between the seed stitch border and each pattern segment.

The chart shows every row of the pattern as viewed from the right/public side of the scarf. For even-numbered rows work the stitches the opposite of what is shown on the chart.

This pattern is appropriate for knitting from end-to-end as explained in "Knitting a Seamen's Scarf in the Traditional Fashion – From End-to-end" (page 100).

This pattern may be worked on any multiple of 12 stitches, plus one stitch.

Haneke Select
merino/alpaca
medium weight

Use stitch markers between the seed stitch border and each pattern segment.

This pattern may be worked on any multiple of 12 stitches.

The Jeffrey Seamen's Scarf

Tail #1:

Using a provisional cast-on (page 13), cast on 36 stitches.

Using Jeffrey Chart S, or the written instructions below, work as many repeats of rows 1-22 as necessary to obtain the length you desire.

End the pattern after working row 11 or row 22; on the final row [11 or 22], work across to the last seven stitches, k2tog, (p1, k1) two times, k1. [35 sts]

Finish tail #1 by working eight rows of seed stitch. Bind off on the ninth row, using the knit-in-pattern bind-off (page 21).

Neckline ribbing:

Remove the provisional cast-on, picking up the 36 stitches.

Set-up row 1: With the public/right side of your scarf facing you, slip the first stitch as if to knit, k3, (p4, k4) four times.

Set-up row 2: Slip the first stitch as if to purl, p3, (k4 p4) four times ending the last repeat p3, k1.

Row 1: Slip the first stitch as if to purl, k3, (p4, k4) four times.

Row 2: Slip the first stitch as if to purl, p3, (k4, p4) four times, ending the last repeat p3, k1.

Repeat Rows 1 & 2 until the neckline ribbing measures approximately the neck measurement of the intended wearer, between 14 inches/35.5 cm and 17 inches/43 cm.

Tail #2:

Work the same as for tail #1, beginning with "Using Jeffrey Chart S."

Worked From End-to-End:

Tail #1: Using your favorite cast-on, cast on 37 stitches and work the following seed stitch border:

Rows 1 - 8: Slip the first stitch as if to purl, (k1, p1) across, ending k2.

Row 9: Slip the first stitch as if to purl, (k1, p1) to the last seven stitches, k2tog, (p1, k1) twice, k1. [36 sts]

Using Jeffrey Chart S or the written instructions, work as many repeats of rows 1-22 as necessary to obtain the length you desire.

Neckline ribbing: Follow the instructions above, beginning with "Set-up row 1."

Tail #1: Using Jeffrey Chart S or the written instructions, work as many repeats of rows 1-22 as worked for Tail #1. Work eight rows of seed stitch, followed by your favorite bind-off.

Row 1: B6, *k1, p1; repeat from *, B6.
Row 2: B6, *(p1, k1) twice, p2, k2, (p1, k1) twice; repeat from * , B6.
Row 3: B6, *k1, p1, k1, p3, k3, p1, k1, p1; repeat from * , B6.
Row 4: B6, *p1, k1, p4, k4, p1, k1; repeat from * , B6.
Row 5: B6, *k1, p5, k5, p1; repeat from * , B6.
Row 6: B6, *p6, k6; repeat from * , B6.
Row 7: B6, *p5, k1, p1, k5; repeat from * , B6.
Row 8: B6, *p4, (k1, p1) twice, k4; repeat from * , B6.
Row 9: B6, *p3, (k1, p1) 3 times, k3; repeat from * , B6.
Row 10: B6, *p2, (k1, p1) 4 times, k2; repeat from * , B6.
Row 11: B6, *p1, k1; repeat from * , B6.
Row 12: B6, *k1, p1; repeat from * , B6.
Row 13: B6, *k2, (p1, k1) 4 times, p2; repeat from * , B6.
Row 14: B6, *k3, (p1, k1) 3 times, p3; repeat from * , B6.
Row 15: B6, *k4, (p1, k1) 2 times, p4; repeat from * , B6.
Row 16: B6, *k5, p1, k1, p5; repeat from * , B6.
Row 17: B6, *k6, p6; repeat from * , B6.
Row 18: B6, *p1, k5, p5, k1; repeat from * , B6.
Row 19: B6, *k1, p1, k4, p4, k1, p1; repeat from * , B6.
Row 20: B6, *p1, k1, p1, k3, p3, k1, p1, k1; repeat from * , B6.
Row 21: B6, *(k1, p1) twice, k2, p2, (k1, p1) twice; repeat from * , B6.
Row 22: B6, *p1, k1; repeat from * , B6.

Jeffrey Scarf – Chart S

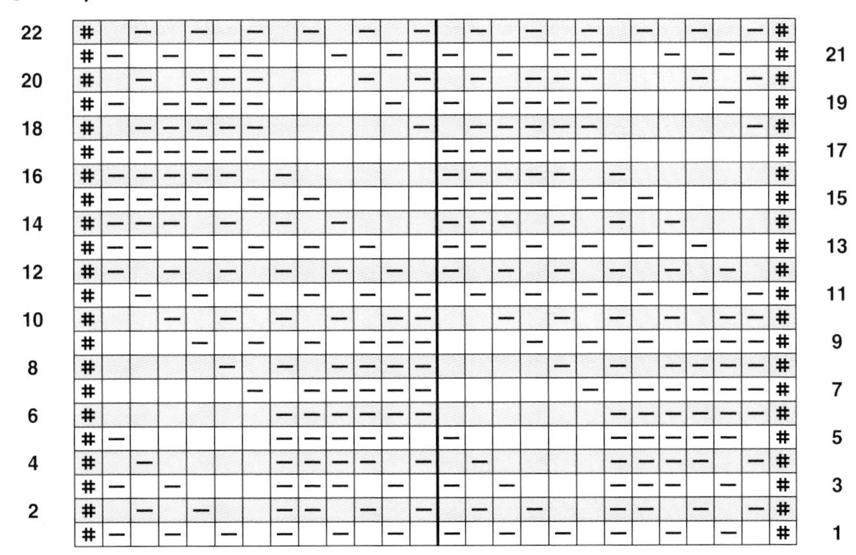

The chart shows every row of the pattern as viewed from the right/public side of the scarf. For even-numbered rows work the stitches the opposite of what is shown on the chart, working from left to right.

Haneke Select merino/alpaca sport weight

The Chevron Christmas Tree Seamen's Scarf

Tail #1:

Using a provisional cast-on (page 13), cast on 45 stitches.

Set-up row: K2, pl, kl, pl, kl, place a marker on your needle, purl 33, place a marker on your needle, B6 (page 23).

Using Chevron Christmas Tree Chart S, work rows la - 4a, followed by three repeats of rows 1-36 separated by as many stockinette stitch rows needed to give you the length you desire.

Finish the tail by working four rows of stockinette stitch body bordered by the six-stitch seed stitch side borders, and then eight rows of seed stitch bottom border. Bind off on the ninth row, using the knit-in-pattern bind-off (page 21).

Neckline ribbing:

Remove the provisional cast-on, picking up the 45 stitches.

Set-up row 1: With the private/wrong side of your scarf facing you, slip the first stitch as if to knit, p4, k4, p4, k4, p4, k3, p4, k4, p4, k4, p4, kl.

Row 1: Slip the first stitch as if to purl, k4, p4, k4, p4, k4, p3, k4, p4, k4, p4, k5.

Row 2: Slip the first stitch as if to purl, p4, k4, p4, k4, p4, k3, p4, k4, p4, k4, p4, kl.

Repeat Rows 1 & 2 until the neckline ribbing measures approximately the neck measurement of the intended wearer, between 14 inches/35.5 cm and 17 inches/43 cm. End after working row 1.

Tail #2:

Set-up row: B6, place a marker on your needle, purl 33, place a marker on your needle, B6.

Work the same as for Tail #1, beginning with "Using Chevron Christmas Tree Chart S."

Chevron Christmas Tree Scarf – Chart S

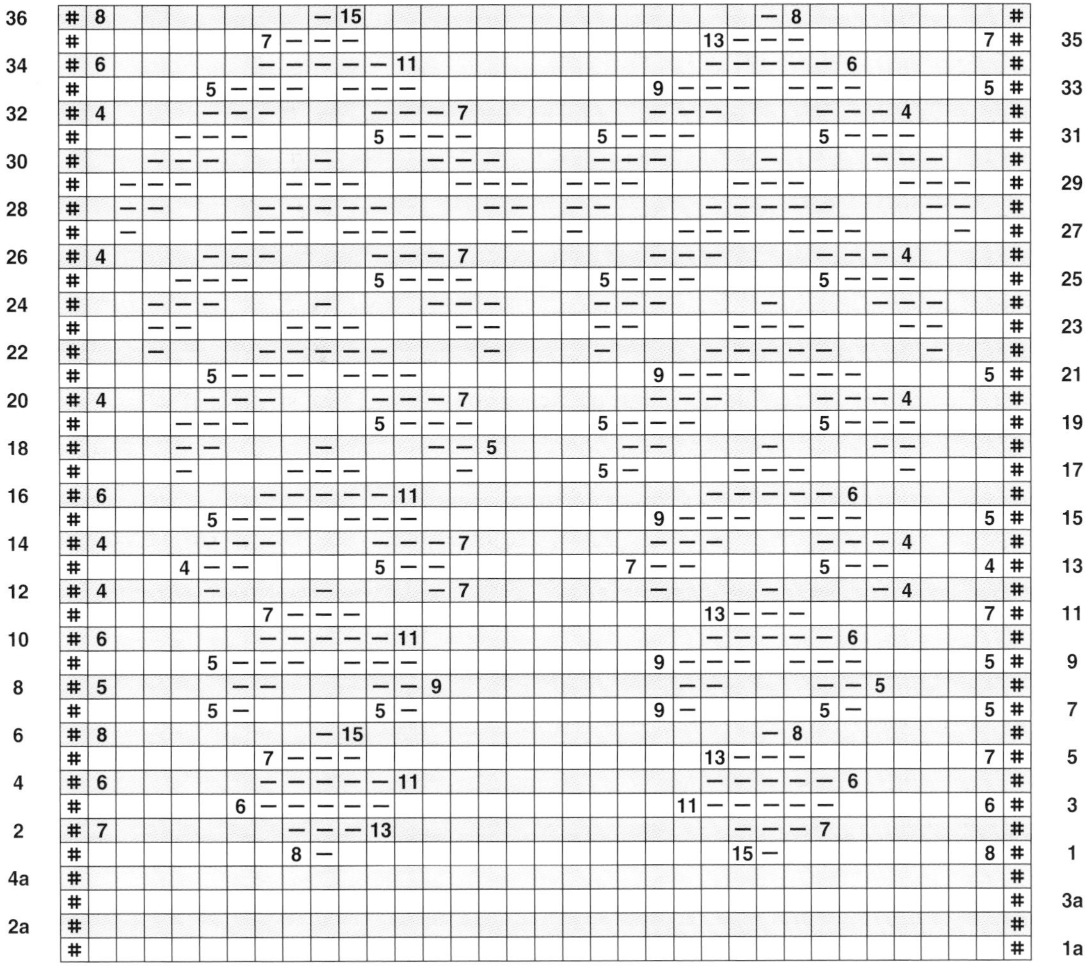

36	#	8								—	15															—	8								#	
	#							7	—	—	—													13	—	—	—							7	#	35
34	#	6						—	—	—	—	—	11											—	—	—	—	—	6						#	
	#					5	—	—	—		—	—	—									9	—	—	—		—	—	—					5	#	33
32	#	4				—	—	—				—	—	—	7							—	—	—				—	—	—	4				#	
	#				—	—	—					5	—	—	—					5	—	—	—					5	—	—	—				#	31
30	#			—	—	—				—				—	—	—				—	—	—				—				—	—	—			#	
	#		—	—	—				—	—	—				—	—	—		—	—	—				—	—	—				—	—	—		#	29
28	#		—	—				—	—	—	—	—				—	—		—	—				—	—	—	—	—				—	—		#	
	#		—				—	—	—		—	—	—				—		—				—	—	—		—	—	—				—		#	27
26	#	4				—	—	—				—	—	—	7							—	—	—				—	—	—	4				#	
	#				—	—	—					5	—	—	—					5	—	—	—					5	—	—	—				#	25
24	#			—	—	—				—				—	—	—				—	—	—				—				—	—	—			#	
	#			—	—				—	—	—				—	—				—	—				—	—	—				—	—			#	23
22	#			—				—	—	—	—	—				—				—				—	—	—	—	—				—			#	
	#					5	—	—	—		—	—	—									9	—	—	—		—	—	—					5	#	21
20	#	4				—	—	—				—	—	—	7							—	—	—				—	—	—	4				#	
	#				—	—	—					5	—	—	—					5	—	—	—					5	—	—	—				#	19
18	#				—	—				—				—	—	5					—	—				—				—	—				#	
	#				—				—	—	—				—					5	—				—	—	—				—				#	17
16	#	6						—	—	—	—	—	11											—	—	—	—	—	6						#	
	#					5	—	—	—		—	—	—									9	—	—	—		—	—	—					5	#	15
14	#	4				—	—	—				—	—	—	7							—	—	—				—	—	—	4				#	
	#				4	—	—					5	—	—							7	—	—					5	—	—				4	#	13
12	#	4				—				—				—	7							—				—				—	4				#	
	#							7	—	—	—													13	—	—	—							7	#	11
10	#	6						—	—	—	—	—	11											—	—	—	—	—	6						#	
	#					5	—	—	—		—	—	—									9	—	—	—		—	—	—					5	#	9
8	#	5					—	—				—	—	9									—	—				—	—	5					#	
	#					5	—					5	—									9	—					5	—					5	#	7
6	#	8								—	15															—	8								#	
	#							7	—	—	—													13	—	—	—							7	#	5
4	#	6						—	—	—	—	—	11											—	—	—	—	—	6						#	
	#						6	—	—	—	—	—											11	—	—	—	—	—						6	#	3
2	#	7							—	—	—	13														—	—	—	7							#	
	#								8	—															15	—								8	#	1
4a	#																																		#	
	#																																		#	3a
2a	#																																		#	
	#																																		#	1a

For the scarf pictured, work rows 1 through 36, then work thirty-six rows with just one motif by centering the motif, then work rows 1 through 36 one more time, followed by the seed stitch border.

To center the motif, work the border stitches and then eight stitches at the beginning of each row before following the chart. In words;

Row 37; B6, k 16, p1, k 16, B6.

Row 38: B6, p 15, k3, p 15, B6.

Row 39: B6, k 14, p5, k 14, B6.

Row 40: B6, p 14, k5, p 14, B6.

Row 41: B6, k 15, p3, k 15, B6.

Row 42: B6, p 16, k1, p 16, B6.

Continue, always adding eight stitches at the beginning of each row before following the chart.

The chart shows every row of the pattern, as viewed from the public/right side of the scarf. For odd-numbered rows read the pattern from right to left; for even-numbered rows read the pattern from left to right and work the stitches the opposite of what is shown on the chart.

The Ginger Seamen's Scarf

Creature Comforts
Hand spun by Carolyn Smith
buffalo/merino/silk
fingering weight

The chart shows every row of the pattern, as viewed from the public/right side of the scarf. For odd-numbered rows read the pattern from right to left; for even-numbered rows read the pattern from left to right and work the stitches the opposite of what is shown on the chart.

Tail #1:

Using a provisional cast-on (page 13), cast on 50 stitches.

Set-up row: K2, p1, k1, p1, k1, place a marker on your needle, purl 38, place a marker on your needle, B6 (page 23).

Using Ginger Chart S, work as many repeats of rows 1-10 as necessary to make the scarf the length you desire.

Finish tail #1 as follows:

Row 1: Slip the first stitch as if to purl, (k1, p1) 11 times, k1, p2tog, k1, (p1, k1) 11 times, k1. [49 sts]

Rows 2-8: Slip the first stitch as if to purl, *k1, p1, repeat from *, ending k2.

Bind off on the ninth row, using the knit-in-pattern bind-off (page 21).

Neckline ribbing:

Remove the provisional cast-on, picking up the 50 stitches.

Set-up row: With the private/wrong side of your scarf facing you, slip the first stitch as if to knit, p5, k5, p4, k4, p4, k4, p4, k4, p4, k5, p5, k1.

Row 1: Slip the first stitch as if to purl, k5, p5, k4, p4, k4, p4, k4, p4, k4, p5, k6.

Row 2: Slip the first stitch as if to purl, p5, k5, p4, k4, p4, k4, p4, k4, p4, k5, p5, k1.

Repeat Rows 1 & 2 until the neckline ribbing measures approximately 70% of the neck measurement of the intended wearer, between 10 inches/25 cm and 12 inches/30 cm. End after working row 1.

Tail #2:

Set-up row: B6, place a marker on your needle, purl 38, place a marker on your needle, B6.

Work the same as for Tail #1, beginning with "Using Ginger Chart S."

Ginger Scarf – Chart S

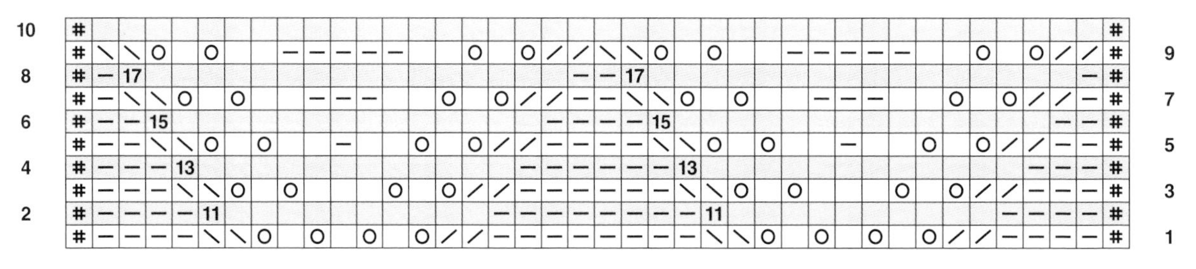

Row 1: [B6, which at the beginning of the row is slip the first stitch as if to purl, k1, p1, k1, p1, k1] [(p4, k2tog, k2tog, yo, k1, yo, k1, yo, k1, yo, ssk, ssk, p4) twice] [B6, which at the end of the row is k1, p1, k1, p1, k2].

Row 2 and all even-numbered rows: B6, work the stitches as they are presented; i.e., knit the knit stitches and purl the purl stitches, B6.

Row 3: B6, (p3, k2tog, k2tog, yo, k1, yo, k3, yo, k1, yo, ssk, ssk, p3) twice, B6.

Row 5: B6, (p2, k2tog, k2tog, yo, k1, yo, k2, p1, k2, yo, k1, yo, ssk, ssk, p2) twice, B6.

Row 7: B6, (p1, k2tog, k2tog, yo, k1, yo, k2, p3, k2, yo, k1, yo, ssk, ssk, p1) twice, B6.

Row 9: B6, (k2tog, k2tog, yo, k1, yo, k2, p5, k2, yo, k1, yo, ssk, ssk) twice, B6.

D. "Let's Make the World a Better Place for All" Seamen's Scarves

In 1998, Matthew Shepard, a gay student at the University of Wyoming, was beaten, tied to a fence and left for dead. He was unconscious when his limp body was discovered by a passing cyclist the day after this vicious crime. Five days later Matthew died, never regaining consciousness. At Matthew's funeral his cousin, the Rev. Anne Kitch, asked the world to find in Matthew's life a lesson that transcends the evil of his death.

Following the directive of Rev. Kitch, I designed two Seamen's scarves in memory of Matthew as gifts to my knitting friends. These patterns subsequently were published as "Knitting Community – More Seamen's Scarves" by Interweave Press in *Knits News*, Volume 4, Number 1 (1999).

As you knit the "Matthew" and "Matt" patterns, remember Matthew, who, in the words of his father, would have been overwhelmed by what his murder has done to the hearts and souls of people around the world. Matthew was the type of person who, if this had happened to another, would have been the first on the scene to offer his help, his hope and his heart.

In 1999 two students from Columbine High School shot and killed 12 classmates and a teacher and wounded 23 other people before committing suicide. Is it possible for us to follow the directive of Rev. Kitch and find a lesson that transcends the evil of the murders of the teacher and students at Columbine High School in Littleton, Colorado? The Columbine series of Seamen's Scarves is designed in memory of the teacher and students of Columbine High School who died. A number of knitters have knit Seamen's Scarves for the family members of those who died at Columbine High.

These patterns are a gift to you, with the request that you offer your help, your hope, and your heart to make the world a better place for all. Permission is granted to copy the instructions and charts for Matthew, Matt, Columbine I, Columbine II, and Columbine III for noncommercial purposes. Give these patterns to your knitting friends. Each time you use one of these patterns, please take some action that will foster an understanding of people who are different from yourself. Knit an extra scarf and donate it to a fund raiser for a worthy cause. Work to find in these tragedies a lesson that transcends the evil of Matthew's death and the deaths at Columbine High School. Please offer your help, your hope and your heart to make the world a better place for all.

Haneke Heaven Sent
baby alpaca/merino
fingering weight

Matthew Chart S shows only the odd-numbered rows. For the even-numbered rows work the seed stitch borders in pattern, and work the center stitches as they present themselves.

The Matthew Seamen's Scarf

Tail #1:
Using a provisional cast-on (page 13), cast on 37 stitches.
Set-up row: K2, p1, k1, p1, k1, place a marker on your needle, purl 25, place a marker on your needle, B6 (page 23).
Using Matthew Chart S, work as many repeats of rows 1-12 as necessary to obtain the length you desire.
Finish tail #1 by working eight rows of seed stitch. Bind off on the ninth row, using the knit-in-pattern bind-off (page 21).

Neckline ribbing:
Remove the provisional cast-on, picking up the 37 stitches.
Set-up row: With the private/wrong side of your scarf facing you, slip the first stitch as if to knit, p4, k4, p4, k4, p3, k4, p4, k4, ending p4, k1.
Row 1: Slip the first stitch as if to purl, k4, p4, k4, p4, k3, p4, k4, p4, k5.
Row 2: Slip the first stitch as if to purl, p4, k4, p4, k4, p3, k4, p4, k4, ending p4, k1.
Repeat Rows 1 & 2 until the neckline ribbing measures approximately 70% of the neck measurement of the intended wearer, between 10 inches/25 cm and 12 inches/30 cm. End after working row 1.

Tail #2:
Set-up row: B6, place a marker on your needle, purl 25, place a marker on your needle, B6. Follow the instructions for Tail #1, beginning with "Using Matthew Chart S."

Matthew Scarf – Chart S

#	—	O	ℓ	—	ℓ	—	ℓ	—	ℓ	—	ℓ	—	↑	—	ℓ	—	ℓ	—	ℓ	—	ℓ	—	ℓ	O	—	#	11
#	—	ℓ	—	ℓ	—	ℓ	O	ℓ	—	ℓ	—	ℓ/	ℓ	ℓ\	—	ℓ	—	ℓ	O	ℓ	—	ℓ	—	ℓ	—	#	9
#	—	ℓ	—	ℓ	—	O	ℓ	—	ℓ	—	ℓ/	—	ℓ	—	ℓ\	—	ℓ	—	ℓ	O	—	ℓ	—	ℓ	—	#	7
#	—	ℓ	—	ℓ	O	ℓ	—	ℓ	—	ℓ/	ℓ	—	ℓ	—	ℓ	ℓ\	—	ℓ	—	ℓ	O	ℓ	—	ℓ	—	#	5
#	—	ℓ	—	O	ℓ	—	ℓ	—	ℓ/	—	ℓ	—	ℓ	—	ℓ	—	ℓ\	—	ℓ	—	ℓ	O	—	ℓ	—	#	3
#	—	ℓ	O	ℓ	—	ℓ	—	ℓ/	ℓ	—	ℓ	—	ℓ	—	ℓ	—	ℓ	ℓ\	—	ℓ	—	ℓ	O	ℓ	—	#	1
#	—	O	ℓ	—	ℓ	—	ℓ	—	ℓ	—	ℓ	—	↑	—	ℓ	—	ℓ	—	ℓ	—	ℓ	—	ℓ	O	—	#	11
#	—	ℓ	—	ℓ	—	ℓ	O	ℓ	—	ℓ	—	ℓ/	ℓ	ℓ\	—	ℓ	—	ℓ	O	ℓ	—	ℓ	—	ℓ	—	#	9
#	—	ℓ	—	ℓ	—	O	ℓ	—	ℓ	—	ℓ/	—	ℓ	—	ℓ\	—	ℓ	—	ℓ	O	—	ℓ	—	ℓ	—	#	7
#	—	ℓ	—	ℓ	O	ℓ	—	ℓ	—	ℓ/	ℓ	—	ℓ	—	ℓ	ℓ\	—	ℓ	—	ℓ	O	ℓ	—	ℓ	—	#	5
#	—	ℓ	—	O	ℓ	—	ℓ	—	ℓ/	—	ℓ	—	ℓ	—	ℓ	—	ℓ\	—	ℓ	—	ℓ	O	—	ℓ	—	#	3
#	—	ℓ	O	ℓ	—	ℓ	—	ℓ/	ℓ	—	ℓ	—	ℓ	—	ℓ	—	ℓ	ℓ\	—	ℓ	—	ℓ	O	ℓ	—	#	1

Encouragement: The twisted ssk and k2tog stitches really are easier to work than the written word makes it sound. Here are the instructions. Stitch 1 is the first stitch on your left needle; stitch 2 is the second stitch on your left needle.
ℓ\ = twisted ssk - keeping your yarn in back of your work,
- insert your right needle as if to purl into stitch 1 and slip stitch 1 onto your right needle;
- insert your right needle as if to knit into stitch 2 and slip stitch 2 off your left needle onto your right needle;
- knit stitches 1 & 2 together.

ℓ/ = twisted k2tog - keeping your yarn in back of your work,
- insert your right needle as if to purl into stitch 1 and slip stitch 1 onto your right needle;
- insert your right needle as if to purl into stitch 2 and slip stitch 2 onto your right needle;
- insert your left needle into the front/right leg of stitch 2 and move stitch 2 from your right needle to your left needle (this results in a twist to the stitch);
- slip stitch 1 back onto your left needle, with the right leg in front;
- knit stitches 1 & 2 together.

The Matt Seamen's Scarf

Haneke Select
merino/alpaca
sport weight

Tail #1:
Using a provisional cast-on (page 13), cast on 41 stitches.
Set-up row: K2, p1, k1, p1, k1, place a marker on your needle, purl 29, place a marker on your needle, B6 (page 23).
Using Matt Chart S, work as many repeats of rows 1-20 as necessary to obtain the length you desire.
Finish tail #1 by working eight rows of seed stitch. Bind off on the ninth row, using the knit-in-pattern bind-off (page 21).

Neckline ribbing:
Remove the provisional cast-on, picking up the 41 stitches.
Set-up row: With the private side of your scarf facing you, slip the first stitch as if to knit, p3, k4, p3, k4, p3, k5, p3, k4, p3, k4, p3, k1.
Row 1: Slip the first stitch as if to purl, k3, p4, k3, p4, k3, p5, k3, p4, k3, p4, k4.
Row 2: Slip the first stitch as if to purl, p3, k4, p3, k4, p3, k5, p3, k4, p3, k4, p3, k1.
Repeat Rows 1 & 2 until the neckline ribbing measures approximately the neck measurement of the intended wearer – generally between 14 inches/35.5 cm and 17 inches/43 cm. End after working row 1.

Tail #2:
Set-up row: B6, place a marker on your needle, purl 29, place a marker on your needle, B6.
Follow the instructions for Tail #1, beginning with "Using Matt Chart S."

Matt Scarf – Chart S

#	—		—		—		—		—	—		—		—		—		—		—	—		—		—		—		—	#	19
#		—		—		—		—		—		—		—		—		—		—		—		—		—		—		#	17
#	—		—		—		—		—	—		—		—		—		—		—	—		—		—		—		—	#	15
#		—		—		—		—		—		—		—		—		—		—		—		—		—		—		#	13
#	—		—		—		—		—	—		—		—		—		—		—	—		—		—		—		—	#	11
#		—		—		—		—		—	—		—		—		—		—	—		—		—		—		—		#	9
#		—		—		—		—		—		—		—		—		—		—		—		—		—		—		#	7
#		—		—		—		—		—	—		—		—		—		—	—		—		—		—		—		#	5
#		—		—		—		—		—		—		—		—		—		—		—		—		—		—		#	3
#		—		—		—		—		—	—		—		—		—		—	—		—		—		—		—		#	1

Rows 1, 5 & 9: [B6, which at the beginning of the row is slip the first stitch as if to purl, k1, p1, k1, p1, k1] [(k1, p1) five times, (p1, k1) four times, p1, (p1, k1) five times] [B6, which at the end of the row is k1, p1, k1, p1, k2].
Rows 2, 6 & 10: B6, (p1, k1) five times, (k1, p1) four times, k1, (k1, p1) five times, B6.
Rows 3 & 7: B6, (k1, p1) across, B6.
Rows 4 & 8: B6, (p1, k1) across, B6.
Rows 11, 15 & 19: B6, (p1, k1) four times, p1, (p1, k1) five times, p1, (p1, k1) four times, p1, B6.
Rows 12, 15 & 20: B6, (k1, p1) four times, k1, (k1, p1) five times, k1, (k1, p1) four times, k1, B6.
Rows 13 & 17: B6, (k1, p1) across, B6.
Rows 14 & 18: B6, (p1, k1) across, B6.

Use stitch markers between the seed stitch border and each pattern segment.

The chart shows the odd-numbered rows only. Work the even-numbered rows as the stitches present themselves.

This pattern is appropriate for knitting from end-to-end as explained in "Knitting a Seamen's Scarf in the Traditional Fashion – From End-to-End" (page 100).

Haneke Select
merino/kid mohair
lace weight

This scarf may be knit using 12 plus any multiple of nine. See "Neckline Ribbing" (pages 135-136) for instructions.

The Columbine I Seamen's Scarf

Tail #1:
Using a provisional cast-on (page 13), cast on 48 stitches.
Set-up row: K2, pl, kl, pl, kl, place a marker on your needle, p 36, place a marker on your needle, B6.
Go to Columbine I Chart S and work as many repeats of rows 1-4 as necessary to obtain the length you desire.

Finish Tail #1 as follows:
Row 1: Slip the first stitch as if to purl, (kl, pl) 11 times, k2tog, (pl, kl) 11 times, kl.
Rows 2-8: Slip the first stitch as if to purl, *kl, pl, repeat from *, ending k2.
Bind off on the ninth row, using the knit-in-pattern bind-off (page 21).

Neckline ribbing:
Remove the provisional cast-on, picking up the 48 stitches.
Set-up row: With the private/wrong side of your scarf facing you, slip the first stitch as if to knit, p5, (k4, p4) a total of five times, ending the last repeat p5, kl.
Row 1: Slip the first stitch as if to purl, k5, (p4, k4) a total of five times, ending the last repeat k6.
Row 2: Slip the first stitch as if to purl, p5, (k4, p4) a total of five times, ending the last repeat p5, kl.
Repeat Rows 1 & 2 until the neckline ribbing measures approximately 70% of the neck measurement of the intended wearer, between 10 inches/25.5 cm and 13 inches/33 cm. End after working row 1.

Tail #2:
Set-up row: With the private/wrong side of your scarf facing you, B6, place a marker on your needle, p 36, place a marker on your needle, B6.
Work the same as for Tail #1, beginning with row 1.

Columbine I Scarf – Chart S

#		O			/	\			O		O			/	\			O		O			/	\			O		O			/	\			O	#	3
#	O			/	\			O		O			/	\			O		O			/	\			O		O			/	\			O		#	1
#		O			/	\			O		O			/	\			O		O			/	\			O		O			/	\			O	#	3
#	O			/	\			O		O			/	\			O		O			/	\			O		O			/	\			O		#	1
																		II									I											

Row 1: B6, kl, *yo, k2, ssk, k2tog, k2, yo, kl, repeat from * ending last repeat yo, B6.
Rows 2 & 4: B6, p 36, B6.
Row 3: B6, *yo, k2, ssk, k2tog, k2, yo, kl, repeat from * ending B6.

The Columbine II Seamen's Scarf

Tail #1:

Using a provisional cast-on (page 13), cast on 45 stitches.

Row 1: K2, p1, k1, p1, k1, place a marker on your needle, (k1, p3) 8 times, k1, place a marker on your needle, B6.

Rows 2 and 3: B6, *p1, k3, repeat from *, ending p1, B6.

Row 4: B6,* (k1, yo, k1) in same stitch, p3tog, repeat from *, ending (k1, yo, k1) in same stitch, B6.

Row 5: B6, *p3, k1, repeat from *, ending p3, B6.

Rows 6 and 7: B6, *k3, p1, repeat from *, ending k3, B6.

Row 8: B6, *p3tog, (k1, yo, k1) in same stitch, repeat from *, ending p3tog, B6.

Repeat rows 1-8 to obtain approximately the length you desire.

Work rows 1-3 once more.

Next row: B6, p2tog, (k1, p1) 3 times, p2tog, (p1, k1) 2 times, p1, p3tog, (p1, k1) 2 times, p1, p2tog, (p1, k1) 3 times, p2tog, B6. [45 stitches reduced to 39 stitches]

Finish tail #1 by working seven rows of seed stitch. Bind off on the eighth row, using the knit-in-pattern bind-off (page 21).

Neckline ribbing:

Remove the provisional cast-on, picking up the 45 stitches.

Set-up row 1: With the public/right side of your scarf facing you, slip the first stitch as if to knit, k4, p4, k4, p4, k4, p3, k4, p4, k4, p4, k5.

Set-up row 2: Slip the first stitch as if to purl, p4, k4, p4, k4, p4, k3, p4, k4, p4, k4, p4, k1.

Row 1: Slip the first stitch as if to purl, k4, p4, k4, p4, k4, p3, k4, p4, k4, p4, k5.

Row 2: Slip the first stitch as if to purl, p4, k4, p4, k4, p4, k3, p4, k4, p4, k4, p4, k1.

Repeat Rows 1 & 2 until the neckline ribbing measures approximately the neck measurement of the intended wearer, between 14 inches/35.5 cm and 17 inches/43 cm. End after working row 2.

Tail #2:

Row 1: Slip the first stitch as if to purl, k1, p1, k1, p1, k1, place a marker on your needle, *k1, p3, repeat from *, ending k1, place a marker on your needle, B6.

Work the same as for Tail #1, beginning with Row 2.

Haneke Select
merino/alpaca
sport weight

Haneke Select
merino/kid mohair
lace weight

Columbine III Chart S shows only the odd-numbered rows. For the even-numbered rows work the seed stitch borders in pattern, and work the center stitches as they present themselves.

The Columbine III Seamen's Scarf

Tail #1: Using a provisional cast-on (page 13), cast on 43 stitches.

Set-up row: K2, pl, kl, pl, kl, place a marker on your needle, purl 31, place a marker on your needle, B6.

Using the Columbine III Chart S, work as many repeats of rows 1-12 as necessary to obtain the length you desire.

Next row: Slip the first stitch as if to purl, (kl, pl) 3 times, (sl 1, k2tog, psso), pl, (kl, pl) 11 times, k3tog, (pl, kl) 3 times, kl.

Finish tail #1 by working seven rows of seed stitch. Bind off on the eighth row, using the knit-in-pattern bind-off (page 21).

Neckline ribbing:

Remove the provisional cast-on, picking up the 43 stitches.

Set-up row 1: With the private/wrong side of your scarf facing you, p4, k4, p4, k4, p4, k3, p4, k4, p4, k4, p3, kl.

Row 1: Slip the first stitch as if to purl, k3, p4, k4, p4, k4, p3, k4, p4, k4, p4, k4.

Row 2: Slip the first stitch as if to purl, p3, k4, p4, k4, p4, k3, p4, k4, p4, k4, p3, kl.

Repeat Rows 1 & 2 until the neckline ribbing measures approximately 70% of the neck measurement of the intended wearer, between 10 inches/25.5 cm and 13 inches/33 cm. End after working row 1.

Tail #2:

Set-up row: B6, place a marker on your needle, purl 31, place a marker on your needle, B6.

Work the same as for Tail #1, beginning with "Using the Columbine III Chart S."

Columbine III Scarf – Chart S

#	–				–	\	O						O	/	O	⋏	O	\	O						O	/	–				–	#	11
#	–				–		\	O				O	/	O	/	O	⋏	O	\	O				O	/		–				–	#	9
#	–				–			\	O		O	/	O	/	O	⋏	O	\	O	\	O		O	/			–				–	#	7
#	–				–					O	/	O	/	O	/	O	⋏	O	\	O	\	O					–				–	#	5
#	–				–				O	/	O	/	O	/	O	⋏	O	\	O	\	O	\	O				–				–	#	3
#	–				–			O	/	O	/	O	/	O	/	O	⋏	O	\	O	\	O	\	O			–				–	#	1

Row 1: [B6, which at the beginning of the row is slip the first stitch as if to purl, kl, pl, kl, pl, kl] [pl, (CF, which is slip the first stitch onto a cable needle and hold in front, knit the next two stitches, knit the stitch from the cable needle), pl, k2, (yo, ssk) three times, yo, sll-k2tog-psso, (yo, k2tog) four times, yo, k2, pl, (CB, which is put two stitches on a cable needle and hold in back, knit the next stitch, knit the two stitches from the cable needle), pl] [B6, which at the end of the row is kl, pl, kl, pl, k2].

Row 2 and all even-numbered rows: B6, kl, p3, kl, p 21, kl, p3, kl, B6.

Row 3: B6, pl, CF, pl, k3, (yo, ssk) three times, yo, sll-k2tog-psso, (yo, k2tog) three times, yo, k3, pl, CB, pl, B6.

Row 5: B6, pl, CF, pl, k4, (yo, ssk) twice, yo, sll-k2tog-psso, (yo, k2tog) three times, yo, k4, pl, CB, pl, B6.

Row 7: B6, pl, CF, pl, k2, k2tog, yo, kl, (yo, ssk) twice, yo, sll-k2tog-psso, (yo, k2tog) twice, yo, kl, yo, ssk, k2, pl, CB, pl, B6.

Row 9: B6, pl, CF, pl, kl, k2tog, yo, k3, yo, ssk, yo, sll-k2tog-psso, (yo, k2tog) twice, yo, k3, yo, ssk, kl, pl, CB, pl, B6.

Row 11: B6, pl, CF, pl, k2tog, yo, k5, yo, ssk, yo, sll-k2tog-psso, yo, k2tog, yo, k5, yo, ssk, pl, CB, pl, B6.

Chapter 3: Design Your Own Seamen's Scarves

Stitch Pattern Choices Are Virtually Endless

The pattern stitches that can be used for knitting a Seamen's scarf are virtually endless. Take a stroll through the lace books included in the Bibliography. Or use one of your favorite stitch patterns to design your own Seamen's scarf.

How Will This Stitch Pattern Look?

Look at the stitch pattern as it appears in the picture or garment. Then turn the picture or garment upside down. If the stitch pattern appears the same, it is suitable for knitting a scarf from end-to-end. If it is different upside down than right side up, use the Stahman method of construction, realizing that because you are knitting from the neck down, the pattern will appear as it looks when viewing the picture or garment upside down.

Will This Stitch Pattern Work Width- and Length-Wise?

Two factors to consider when selecting a stitch pattern are the number of rows and the number of stitches in each pattern repeat. An additional important factor is the border treatment you select, whether it be seed stitch, garter stitch, mock rib, I-cord, or a border of your own design.

The number of rows per pattern repeat is generally the number of rows contained in the instructions. Some, but not many, stitch patterns do require some "set-up" rows that are not repeated thereafter. The more rows to a pattern, the more planning you must do to ensure that you will be happy with the length of your scarf. With a four-row repeat it is easy to end your scarf at the conclusion of a pattern repeat; with a 36-row repeat it is much more difficult to ensure that you will be happy with the length.

Most stitch patterns will tell you the number of stitches in a multiple and whether you need any additional stitches. This will often be phrased as "multiple of X stitches plus Y," with X being the number of stitches in each pattern repeat, and Y being the number of additional stitches recommended for the edges. Sometimes those "additional" stitches are neither necessary nor desired when designing a Seamen's scarf, depending upon the border you have selected. Charting a written pattern will give you a great picture of the pattern design you have selected, and will help you decide whether the additional stitches are necessary for your scarf. Remember to add the stitches in the border you have selected to the stitches in the stitch pattern you have selected. Consider also the weight of the yarn and the needle size you will use. The scarves I have designed vary from 29 stitches to 51 stitches in width. When using bulky yarn and large needles, you will use fewer stitches than when using cobweb yarn and tiny needles.

Side and Bottom Border Selection

Because of the nature of knit fabric, side and bottom borders help a scarf to lay flat. My favorite border is seed stitch worked over six stitches, including the selvedge stitch. Other borders I sometimes use include garter stitch, mock ribbing, and I-cord. Select the border that complements the stitch pattern you have selected and that pleases you.

When using a seed stitch border, it is necessary to have an odd number of stitches when working the bottom borders of the tails. When the stitch pattern I have selected uses an even number of stitches, I generally decrease one stitch directly in the middle of the first row of my seed stitch bottom border. Sometimes this is done by k2tog, other times by p2tog, depending entirely on the number of stitches in the scarf.

Neckline Ribbing

Stitch Sequence

The traditional Seamen's scarf pattern, using a knit four, purl four ribbing, produces a scarf which nicely hugs the neck of the wearer. It is my favorite. But not all stitch patterns are made up of a multiple of four. Although I have tried knit one, purl one ribbing and knit two, purl two ribbing, I believe these ribbings don't produce the wonderfully comfortable "hugging" produced by the knit four, purl four ribbing. A ribbing of knit three, purl three, or of a combination of three and four stitches gives a very similar fit as the knit four, purl four ribbing.

I recommend the following sequences of knits and purls. These sequences always are an odd multiple of knits and purls, so that the public side of the neck ribbing will be bordered with a band of knit stitches on each edge. The following stitch instructions are written as you view the public/right side of your scarf.

For **29** stitches: kl, (k3, p3) four times, k4; or k5, p4, k4, p3, k4, p4, k5.
For **30** stitches: k5, (p4, k4) twice, p4, k5.
For **31** stitches: k5, (p3, k3) three times, p3, k5; or k5, p4, k4, p5, k4, p4, k5.
For **32** stitches: (k4, p3) four times, k4; or k5, p3, k3, p3, k4, p3, k3, p3, k5.
For **33** stitches: k4, (p4, k3) four times, ending k4.
For **34** stitches: k5, (p3, k4) three times, p3, k5.
For **35** stitches: k5, (p4, k3) four times, ending k5; or (k4, p4) twice. k3, (p4, k4) twice.
For **36** stitches: k4, (p4, k4) four times.
For **37** stitches: k5, p4, k4, p4, k3, p4, k4, p4, k5.
For **38** stitches: k5, (p4, k4) three times, p4, k5.
For **39** stitches: k5, p4, k4, p4, k5, p4, k4, p4, k5.
For **40** stitches: k5, p5, (k4, p4) twice, k4, p5, k5; or k4, (p4, k3) four times, p4, k4.
For **41** stitches: k5, p5, k4, p5, k3, p5, k4, p5, k5 Or k4, p4, k3, p4, k3, p5, k3, p4, k3, p4, k4.
For **42** stitches: k4, p4, k3, p4, (k4, p4) twice, k3, p4, k4.
For **43** stitches: (k4, p4) twice, k4, p3, (k4, p4) twice, k4.
For **44** stitches: (k4, p4) five times, k4.
For **45** stitches: k5, (p4, k4) twice, p3, (k4, p4) twice, k5.
For **46** stitches: k5, (p4, k4) four times, p4, k5.
For **47** stitches: k5, (p4, k4) twice, p5, (k4, p4) twice, k5.
For **48** stitches: k6, (p4, k4) four times, p4, k6.
For **49** stitches: k6, (p4, k4) twice, p5, (k4, p4) twice, k6.
For **50** stitches: k6, p5, (k4, p4) three times, k4, p5, k6.
For **51** stitches: k6, p4, k4, p4, k5, p5, k5, p4, k4, p4, k6.
For **52** stitches: (k4, p4) six times, k4.
For **53** stitches: (k4, p4) three times, k5, (p4, k4) three times.

Length of Neckline Ribbing

The traditional Seamen's garter stitch scarf calls for a neckline ribbing of 18 inches.

For Seamen's scarves using a solid pattern, I recommend working the ribbing for 100% of the size of the neck of the intended wearer.

For Seamen's scarves using a lace design, I recommend working the ribbing for 70% of the size of the neck of the intended wearer. Using this formula results in the beauty of the lace pattern showing from the front view combined with the wonderful fit of the neckline ribbing.

Beginning Your Scarf Using the Stahman Method of Construction

When using a lace pattern with yarnovers in the first row, it is generally a good idea to work one plain row after completing the provisional cast-on, rather than beginning immediately with a pattern row. So, for the very first row of your scarf, work the side border stitches in the border pattern you have selected, place a marker on your needle, purl across, place a marker on your needle, work the side border stitches in pattern. On the next row insert the first row of your stitch pattern between the borders.

When using a pattern stitch that does not have yarnovers in the first row, it works great to begin immediately with row 1 of your stitch pattern.

Picking Up Stitches from the Provisional Cast-On

When you are ready to work the neckline ribbing stitches, remove the provisional cast-on and pick up each stitch as it is released. With the tail from the beginning of your scarf hanging on the right end of your needle as you hold your work, look at your scarf. Is the public/right side of your scarf facing you? If so, use the stitch sequence as written above, beginning with a group of knit stitches. If the private/wrong side of your scarf is facing you, simply substitute purl for knit and knit for purl in the stitch sequence as written above, always slipping the first stitch as if to purl and always knitting the last stitch, to maintain the chain selvedge.

Have a great time as a designer of Seamen's scarves! Do share your creations with others, helping to make this world a better place for all.

Appendices

Appendix A

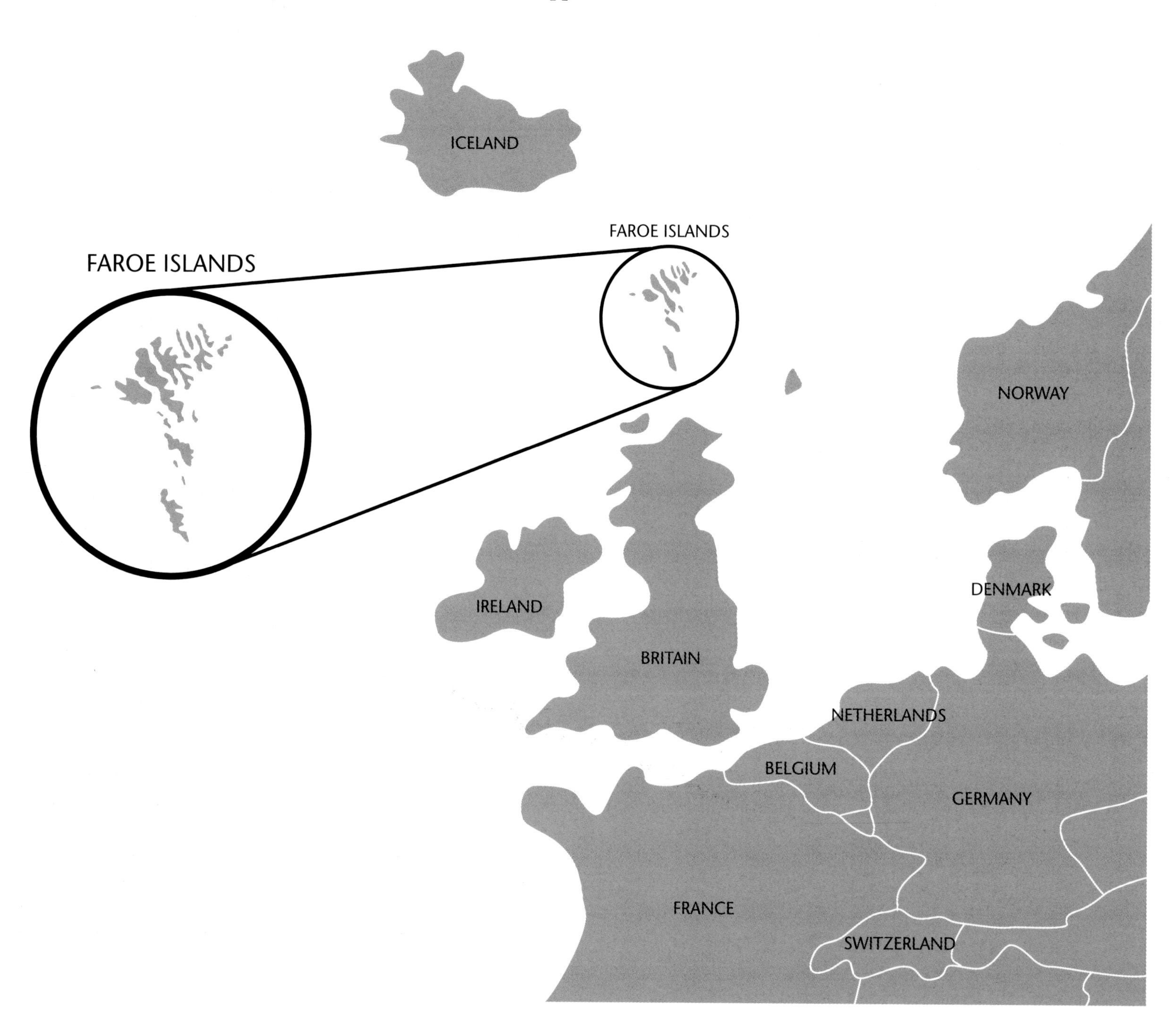
ICELAND
FAROE ISLANDS
FAROE ISLANDS
NORWAY
IRELAND
BRITAIN
DENMARK
NETHERLANDS
BELGIUM
GERMANY
FRANCE
SWITZERLAND

Appendix B

SWATCH RECORD

Pattern Name: ______________________ Date: ____________________________

Yarn Brand: ____

Yarn Weight: ____

Fiber Content: ____

Wraps per inch/2.5cm: ____

Skein size (weight and length): ____

Swatch #1:

Needle used: ______________________ Number of stitches cast on: _______

Gauge before dressing:

One pattern repeat consists of ___ stitches and measures ___ inches/cm across.

One pattern repeat consists of ___ rows and measures ___ inches/cm in height.

Gauge after dressing:

One pattern repeat consists of ___ stitches and measures ___ inches/cm across.

One pattern repeat consists of ___ rows and measures ___ inches/cm in height.

Thoughts on this swatch: ____

____

____

____

____

Swatch #2:

Needle used: ______________________ Number of stitches cast on: _______

Gauge before dressing:

One pattern repeat consists of ___ stitches and measures ___ inches/cm across.

One pattern repeat consists of ___ rows and measures ___ inches/cm in height.

Gauge after dressing:

One pattern repeat consists of ___ stitches and measures ___ inches/cm across.

One pattern repeat consists of ___ rows and measures ___ inches/cm in height.

Thoughts on this swatch: ____

____

____

____

____

Appendix C

SCARF RECORD

Scarf Name: ____

For whom: ____

Date begun: ______________________ Date completed: _________________

Approximate hours of knitting: ____

Yarn Brand: ____

Fiber Content: ____

Yarn Weight: ____

Wraps per inch/2.5cm: ____

Skein size (weight and length): ____

Number of skeins begun with: _______ Number of skeins used: _________

Needles used: ____

Gauge before dressing:

One pattern repeat consists of ___ stitches and measures ___ inches/cm across.

One pattern repeat consists of ___ rows and measures ___ inches/cm in height.

Gauge after dressing:

One pattern repeat consists of ___ stitches and measures ___ inches/cm across.

One pattern repeat consists of ___ rows and measures ___ inches/cm in height.

Weight of finished scarf: ____

Measurements of finished scarf before dressing: width: ___ length: _______

Actual measurement of finished scarf after dressing: width: ___ length: _____

Things to remember for next time I use this pattern: ____________________

____

____

____

____

____

Things I would do differently when I use this pattern again: ______________

____

____

____

____

____

____

Appendix D

SHAWL RECORD

Shawl Name:____
For whom: ____
Date begun: ____
Date completed: ____________________________________
Approximate hours of knitting: ____________________________
Yarn Brand: ____
Fiber Content: ______________________________________
Yarn Weight: _______________________________________
Wraps per inch/2.5cm: ________________________________
Skein size (weight and length): ___________________________
Number of skeins begun with: ________ Number of skeins used: _________
Needles used: _______________________________________
Gauge before dressing:
One pattern repeat consists of ____ stitches and measures ____ inches/cm across.
One pattern repeat consists of ____ rows and measures ____ inches/cm in height.
Gauge after dressing:
One pattern repeat consists of ____ stitches and measures ____ inches/cm across.
One pattern repeat consists of ____ rows and measures ____ inches/cm in height.
Weight of finished shawl: ________________________________
Measurement of finished shawl from back of neck to bottom of shawl before dressing: ________________________________
Actual measurement of finished shawl from back of neck to bottom of shawl after dressing: ________________________________
Things to remember for next time I use this pattern: ____________________
____
____
____
____
____

Things I would do differently when I use this pattern again: ____________
____
____
____
____
____
____

Appendix E

Caring for Me, Your Hand Knit [Shawl] [Scarf]

I have been knit specially for you by *. Please use me often. With proper care, I will be a lasting heirloom.

I am knit from * yarn. I am washable in a wool-friendly washing product, a small bottle of which I have enclosed.

First fill your sink or your washing machine with warm water – yes, I do like warm water – so that I have plenty of water in which to swim. Put in the wool-friendly washing product. Put me in and let me soak for about ten minutes. If you are putting me in your washing machine, be sure to turn the machine off. I do not want to be agitated, as that really bends me out of shape!

After I have soaked for about ten minutes, empty the sink and squeeze out the excess water, or turn the washing machine to spin and gently spin the water out of me. Do be gentle – I like to be handled with care. Rinse me in the same temperature water to remove all suds.

Take me out and lay me out flat to dry. If you have floor space, put a clean bed sheet on the floor and put me on it. Just make sure your favorite dog or cat doesn't get to me while I am drying. Or you can even put me on your bed.

When I am dry, pick me up, cuddle me, and use me – that's what I am for.

If you have any questions about my care, please feel free to contact my creator at *.

Appendix F

The Seamen's Church Institute Christmas-at-Sea Watch Cap

MATERIALS: 4-ply yarn - 3 ounces makes 2 caps
NEEDLES: Pair No. 6
Wool needle for joining seam and crown.
GAUGE: IMPORTANT - CHECK GAUGE 5 STS = 1"; 7 ROWS = 1" (Garter Stitch)

BORDER OF CAP: Cast on 84 sts. K2, P2 for 4 inches.
BODY OF CAP: Knit even for 40 rows (20 ridges).
TO FORM CROWN:
*K 10, K2tog, repeat from * across - Knit back even.
*K9, K2tog, repeat from * across - Knit back even.
*K8, K2tog, repeat from * across - Knit back even.
*K7, K2tog, repeat from * across - Knit back even.
*K6, K2tog, repeat from * across - Knit back even.
*K5, K2tog, repeat from * across - Knit back even.
*K4, K2tog, repeat from * across - Knit back even.
*K3, K2tog, repeat from * across - Knit back even.
*K2, K2tog, repeat from * across - Knit back even.
*K1, K2tog, repeat from * across - Knit back even.
You now have 14 stitches remaining on needle. Knit back even to middle of row.
TO JOIN CROWN: With half the stitches on each needle, break yarn, leaving a 15" length and thread into wool needle.
Fold cap so that both needles are even and parallel (one in back of the other), with free yarn extending from right-hand end of back needle (or the one farthest from you). While working always keep yarn under knitting needles. Weave sts from front and back needles together with KITCHENER stitch, or as follows: (This easy method makes garter stitch pattern.) Start on front needle.
* Pass wool needle through first st on knitting needle (enter from left to right) as if to knit. Slip st off needle. Pass through second st on same needle (enter from right to left as if to purl. Pull yarn through but leave on needle. Repeat from * on back needle. Weave sts together alternating from front to back until all sts are off needles. Pull yarn through and fasten securely, leaving extra length to sew up seam.
TO SEW SEAM: Place edges of cap adjacent to each other, pattern matching. Secure edges with safety pins. Picking up outside loop of stitch from each side, sew back & forth, drawing two edges securely together from top of crown to bottom of cuff. DO NOT SEW THROUGH DOUBLE THICKNESS. DO NOT BLOCK CAP.

Appendix G

Bonus: A Cotton Diamond Dish Cloth or Face Cloth

This hand knit cloth makes a great gift. Give dish cloths to those individuals who have touched your life in a special way and to those who need a little something to brighten up their day.

Materials:

Size 7, 8 or 9 circular knitting needle
Approximately 2 ounces of 100% cotton worsted-weight yarn

Instructions:

Cast on 4 stitches using the "knit-on" cast-on.
Row 1: Knit 3, yarn over, knit to the end.
Next rows: Continue in the pattern of Row 1 until you have 45 stitches on your needle.
Decrease row: Knit 2, knit 2 together, yarn over, knit 2 together, knit to the end of the row.
Next rows: Continue in the pattern of the decrease row until you have eight stitches left.
Next row: Knit 2, knit 2 together, knit 2 together, knit 2.
Next row: Knit 2, knit 2 together, knit 2.
Next row: Knit 2, knit 2 together , knit 1.
Next row: Bind off. (There should be four stitches left to bind off. I use the "knit off" bind-off.)

Notes:

- Finish off the ends of the yarn by working three or four knots down the side of the cloth from the end.
- If there is a knot in the skein of yarn, or for some other reason you need to join the yarn, join at the beginning of a row. Later tie the two ends and then finish off the ends by working three or four knots up and down the side of the cloth from the knot. Don't join the yarns in the middle of the dish cloth.
- Use a sport weight 100% cotton for face cloths or for a great gift for a new baby.

Yarns Used For Shawls and Scarves Pictured

Every yarn manufacturer has the freedom to call its yarn as it wishes. What one yarn manufacturer designates as lace weight may be equivalent in wraps per inch [2.5cm] and yards per ounce [meters per 50 grams] to what another manufacturer designates as fingering weight. I have used below the designations provided by the manufacturer. See page 8 for more guidance on my classification of yarn weights.

Information on the approximate wraps per inch [2.5cm] is provided for each yarn used for the shawls and scarves pictured in this book. Wraps-per-inch [2.5cm] varies greatly from person to person because this measurement is dependent upon how much tension is put on the fiber and how tightly one places the fibers together when measuring. This information is provided as a guide, not as a hard-and-fast rule.

Information is also provided on yards per ounce [meters per 50 grams] for each yarn used. These measurements are approximations. Yards per ounce [meters per 50 grams] may vary from one spinning to another and from one climate to another. Where the manufacturer has not provided this information, I have used a McMorran Yarn Balance to determine these measurements.

The finished measurement of each shawl is provided, both in inches and in centimeters, measured from the top of the back neck band to the bottom of the border. This is followed by the actual weight of the finished shawl. Because this is the actual weight of the finished shawl, I recommend you purchase additional yarn to ensure that, for your knitting tension, you have sufficient yarn. It is always better to have a bit too much yarn than to run out before your shawl is completed.

The finished size of each scarf includes the width and length of a tail, followed by the length of the neck ribbing. The actual weight of the finished scarf is provided both in ounces and in grams.

This information is provided for guidance. Because you and your knitting are unique, and because scarves and shawls are beautiful no matter what their size, do realize that your shawl or scarf likely will have different finished measurements.

Haneke Wool Fashions, 630 North Black Cat Road, Meridian, ID 83642
800-523-9665 [WOOL] http://hanekewoolfashions.com

Margaret Stove's Artisan New Zealand lace weight; 38-40 wpi/2.5cm; 461 yards per ounce; 750 meters per 50 grams
Margaret scarf, page 118; 6" x 13.5" [15cm x 34cm]; 9" [23cm]; 0.6 ounces [18 grams]

Haneke Select 75% merino, 25% kid mohair lace weight; 24wpi/2.5cm; 128 yards per ounce; 207 meters per 50 grams
Alberta scarf, page 63; 7.5" x 20.5" [19cm x 52cm]; 9.5" [24cm]; 2.0 ounces [56 grams]
Columbine I scarf, page 132; 8" x 18" [20.5cm x 46cm]; 9.5" [24cm]; 1.8 ounces [51 grams]
Columbine III scarf, page 134; 7.5" x 17" [19cm x 43cm]; 10" [25.5cm]; 2.2 ounces [63 grams]

Frances scarf, page 87; 8" x 15"[20.5cm x 38cm]; 10.5" [26.5cm]; 1.8 ounces [51 grams]
Marialis scarf Variation I, page 49; 8" x 17" [20.5cm x 43cm]; 9" [23cm]; 1.8 ounces [51 grams]
Marilyn scarf, page 113; 7.5" x 20.5" [19cm x 52cm]; 10" [25.5cm]; 1.8 ounces [51 grams]
Robert scarf, page 7; 8" x 19.5" [20.5cm x 49.4cm]; 10" [25.5cm]; 1.5 ounces [43 grams]

Haneke 100% merino lace weight; 26 wpi/2.5cm; 2800 yards per pound; 175 yards per ounce; 383 meters per 50 grams
Alka scarf, page 67; three pattern repeats; 9" x 17" [23cm x 43cm]; 10" [25.5 cm]; 2.6 ounces [74 grams]
Anne scarf, page 83; 7.5" x 20" [19cm x 51cm]; 10.5" [26.5cm]; 2.0 ounces [56 grams]
Marialis B shawl, page 51; 27.5" [70.cm]; 7.4 ounces [211 grams]

Haneke 100% merino singles; 24 wpi/2.5cm; 137.5 yards per ounce; 222 meters per 50 grams
Anne shawl, pearl gray, page 82; 27.5" [70cm]; 6.2 ounces [176 grams]

Haneke Exotics 50% super fine alpaca, 50% tencel fingering weight; 24 wpi/2.5cm; 120 yards per ounce; 194 meters per 50 grams
Josephine shawl, cover photo and pages 9 and 94; on smaller needle, 28" [71cm]; 8.9 ounces [253 grams]
Josephine shawl, pages 9 and 35; on larger needle, 28" [71cm]; 7.2 ounces [204 grams]

Haneke Heaven Sent 70% baby alpaca, 30% merino fingering weight; 24 wpi/2.5cm; 115 yards per ounce; 186 meters per 50 grams
Elizabeth scarf, pages 36 and 91; 7.5" x 18" [19cm x 46cm]; 10.5" [27cm]; 3 ounces [85 grams]
Matthew scarf, page 130; 6" x 18" [15cm x 46cm]; 10.5" [27cm]; 2.2 ounces [62 grams]
Patricia scarf, page 117; 7" x 13" [18cm x 33cm]; 10" [25.5cm]; 2.2 ounces [62 grams]
Susan scarf, page 75; 7.5" x 16" [19cm x 40.5cm]; 10" [25.5cm]; 2.4 ounces [68 grams]

Haneke Heaven Sent 100% alpaca fingering weight; 24 wpi/2.5cm; 115 yards per ounce; 186 meters per 50 grams
Marialis scarf Variation II, page 49; 6.5" x 18" [16.5cm x 45.5cm]; 10" [25.5cm]; 2.4 ounces [68 grams]

Haneke 100% alpaca melange fingering weight; 24 wpi/2.5cm; 109 yards per ounce; 176 meters per 50 grams
Lace Christmas Tree scarf, green, page 121; 6.5" x 19.5" [16.5cm x 49.5cm]; 11" [28cm]; 2.6 ounces [74 grams]
Susan shawl, green, page 74; 27.5" [70cm]; 8.4 ounces [238 grams]

Haneke 100% merino thin spin; 24 wpi/2.5cm; 110 yards per ounce; 178 meters per 50 grams
GS Catharina scarf, wild raspberry, page 45; 6" x 14.5" [15cm x 37cm]; 10" [25.5cm]; 1.4 ounces [40 grams]
Marialis A shawl, page 51; 29" [73.5cm]; 7.6 ounces [216 grams]

Haneke 100% merino fingering weight; 17 to 20 wpi/2.5cm; 130 yards per ounce; 210 meters per 50 grams
Gracie scarf, page 79; 9" x 19" [23cm x 48cm]; 11" [28cm]; 2.4 ounces [68 grams]

Haneke Select 75% merino, 25% alpaca fingering weight; 17 to 20 wpi/2.5cm; 130 yards per ounce; 210 meters per 50 grams

Alka shawl, fawn, cover photo; 26" [66cm]; 8.2 ounces [233 grams]

Alka scarf, fawn, page 67; two pattern repeats: 6.5" x 19" [16.5cm x 48cm]; 11" [28cm]; 1.8 ounces [51 grams]

Barbara scarf, page 71; 8.5" x 17" [21.5cm x 43cm]; 10.5" [26.5cm]; 2.2 ounces [62 grams]

Charles' Diamonds scarf, page 123; 9" x 17.5" [23cm x 44.5cm]; 15" [38cm]; 3.2 ounces [91 grams]

Frances shawl, pewter, pages 3 and 86; 27.5: [70cm]; 6.9 ounces [196 grams]

Gracie shawl, smokey, page 78; 29" [73.5cm]; 7.0 ounces [199 grams]

GS Gracie scarf, page 41; 7.5" x 16" [19cm x 40.5cm]; 10.5" [26.5cm]; 1.5 ounces [43 grams]

Marialis C shawl, white, fawn & cocoa, pages 48 and 51; 29" [73.5cm]; 6.4 ounces [182 grams]

Robert scarf, cocoa, page 7; 8" x 18.5" [20.5cm x 47cm]; 10" [25.5cm]; 2.2 ounces [62 grams]

Haneke Select 75% merino, 25% mohair fingering; 17 to 20 wpi/2.5cm; 125 yards per ounce; 202 meters per 50 grams

Idella shawl, page 58; 25.5" [65cm]; 6.3 ounces [179 grams]

Haneke Select 75% merino, 25% alpaca, sport weight; 15 to 17 wpi/2.5cm; 90 yards per ounce; 145 meters per 50 grams

Alka shawl, fawn, cover photo; 26" [66cm]; 8.0 ounces [227 grams]

Chevron Christmas Tree scarf, page 126; 9.5" x 19" [24 cm x 48cm]; 14.5" [37cm]; 4.2 ounces [119 grams]

Columbine II scarf, page 133; 9" x 18" [23cm x 45.5cm]; 10" [25.5cm]; 3.8 ounces [108 grams]

GS Gracie shawl, page 40; 28.5" [72.5cm]; 9.5 ounces [270 grams]

Irling's Half Diamond scarf, page 115; 8.5 " x 17.5" [21.5cm x 44.5cm]; 3.4 ounces [96 grams]

Jerrold's Basket Weave scarf, page 122; 7" x 19" [18cm x 48cm]; 15.5" [39.5cm]; 3.4 ounces [96 grams]

Matt scarf, page 131; 8" x 15.5" [20.5cm x 39.5cm]; 14.5" [37cm]; 2.8 ounces [79 grams]

Haneke Select 50% merino, 50% angora sport weight; 15 wpi/2.5cm; 57 yards per ounce; 92 meters per 50 grams

Beth's candy cane scarf, page 111; 8.5" x 16" [21.5cm x 40.5cm]; 10" [25.5cm]; 3.9 ounces [111 grams}

Haneke Exotics 50% baby alpaca, 25% merino, 25% angora; sport weight; 14 wpi/2.5cm; 70 yards per ounce; 113 meters per 50 grams

GS Catharina shawl, burgundy; page 44; 35.5" [90cm]; 15 ounces [426 grams]

Robert scarf, denim, page 7; 8.5" x 19" [21.5cm x 48cm]; 10" [25.5cm]; 5 ounces [142 grams}

Haneke Select 75% merino, 25% alpaca medium weight; 12 to 14 wpi/2.5cm; 62 yards per ounce; 100 meters per 50 grams

Alka shawl, cocoa, cover photo; 29" [73.5cm]; 9.9 ounces [281 grams]

Fenna scarf, white, page 105; 6" x 17" [15cm x 43cm]; 16" [40.5cm]; 2.6 ounces [74 grams]

I.J. scarf, cocoa. pages 4 and 104; 7.5" x 16" [19cm x 40.5cm]; 17" [43cm]; 3.4 ounces [97 grams]

Jeffrey scarf, page 124; 8" x 15" [20.5cm x 38cm]; 15" [38cm]; 3.2 ounces [91 grams]

Robert scarf, fawn, pages 7 and 24; 7.5" x 19" [19cm x 49cm]; 2.8 ounces [80 grams]

Walter scarf, fawn, cover photo and page 116; 8" x 17" [20.5cm x 43cm]; 14.5" [35.5cm]; 4.0 ounces [113 grams]

Haneke 100% merino three-ply bulky; 10 wpi/2.5cm; 46 yards per ounce; 74 meters per 50 grams
Alka shawl, chocolate, cover photo and page 33; 27" [68.5cm]; 13.0 ounces [369 grams]
Robert scarf, white, pages 7, 24 and 106; 8" x 17.5" [20.5cm x 44.5cm]; 12.5: [32cm]; 3.9 ounces [111 grams]

Creature Comforts, P.O. Box 606, Vashon, WA 98070
206-463-2004 viva@csn.org www.nwrain.net/~viva
Buffalo, merino, silk fingering weight, 22 wpi/2.5cm; 2400 yards per pound; 150 yards per ounce; 242 meters per 50 grams
Ginger scarf, page 128; 8" x 13" [20.3cm x 33cm]; 9" [23cm]; 1.8 ounces [51 grams]
75% merino, 15% chinchilla, 10% silk fingering weight, 20 wpi/2.5cm; 2400 yards per pound; 150 yards per ounce; 242 meters per 50 grams
Barbara shawl, page 70; 32" [81cm]; 6.2 ounces [176 grams]
Berdien's Boxes scarf, page 114; 7" x 18.5" [17cm x 47cm]; 11" [28cm]; 1.6 ounces [46 grams]
Carolyn's Rosebuds and Hearts scarf, page 112; 9" x 17" [23cm x 43cm]; 10" [25.5cm]; 2.2 ounces [63 grams]
75% targhee, 15% chinchilla, 10% silk fingering weight, 20 wpi/2.5cm; 2400 yards per pound; 150 yards per ounce; 242 meters per 50 grams
Joan scarf, page 109; 8" x 19" [20.3cm x 48cm]; 10.5" [26.5cm]; 2.2 ounces [63 grams]
Chinchilla, merino, silk medium weight, 14 wpi/2.5cm; 950 yards per pound; 59 yards per ounce; 95 meters per 50 grams
Berdien's Boxes scarf, page 114; 8.5" x 18" [21.5cm x 46cm]; 10" [25.5cm]; 3.8 ounces [108 grams]

MOCO Yarns, 633 Fish Hatchery Road, Hamilton, MT 59840
406-363-6287 muskox@bitterroot.net
100% qiviut lace weight, 42 wpi/2.5cm; 300 yards per ounce; 485 meters per 50 grams
Catharina scarf, page 119; 7.5" x 16" [19cm x 40.5cm]; 10" [25cm]; 0.9 ounce [26 grams]
Josephine scarf, page 95; 6.5" x 16" [16.5cm x 40.5cm]; 12" [30.5cm]; 0.9 ounce [26 grams]
Nancy scarf, page 120; 6.5" x 16" [16.5cm x 40.5cm; 9.5" [24cm]; 0.9 ounce [26 grams]

Ozark Carding Mill, RR#4, Box 130B, Warsaw, Missouri 65355
660-438-2308 whitegj@iland.net
Handspun 100% angora sport weight, 17 wpi/2.5cm; [1625 yards per pound] 101 yards per ounce; 163 meters per 50 grams
Alberta shawl, page 62; 10.4 ounces [295 grams]
Handspun Romney, medium weight, 12 wpi/2.5cm; [740 yards per pound] 46 yards per ounce; 74 meters per 50 grams
Fenna shawl, variegated, page 38; 32.5 inches [82.5cm]; 16 ounces [454 grams]

Cashmere America Cooperative, P.O. Box 1126, Sonora, TX 76950 915-387-6052 or 360-424-7935 or 207-336-2948
2-ply 100% cashmere, fingering weight; 31 wpi/2.5cm; 248 yards per ounce; 403 meters per 50 grams
Idella scarf, page 59; 5" x 18" [12.5cm x 45.5cm]; 12" [30.5cm]; 1.0 ounces [28 grams]

Cotton Clouds, 5176 South 14th Ave., Safford, Arizona 85546; 800-322-7888
3/2 pearle cotton sport weight; 20 wpi; 1360 yards per pound; 85 yards per ounce; 137 meters per 50 grams
Alka shawl, deep blue, cover photo; 31" [79cm]; 12.0 ounces [340 grams]

Hayfield Textiles, LTC, Glusburn, England

Hayfield Exquisite Shimmer, 61% acrylic, 39% nylon sport weight; 16 wpi; 88 yards per ounce; 144 meters per 50 grams

Alka shawl, emerald, cover photo; 26" plus 9.5" fringe [66cm plus 24cm fringe]; 8.4 ounces [239 grams]

Hunt Valley Cashmere, 6747 White Stone Road, Baltimore, Maryland 21207-4173

410-298-8244 (weekdays); 410-527-0262 (weekends)

Two-ply cashmere; 26 wpi/2.5cm; 200 yards per ounce; 323 meters per 50 grams

Elizabeth shawl, page 90; 29.5" [75cm]; 5.4 ounces [154 grams]

Jagger Brothers, Inc., Water Street, Springvale, Maine 04083

207-324-4455 jaggers@waveinter.com

JaggerSpun 50% merino, 50% silk lace weight; 32 wpi; 310 yards per ounce; 501 meters per 50 grams

Alka shawl, cover photo and page 33; 27" [68.5cm]; 2.8 ounces [80 grams]

Enchanted Lace Yarns, Susan Emerson

502-753-4634 Lacelady@mindspring.com Lacelady@slye.net

100% angora handspun cobweb weight; 55 wpi/2.5cm; 440 yards per ounce; 715 meters per 50 grams

Robert scarf, pages 7 and 107; 8" x 18" [20.5cm x 45.5cm]; 9.5" [24cm]; 0.7 ounces [20 grams]

Louet Sales, P.O. Box 267, Ogdensburg, NY 13669

1-613-925-4502 info@louet.com

Euroflax 4/14 linen; 23 wpi; 1325 yards per pound; 82 yards per ounce; 132 meters per 50 grams

Alka shawl, eggplant, cover photo and page 66; 30" [76cm]; 11.8 ounces [335 grams]

Windsor Farms Rabbitry, 4151 Mountain View Road, Silverton, OR 97381

503-873-3128 angoralady@aol.com http://members.aol.com/angoralady/index.htm

33.3 angora, 33.3 merino, 33.3 silk, handspun, sport weight; 16 wpi/2.5cm; [725 yards to the pound] 45 yards per ounce; 72 meters per 50 grams

Anastasia scarf, page 108; 8.5" x 18" [21.5cm x 45.5cm]; 9.5" [24cm]; 3.4 ounces [97 grams]

Wool, Yarns and Fibres, Christchurch, New Zealand

Handspun Romney by Diane Sullivan; 13 wpi/2.5cm; 1150 yards per pound; 71 yards per ounce; 114 meters per 50 grams

GS Gracie shawl, charcoal, pages 3 and 43 and back cover; 35" [89cm]; 18.4 ounces [522 grams]

Sirdar Highlands & Islands Balmoral double knitting, 72% wool, 25% alpaca, 3% silk, 14 wpi/2.5cm; 72 yards per ounce; 117 meters per 50 grams

GS Catharina shawl, page 47; 35" [89cm]; 13.7 ounces [389 grams]

New Zealand merino, possum; not commercially available; 22 wpi/2.5cm; 3600 yards per pound; 225 yards per ounce; 364 meters per 50 grams

Peter scarf, page 110; 6" x 18" [15.5cm x 46cm]; 11.5" [29cm]; 1.2 ounces [34 grams]

Selected Bibliography

Basic Skills

Hiatt, June Hemmons, *The Principles of Knitting*, Simon and Schuster, Inc., New York (1988)

Stanley, Montse, *The Handknitter's Handbook*, David & Charles Craft (1990)

Thomas, Mary, *Mary Thomas's Knitting Book*, Dover Publications, Inc. New York (1972)

Vogue Knitting, Pantheon Books, New York (1989)

Zimmermann, Elizabeth, *Knitting Without Tears*, Charles Scribner's Sons, New York (1971)

Knitting To and Purling Fro, also known as Knitting Back Backwards and Left-Handed Knitting

Phillips, Mary Walker, *Step by Step Knitting*, Golden Press, New York (1967)

Hurlburt, Regina, *Left-Handed Knitting*, Van Nostrand Reinhold, New York (1977)

Stanley, Montse, *The Handknitter's Handbook*, David & Charles Craft (1990) at pp.26-27

Bates, Susan, *Learn to Knit, Knitting for Beginners*, Coats Patons, Toronto (1987) at pp.10 & 16

Charting Aids

Selfridge, Gail, *Graph It!*, Interweave Press (1991)

Stitch Painter, Cochenille Design Studio, P.O. Box 4276, Encinitas, CA 92023

Books Which Include Lace

Abbey, Barbara, *Barbara Abbey's Knitting Lace*, The Viking Press, New York (1974), reprinted Schoolhouse Press, Pittsville, WI (1993)

Abbey, Barbara, *The Complete Book of Knitting*, The Viking Press, Inc., New York (1971)

Amedro, Gladys, *Shetland Lace*, The Shetland Times Ltd, Lerwick, Shetland (1993)

Carter, Hazel, *Shetland Lace Knitting From Charts*, Hazel Carter, Madison, WI (1988)

Don, Sarah, *The Art of Shetland Lace*, Lacis, Berkeley, CA (1991)

Eaton, Jan, *Country Crochet & Knitted Lace*, New Holland Publishers Ltd, London (1994)

Eaton, Jan, *A Creative Guide to Knitted Lace*, New Holland Publishers Ltd, London (1994)

Halldorsdottir, Sigridur, *Prihyrnur Og Langsjol (Three Cornered and Long Shawls)*, Icelandic Home Industries Council, Utgefandi: Heimilisionaoarfelag Islands, Reykjavik (1988)

The Harmony Guide to Knitting Stitches, Lyric Books Limited, London (1983)

Harmony, *Knitting Sensational Stitches*, Lyric Books, Limited, London (1994)

Hewitt, Furze, *Heirloom Knitting for Dolls*, Kangaroo Press, Kenthurst, NSW (1992)

Hewitt, Furze, *Traditional Knitting for Children and Bears*, Kangaroo Press, Kenthurst, NSW (1995)

Hewitt, Furze, *Traditional Lace Knitting*, Kangaroo Press, Kenthurst, NSW (1997)

Hewitt Furze & Daley, Billie, *Classic Knitted Cotton Edgings*, Kangaroo Press, Kenthurst, NSW (1987)

Hewitt Furze & Daley, Billie, *Motifs, Borders and Trims in Classic Knitted Cotton*, Kangaroo Press, Kenthurst, NSW (1988)

Hollingworth, Shelagh, *Traditional Victorian White Work to Knit and Crochet for the Home*, St. Martin's Press, New York

Khmeleva, Galina & Noble, Carol R, *Gossamer Webs: The History and Techniques of Orenburg Lace Shawls*, Interweave Press, Loveland, CO (1998)

Kinzel, Marianne, *First Book of Modern Lace Knitting*, Dover Publications, Inc. New York (1972)

Kinzel, Marianne, *Second Book of Modern Lace Knitting*, Dover Publications, Inc. New York (1972)

Kliot, Jules & Kaethe, editors, *The Knitted Lace Patterns of Christine Duchrow - Volume I*, Lacis Publications, Berkeley, CA (1993)
Kliot, Jules & Kaethe, editors, *The Knitted Lace Patterns of Christine Duchrow - Volume II*, Lacis Publications, Berkeley, CA (1994)
Kliot, Jules & Kaethe, editors, *The Knitted Lace Patterns of Christine Duchrow - Volume III*, Lacis Publications, Berkeley, CA (1995)
Lewis, Susanna E., *Knitting Lace - A Workshop with Patterns and Projects*, Taunton Press, Newtown, CT (1992)
Leinhauser, Jean, *101 Knit and Crochet Ripple Stitches*, American School of Needlework, San Marco, CA (1997)
Lorant, Tessa, *Knitted Lace Collars*, The Thorn Press, Somerset, United Kingdom (1983)
Lorant, Tessa, *Knitted Shawls and Wraps*, The Thorn Press, Somerset, United Kingdom (1986)
Matthews, Anne, *Vogue Dictionary of Knitting Stitches*, The Conde Nast Publications Ltd. Hong Kong (1984)
mon tricot, *Knitting Dictionary* (1963) (also published as *1300 Pattern Stitches Advice Hints;* and also as *Knitting Encyclopedia - 1500 Patterns*)
Nehring, Nancy, *The Lacy Knitting of Mary Shiffmann*, Interweave Press, Loveland, CO (1998)
Norbury, James, *Traditional Knitting Patterns from Scandinavia, the British Isles, France, Italy and other European Countries*, Dover Publications, Inc. New York (1973)
Orr, Anne, *Decorative Bedspreads Knitting*, Nashville, Tennessee (1941)
Penning, Gloria, *The Complete Works of Rachel Schnelling — Patterns for the Art of Lace Knitting*, Heirloom Lace Patterns, Hermann, MO (1991)
Penning, Gloria, *Danish Lace Treasures — featuring the work of Anna Marie Jensen*, Heirloom Lace Patterns
Penning, Gloria, *Knitted Heirloom Lace II*, Heirloom Lace, Hermann MO
Penning, Gloria, *Knitted Lace in Miniature*, Heirloom Lace Patterns, Hermann, MO
Penning, Gloria, *Old World Treasures — featuring the work of Lillie Meitler*, Heirloom Lace Patterns
Phillips, Mary Walker, *Knitting Counterpanes — Traditional Coverlet Patterns for Contemporary Knitters*, The Taunton Press, Newtown, CT (1989)
Reade, Dorothy, *25 Original Knitting Designs*, Koke Printing Company, Eugene, OR (1968)
Stanfield, Lesley, *The New Knitting Stitch Library*, Quarto Publishing plc, Chilton Book Company, Radnor, PA (1992)
Stove, Margaret, *Creating Original Hand-knitted Lace*, Lacis Publications, Berkeley, CA (1995)
Terp, Sandy, *The Pruden Knitting Diary - Lace Patterns*, Moonrise, Perkasie, PA (1997)
Thomas, Mary, *Mary Thomas's Book of Knitting Patterns*, Dover Publications, Inc., New York (1972)
Timmons, Susan, *S Before T*, Susan Timmons, Raleigh, NC (1999)
van Schalkwyk, Sarie, *Lace Knitting - A selection of 26 patterns*, Delos, Cape Town (1991)
Walker, Barbara G., *The Craft of Lace Knitting*, Charles Scribner's Sons, Inc. New York (1971)
Walker, Barbara G., *Charted Knitting Designs - A Third Treasury of Knitting Patterns*, Charles Scribner's Sons, New York (1972)
Walker, Barbara G., *A Treasury of Knitting Patterns*, Charles Scribner's Sons, New York (1968)
Walker, Barbara G., *A Second Treasury of Knitting Patterns*, Charles Scribner's Sons, New York (1970)
Waterman, Martha, *Traditional Knitted Lace Shawls*, Interweave Knits, Loveland, CO (1998)
Wiseman, Nancie, *Lace From the Attic: A Victorian Notebook of Knitted Lace Patterns*, Interweave Press, Loveland, CO (1999)

Sources for Faroese Shawl Patterns

Anderson-Shea, Charlene, *A Faroese Shawl in Icelandic Unspun*, knitting NOW, p.5, Winter, Vol. 3, No. 1 (1978)

Bundnaturriklaedid, *Foroysk Bindingarmynstur*, Foroyskt Heimavirki, Torshavn (1983) translated into English by Marilyn van Keppel and titled *Faroese Knitting Patterns* School House Press, Pittsville, WI (1997)

Erickson-Schweitzer, Jackie, individual shawl patterns, HeartStrings, 53 Parlange Drive, Destrehan, LA 70047

Lind, Vibeke, *Knitting in the Nordic Tradition*, translated into English by Annette Allen Jensen, Lark Books, Asheville, North Carolina (1984) at p.78

Myatt, Edward, *Mary's Triangular Shawl*, available direct from Edward for $8.00 Edward Myatt, 1-469 8th St. E, Owen Sound, Ontario, Canada, N4K 1L6

Slayton, E.J. *Lace Leaf Shawl*, Knitting World, p. 32, September (1992) reprinted in *Shawls*, available from E.J. Slayton, Route 1, Box 1346, Cadet, MO 63630

Stahman, Myrna A.I., *Faroese-style Lace*, Knitter's Magazine, p. 42-45, Issue 50, Spring, Vol. 15, No. 1 (1998)

Swansen, Meg, *Faroese Shawls*, Knitter's Magazine, p. 26-29, Issue 9, Winter, Vol. 4, No. 4 (1987)

Thomas, Nancy J., editor, *The Best of Knitter's Magazine: Shawls and Scarves*, XRX, Inc. Sioux Falls, SD (1999)

van Keppel, Marilyn, *Faroese Shawl*, Knitter's Magazine, p. 32-33, Issue 48, Fall, Vol. 14, No. 3 (1997)

Index

Symbols

The charts consist of rectangles which contain symbols. A blank rectangle means knit one. A number within a rectangle tells you how many plain knit stitches are shown; thus, you don't have to count the blank rectangles. Whenever there are three or fewer plain knit stitches, no number will be shown. In the majority of charts, whenever there are four or more plain knit stitches, a number is inserted in the first rectangle.

The symbols are

- (blank) = k = knit one
- O = yo = yarn over
- – = p = purl one
- ∩ = slip as if to purl with yarn in front
- / = k2tog = knit two stitches together
- \ = ssk = slip one stitch as if to knit, slip the second stitch as if to knit, knit the two stitches together
- ℓ = twisted stitch = knit into the back of the stitch
- ℓ/ = twisted stitch k2tog
- ℓ\ = twisted stitch ssk
- < > = twisted yarnover = make one stitch with a left thumb loop (m1L) or make one stitch with a right thumb loop (m1R); when these are used in close proximity, be sure to make mirror-image thumb loops; see page 19
- ⟍ Slip the first stitch onto a cable needle and hold in front, knit the next two stitches, knit the stitch from the cable needle.
- ⟋ Put two stitches on a cable needle and hold in back, knit the next stitch, knit the two stitches from the cable needle.
- ⋌ = 3-to-1 = k3tog = knit three together
- ⋋ = 3-to-1 = Sl1-k2tog-psso = slip the first stitch as if to knit, knit two together, slip the first stitch over the k2tog. This method produces a "crossed" look, which reminds me of chicken feet.
- ↑ = 3-to-1 = slip the first two stitches at the same time as if to knit, knit the third stitch, slip the two slipped stitches over. This gives a very vertical look to the pattern.
- # = the border stitches, knitter's choice of seed stitch, garter stitch, mock ribbing, or I-cord
- **B5** = the five border stitches when working in garter stitch
  - # B5 at the beginning of the row when knitting a shawl in garter stitch = slip the first stitch as if to purl, k 4
  - # B5 at the end of the row when knitting a shawl in garter stitch = k5
  - # B5 at the beginning of the row when knitting a garter stitch Seamen's scarf = slip the first stitch as if to purl, k3, k2tog, yo
  - # B5 at the end of the row when knitting a garter stitch Seamen's scarf = yo, ssk, k4
- **B6** = the six border stitches when working in seed stitch
  - # B6 at the beginning of the row when working in seed stitch is slip the first stitch as if to purl, k1, p1, k1, p1, k1
  - # B6 at the end of the row when working in seed stitch is k1, p1, k1, p1, k2
- **m1R** = increase one stitch with a twisted yarnover increase; see page 19
- **m1L** = increase one stitch with a twisted yarnover increase of a mirror image of the m1R; see page 19